MW00337841

# MY
# FATHER
## THE
# KING

Jubilee Lipsey

Author Photo: Lyndsey Ashmore Photography

Publishing Services provided by Paper Raven Books
Printed in the United States of America
First Printing, 2021

Paperback ISBN= 978-1-7373447-4-2
Hardback ISBN= 978-1-7373447-5-9

*To the princes willing to wrestle*

# THANK YOU

These words have never felt more inadequate, but they're absolutely necessary!

Jesus, my *Yeshu-hah*, my heart cannot contain you. You have been infinitely patient with my wrestling, gently guiding me along the path you equipped me for even when I couldn't see it. I am overwhelmed by your kindness to give me all of this—and yourself. I will gladly spend the rest of my life absorbing and sharing your abundance.

Paper Raven, you didn't know it, but you were the answer to my prayers for a publisher who would understand me and value the words I've worked so hard on. Thank you for helping me get them out to those who need to hear them!

To my family and friends, these books are a testament to you. Your years of love and support are woven into these chapters, and I'm forever grateful.

To my readers, being able to share these books with you is an honor that I will never get over. Thank you for taking this journey with me!

# A NOTE FROM THE AUTHOR

———————◆————————

In the violent aftermath of Saul's and Jonathan's deaths in 2 Samuel, we meet a new character, mentioned briefly in a short paragraph before disappearing from sight for several chapters. Several years. Compared to the giant-killer, David, and his intrepid best friend, the biblical character Mephibosheth doesn't seem to stand out much. His identity as Jonathan's son is the main reason for his significance.

Jonathan was a faithful friend to David, ultimately trusting their covenant enough to place his son in the care of the man who was after God's heart. Even before being crowned king of Israel, David was known far and wide for his successful military exploits and his intense love for God.

Conversely, Mephibosheth boasted little glory in his life. He grew up disabled in a culture that did not have many options for the handicapped. And as a descendent of Saul, the king who had rejected Yahweh, he was destined to live out his days in David's shadow. But Mephibosheth had a purpose, and there is so much we can learn from his life.

His name carried several connotations of purity, integrity, and favor before God, meaning "one who contends against idols" or "one who will destroy the shame of idol worship in Israel." But through no fault of his own, Jonathan's young son was thrust into a set of circumstances that would have seemed in his day to be the most dishonorable and ignoble of all.

Crippled by a fall while escaping the Philistines who'd killed his father, five-year-old Mephibosheth likely grew up in hiding and in poverty, miserably ignorant of the honor and pride that had once been his, long before he had been old enough to appreciate it.

Scripture doesn't give us many details from Mephibosheth's early life, but it's easy to imagine the abandonment and shame he struggled with. We know that he was likely an orphan, cared for by his nurse, his grandfather's servant Ziba, and a wealthy man named Machir ben Ammiel. But the most important thing we know about Mephibosheth is that he was adopted by David and mercifully spared the death that eventually met all of Saul's remaining descendents. From this, we can derive his story's meaning for us today.

Before Christ brought salvation to the world, humanity was in a similar position as Mephibosheth. Steeped in the sin of our ancestors, we were helpless and needy, cut off from the fellowship with God we once had, and unable to get back to it. Jesus the Messiah—the promised, anointed Son of David was and is our only hope. Jesus is the true *Melek,* the King who has given His life for us, canceled the debts against us, and raised us up to His side, giving us the opportunity to become children of God!

Like the kindness granted to Mephibosheth, the favor and mercy we are given is not merited by anything we have done. But it's possible because God now looks at us and sees the righteousness of His Son. As David loved and redeemed Mephibosheth for Jonathan's sake, God accepts us in His Son's precious Name!

As you dive into this novel, I invite you to open your heart to the beautiful depths hidden within Mephi's story. Within your story. Because of Jesus, no matter how broken your past, you have the opportunity to take the hand of your Savior today, and embrace the royalty you were destined for at the King's side!

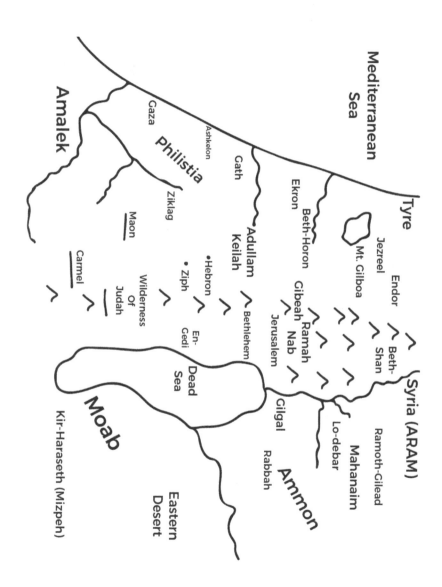

# CHARACTER LIST

———◆◆◆◆◆———

Abiathar—*David's priest and friend*

Abigail—*David's third wife*

Abinadab—*man from Lo Debar*

Abishai—*Joab's second brother*

Abner—*Saul's general and cousin, deceased*

Absalom—*David's third son*

Achish—*Philistine king*

Ahimaaz—*Zadok's son, a young priest*

Ahinoam—*David's second wife*

Ahithophel—*David's advisor, who turns against him*

Amasa—*Absalom's general*

Amnon—*David's firstborn*

Amram—*priest from Lo Debar*

Asahel (Asa)—*Joab's youngest brother, deceased*

Bathsheba—*Uriah's wife, who committed adultery with David*

Becorath—*Gibeonite raider*

Benaiah—*David's chief of staff*

Bosheth—*Saul's youngest son, deceased*

Chileab—*David's second son*

David—*second king of Israel*

Ebenezer—*carpenter from Lo Debar*

Gad—*elder from Lo Debar*

Gimel—*Ziba's Amorite servant*

Hushai—*David's elderly friend*

Iscah—*Ziba's maidservant*

Ittai—*soldier from Gath, who defected to David*

Joab—*David's general and oldest nephew*

Jonadab—*Amnon's friend*

Jonathan—*Abiathar's son, a young priest*

Jonathan—*Mephi's father, deceased prince of Israel*

Kemuel—*Gibeonite elder*

Keziah (Kezi)—*Mephi's wife*

Machir ben Ammiel—*Mephi's father-in-law, a physician*

Mephibosheth (Mephi)—*Jonathan's son, Saul's grandson*

Merab—*Saul's oldest daughter, deceased*

Mica—*Mephi's son*

Michal—*Saul's youngest daughter, David's first wife*

Naamah (Ama)—*Mephi's nurse, Ziba's sister*

Nahash—*Ammonite king who supports David*

Nathan—*prophet who serves David*

Palti of Laish—*Michal's second husband*

Saul—*first king of Israel, deceased*

Shemei—*a Benjaminite who hates David*

Solomon—*David's son by Bathsheba*

Tamar—*David's daughter, Absalom's sister*

Tubal—*Becorath's brother*

Uriah—*David's Hittite soldier, Bathsheba's first husband*

Zadok—*David's priest*

Ziba—*Naamah's brother, Mephi's guardian*

Ziba's oldest sons—*Japhia, Shaphat, Zarethan, Shaalbim, and Azarel*

# GLOSSARY OF HEBREW WORDS

Abba—*father*

Adon—*lord (high-ranking official)*

Adonai—*the Lord God*

Arabah—*eastern plains*

Chesed—*mercy or lovingkindness, favor*

Chuppah—*traditional betrothal/wedding canopy*

Eema—*mother*

Ephod—*ancient priest's garment used to inquire of God*

Geber—*master's title*

Hakkodesh—*Presence of God*

Hassar—*crown prince, a king's oldest son and heir*

Melek—*king*

Nephilim—*offspring of the giants mentioned in Genesis 6; Goliath was one*

Neshama Sheli—*one soul, an expression of kinship*

Roeh—*seer or prophet, messenger of God*

Ruach—*Spirit of God*

Saba—*grandfather*

Sar—*prince*

Sarrah—*princess*

Shabbat—*weekly Hebrew service, day of rest*

Shekel—*ancient Hebrew currency*

Shema—*ancient Hebrew prayer*

Sheol—*ancient Hebrew term for the grave*

Torah—*Law of Moses, sacred Jewish writings*

Yahweh—*God's covenant Name given to Israel*

Yeshu-hah—*salvation or deliverer*

Zion—*name for Jerusalem, the City of David*

# PROLOGUE

*Mephi's fifth year*

⬥

I'm five years old when the screams find me, pulling me out of sleep. The violent cries in the street shake the floors of my father's house, but I don't know what's happening. Curled on my bed in complete darkness, I push cold fingers through the thick blankets to find my bow.

It resembles my father's big one with the detailed carvings around its edges, and I keep it close every night, staring at the outlined claws of the wolf symbol of Benjamin until I fall asleep. Having it in my hands usually makes me feel safe, like I could bend an arrow through it in a split-second, the way my father can. But lying there alone watching the eerie shadows creeping up the wall, I feel powerless.

I'm never afraid at night when Abba's here, when I can climb into bed with him and snuggle into the giant cavern of his chest. But he's gone.

A man in the street yells that the Philistines are coming, and I try to calm down, remembering that Abba's fighting them. He'll save us. We just have to wait here for him. Something shatters in a lower chamber, and I hide my face, terrified by the frantic footsteps devouring the stairs.

"Mephi!" My nurse, Ama bursts into the room, backlit by torches. Her cheeks are wet, her eyes wild within a heavy veil. She lunges over and takes my face in her hands. "Mephi, listen to me; we have to go. Everything's going to be all right." She gasps, struggling to breathe. "You have to be brave. Like your father, yes?"

Barely waiting for me to nod, she pulls me into her arms as more footsteps clatter into the hall.

Servants swarm the room, yanking blankets and clothing and anything of value—the tapestries, the huge shield on the wall, the scrolls Abba reads every morning. A man nearly knocks Ama down in the hallway, and something drops to the floor.

"Ama—my bow!" I cry over her shoulder, but she doesn't stop. People shove past each other to get through the doors, screaming a dozen things.

"Where do we go, Naamah! What do we do?"

"Just run!" she cries over my head. "Get out of the city. My brother's servants are crossing the river to hide. Follow them." She stumbles down the stairs, gripping my back. "Hold tight," she reminds me, but I'm already clasping her neck so hard that my wrists hurt. The lower rooms blur past us, and cold darkness stings my cheeks outside the door.

There are hundreds of people in the streets, but we don't stop until we've reached the back gate of the city. Ama scrambles up into the strip of forest outside Gibeah, where I'm not allowed to go alone. The ground pushes up into hills on all sides, lumping into the rocky wilds where Abba said he would take me hunting one day.

Branches slap our arms and faces. Nothing is flat, and Ama's pace slants wildly, tilting as she starts to climb the brushy ridge over the river. The trees clasp arms over us, thickening the darkness. Men scramble for cover, calling back to us, but their torchlight bobs too far ahead.

"I'm coming! Wait—" Ama's feet shift left and right, balancing my weight against the burden of the pack on her shoulder. The trail is narrow, following a skinny ridgeline of rock that drops down into nothing. The path's crumbling edge keeps pulling at us, tugging our weight towards it. The moon opens over our heads, and Ama's call breaks in the wind. "Wait—"

Then, she stumbles. Her foot slides and her body twists sharply, her shoulder shrugging me off. I barely feel the hiss of alarm shake her chest before the ground drops away, and emptiness grabs me.

At first, it feels like the dozens of times I've jumped from the tree in the garden, higher every year. That half-second where my body leaves the branch, catching air before hitting the ground. But this time, I keep falling. Too long, before wet rock slams into me.

The sharpest fear I've ever felt rears over me in seconds. Teeth bared and claws outstretched, it grabs my limbs and drags me into the dark.

I wake up slowly, blinking into eerie dimness. Shadows from a single torch paint rocky walls with monstrous images, and it's terrifying to feel my mind pulling, trying to remember something. Anything. I can't see Ama, but I can hear her. She's sobbing, moaning Yahweh's Name. Begging Him to forgive her and spare me.

Questions wail beneath my tongue, but I can't reach them through the churning in my head. Or is it rain? Something's pounding on the ceiling above me, and the thunder sounds like an army trying to break in.

I'm so cold, but the fire trapped in my bones is making my body ache. The ground under me is hard and uneven. My clothes are torn apart, sticking to me with rain and mud. I gasp into the dark, my cry hitting the narrow walls.

"Mephi!" Ama's face appears over mine, her hands smoothing my hair. "I'm sorry. I'm so sorry." She kisses my head, her tears dropping onto me.

I try to say her name, but panic holds me down like a fist at my collar, and I can't move out from under it. My fingers are numb, and I don't know where I am. I want water to make my lips stop breaking in half. I want my stomach to stop tossing like a boat on water. Everything's blurry, and the pain in my ankles pushes back and forth like a knife sawing through the bones.

"Where's Abba?" I whimper, remembering. He has to find me. I raise my voice, my lips trembling. "I want my Abba!"

Ama just sobs into her hands. "Oh, God! Oh, God!" She catches her breath when a man stoops through the narrow opening behind her, drenched with the rain. "Oh. Ziba…"

I've only seen her brother a few times. He isn't as tall as my father, but he can still look down on her. And his brows knit together fiercely in a way Abba's never did.

"Keep him quiet!" he snaps. "We're not safe until we make it past the Jordan."

Ama clasps her hands, her shoulders quivering. "What are we supposed to tell him?"

Ziba just sighs, coming over to crouch in front of me. I yelp when his knee touches my leg, but he shushes me.

"You fell; do you remember that? It looks like you broke your ankles. I pulled you out of the bottom of the ravine." Rubbing his face, he pushes a long breath through his fingers, muttering, "Though you may live to wish I hadn't."

My head spins with the pain. Nothing makes sense, but I feel sick when I look at Ziba. He knows everything Ama's not saying. He brought me here so my father can't find me. "Where's my Abba?"

Ziba doesn't answer right away. He chews his lip, watching me. Like he knows I'm going to hate him for what he's about to say. "He's dead."

No.

It's the first word that comes to mind, and I keep thinking it, over and over. Abba's not dead. He wouldn't have left me.

He never liked Ama's brother anyway. He said he wasn't to be trusted, and now I know he was right. Ziba's lying so he can take me away. I start to shake again, afraid of the pain, and the dark, and the tight grip of the man who has my life in his hands.

"You have to be quiet," he tells me. "We can't let the Philistines find us."

I shake my head, tears rolling down my face, even though I don't believe him. "No. No, I want my Abba!"

Ziba just stands up, nearly hitting his head, and pushes his sister at me. "Keep him quiet. I mean it. Achish's scouts will sweep the countryside looking for survivors. If they find us, we're all dead."

Ama's shoulders quake. "What are we going to do? He'll catch his death after being in that cold water. We need a physician; we need…"

"We need to keep hidden," Ziba cuts her off. "We need to find out if my sons have reached safety." His voice drops tightly. "We're not going to find a physician out here. Besides, what's he going to do about broken ankles, anyway? I doubt they're going to heal. Which means we'll have a damaged, wailing prince's son to carry around everywhere. It'll be a miracle if we can keep him from the Philistines."

My heartbeat screams, trying to break through my chest.

Ama wrings her hands. "Then, we have to find Abner. The general always said he would make Mephi king if anything happened."

"It's too late for that," Ziba interrupts. "If his legs are useless, so is his royal blood. Even if he wasn't crippled…" He sighs, frustrated. "Israel will never be the same. We all knew Saul's sins would destroy everyone connected to him. Now you see what's happened. Yahweh has rejected Saul's clan outright." He gestures toward me. "It would've been kinder if he'd died with them."

Ama breathes in sharply. "What will happen to Saul's last son? And Abner?"

Ziba folds his arms. "Abner will wait to see who's left alive and who's loyal. When things die down, he will try to place the kingdom in Bosheth's hands."

Ama twists her shawl. "Ish-Bosheth was not Saul's choice. He wanted Jonathan's line to…"

"I told you, that's over," Ziba retorts. "Israel doesn't need a five-year-old king with no family and no legs to stand on. If Abner survives, we'll see who follows him."

"He has family," Ama declares tightly.

Ziba stiffens, pointing at her. "You and I are family. Saul's son did nothing for you except make you the servant of a man who ruined you. Now, it's time to do what we should have done years ago. Look out for ourselves."

Ama wilts, weeping into her shawl. "He's the prince's son."

"Not anymore." Her brother grimaces. "Which reminds me, we should call him something else. His name is too widely known."

Ama's head comes up. "Change his name? His father wouldn't…"

"His father is dead," Ziba says again. "And thanks to your pathetic preference for Jonathan, I get to decide what happens to the boy. The Philistines are not the only ones who would harm a grandson of Saul's if they had him in their power. If you want to keep him safe, you'll listen to me. And help the boy fall in line."

"Jonathan mentioned David…" Ama ventures, but Ziba jerks violently, clapping a hand over her mouth.

"We are *not* sending word to David; do you hear me? Right now, we'd be in just as much danger from him as the Philistines."

I grip the edges of my sleeves, afraid to hurt this badly. I wish I was dreaming. But I can hear what Ziba's saying. I can feel the rough ground under me. The rain, and the dark, and the pain are all real. Which means…which means…

I think of Abba and start crying again.

Ziba whirls around and grabs my mouth. "Be quiet! Do you hear me? The Philistines want to find you and kill you. Do you understand? Do you want that?"

Ama pulls at his shoulder, telling him to stop, and he pushes her back against the wall.

"Stop it!" I scream, trying to sit up. "Leave her alone!"

I've never been more terrified. He's hurting both of us, and Abba isn't coming to stop him.

Ziba sounds breathless. "Just keep him quiet! Get him out of those clothes and wrap him up in something warmer. And stay packed. We leave as soon as the rain stops."

I try to keep still until Ziba leaves, but by now the sobs are stuck in my chest, and I can't breathe. Ama unwinds her shawl and tucks it under my chin where my teeth are chattering. "Don't cry, Mephi. Don't be afraid."

But I can feel the tears on her face. If she's afraid, why shouldn't I be? I turn my head into her arm. My chest jerks with every other word. "I…want…my Abba."

But he's gone. He's not coming back.

"Listen to me." Ama lifts my shoulders, pulling my head onto her lap. She combs my hair back from my ear and whispers into it. "Yahweh is here with us. Your father trusted Him to keep you safe. If you cry out to Him, Adonai will protect you." She gulps, resisting sobs. "Do you understand?"

I feel frozen. My father always prayed to Yahweh—over my bed, at the feasts, and in the dark alone, when he didn't know I was watching. But Yahweh let him die. Was I supposed to die too, like Ziba said? Does Yahweh hate me the way He hates Saul? Is that why He let me fall?

The thought is suffocating. It roams around inside me, stealing my breath, and I don't know how to make it stop. I just close my eyes and hold onto Ama, hoping she won't disappear. I'm so cold, and everything hurts so much. And there's nowhere in the world I can hide if Yahweh wants me dead.

PART ONE

# ONE

## Mephi

———•◆•◆•◆•———

*Eight years later*

I'm thirteen today.

I flinch away from the thought before it's halfway through my mind. It drifts by with the dust of the road, settling on my skin for a choking breath before wafting into the air to cloud the breeze.

It's a useless thought. Just as irritating as the trail of sweat slowly inching its way down my neck. I reach back and scrape my tunic against it, but all that does is leave another streak of dirt on my clothes. In full sunlight, it's too hot to be directly in the road, but too many other beggars huddle against the gates. I won't be noticed there.

I pull myself farther out into the path of the approaching travelers, adjusting my robe where it's slipped askew again. Too big for my bony shoulders. I reach up to yank it straight, and my hand catches the strand of hemp around my neck. I let my fingers briefly touch the thick circle of metal hanging from the end before shoving it back under my collar. Finding it there still startles me.

Ama had slipped the cord over my head this morning, leaving my father's ring hanging over my chest. "He asked me to keep it for you. You should have it now," she'd said, but I still can't figure out why. Unless I stay perfectly still, it taps my breastbone over and over, coaxing something forbidden to the surface. Something I don't know how to answer.

My father wore the ring as the Hassar, Israel's crown prince. Before he'd died alongside my grandfather, King Saul. And my uncles. Any other heirs have since been slaughtered by the men who've crowned a new king in Judah. And I was never supposed to live this long.

So, the circular band of gold etched with the symbols of Saul should mean nothing. A forgotten relic from a dynasty that no longer exists. But my pulse still scatters out of control when I touch it.

At least it hangs so long that my clothing covers most of it. Annoyed, I pull more of my fraying robe over my chest. I can't get distracted. For months, I've planned what to do, and

I'll need help. Which means I'll need more money. I won't tempt Becorath with the few coins hidden under my cloak. I squint into the afternoon glare, assessing the travelers.

A boy rides ahead of a small caravan several feet off, heading for the gates of Ramoth. Something about the way his head tilts confidently, the way his shoulders arch back, giving him more height, stirs the ache in my stomach. I've gotten used to the gnaw of hunger, but this isn't it.

I'd be that tall if I were on my feet. Huddled on the ground with my broken ankles bent under me, I can barely hide the way my frame has healed crooked, one hip out of joint and one shoulder slightly higher than the other. My childhood injury left permanent marks on me, and that's all anyone sees.

I glance up at the boy on the mule, wondering if he's actually my age. Thirteen is a mile-marker for sons of Israel. It's when the elders start paying attention to what you have to say, watching you with more interest. It's when you're initiated as your own man while taking up the business of your father. If you have one.

If mine had lived, would it have been like that for me? It's all I have to think about, sitting in the shadow of Ramoth-Gilead watching traders and travelers pass me by. But a reality like that is as elusive as the dust of the road. Thirteen means nothing in the streets.

"It helps if you say something."

A hoarse cackle reaches out to me from along the gate. Propped against it in the shade, Ephron looks like a pile of bones. I turn my back to him, wincing. I hate the sight of the wizened old men who lie under ragged tents, their glazed eyes either fixed on the dusty ground or lifted to travelers in an appeal. Their misery is like a nightmare I can see coming.

Paralyzed on one side from an illness, Ephron has been sitting at this gate longer than I've been alive, and he's too old to remember how often he's given me the same advice. Or that I rarely take it.

"People don't know what to do with gifts like ours, other than throw money at them," he often says. "Use that."

But I hate begging. It's humiliating, exposing me to the harshness of the wind and sun, draining dignity away every hour my hands stay idle. And my guardian doesn't need the money.

After decades of service to King Saul's captains, Ziba knows every hidden corner of Benjamin's territory, and he's spent the last several years sending his servants back and forth, regaining what was supposedly his. "What Saul took from me," he always adds for my benefit. He should be a wealthy man soon if he's acquired as much as he says. And he has fifteen sons who will provide for him one day. But Ziba can make me do whatever he wants.

I have nothing else so close to a guardian, but since the day he picked me up out of the ravine where I broke my legs, he's never defended me. Not even when his sons dragged me half a mile into the wasteland and left me to struggle back. My hands and knees were bleeding by the time I made it half a mile. Ziba had barely noticed in enough time to send a servant after me, and then only because of Ama.

Men praise him for taking me on, assuming I'm his sister's bastard, but I'm sure he'd get rid of me if he could. He's threatened before, saying he would only wait until I was thirteen. Which is why I have to leave. Today.

But it's past noon, and Becorath hasn't shown himself. He said he'd be back this way in a month. Did I count the days right? I push onto my knees, resisting agitation. I don't have all the time in the world.

There's only so many weeks that Ziba is gone, out spying with the network he's strung across the land the way rich men spread flocks over the eastern Arabah. But he'll be back any day. Maybe tonight. And he watches me closer when he's here, even though he was the one who'd decided it was worth the risk to expose me. No one ever asks a beggar his name.

"Move! Get out of the way." A man from the caravan strides ahead of the boy on the path, aiming his staff at me.

Travelers reaching Gilead at midday are as hot-tempered as the sun overhead. They're eager to get through the gates and buy food, or head for the well at the center of the marketplace.

Eager to avoid delaying his master, riding several paces behind, the man angles the animals out of my direct path, aiming sour advice up at the boy. "Leave him. Beggars carry diseases."

"I can't walk. I'm starving." The words burn my tongue no matter how many times I say them. I hold up my hands, shame blurring my vision.

"Are you sure?" The servant's sneer turns my chest cold. "Or are you just out here to bleed travelers for some nobleman?"

Smirking, he reaches into the leather pouch at his belt. "Tell your master to feed you with this."

He tosses the coin in my face, and my cheeks ignite.

I fling the *shekel* back at him. "Keep your money."

It's not quite a snarl, but the servant is every bit as offended as I hoped. He springs at me, slashing his riding whip across my torso. "Stupid stray dog!" he yells, kicking dust in my direction.

Sand stabs at the open wound, and the dirt digs into my throat. But I have a plan.

"Can I at least have water?" Bent over, shuddering, I point at the waterskin slung across his shoulder.

Scowling, he hesitates only a second before moving up closer, muttering under his breath. He fills the clay cup attached to the skin while I crouch at his side, my right hand edging up under his robe. The twine looped around his belt is barely knotted. Too easy.

I'm still bent over, hugging my side when he hands me the water. "All right?"

I nod, and the servant's face tightens. "Good. Starve to death for all I care!"

Ignoring him, I stay curled on the ground to hide what's in my fists, crushed under me. Once the caravan has passed by, I push myself up and pry open the leather pouch, pouring ten *shekels* into my palm. For all the man's hotheaded defense, he'd failed to notice what I was doing. And the boy had simply turned away, refusing to watch. *Idiot.*

I swallow, tasting dust while I return the money to the pouch. I've tried to forget the first time I ever stole, reasoning that it wasn't stealing if the man was dead. The old beggar hadn't moved in a day, and Ziba had hit me the night before, demanding to know why I had so little.

Thieving comes easier than begging now. Maybe because it feels like more of a profession, something that requires skill and strategy. It's not hard to justify taking what I can, especially when I lose so much to Ziba's sons and other beggars. I've had to get creative, hiding coins in my clothes and in my mouth. My whole life, Ziba's insisted I'd be useless at a real trade. But there's more I could do.

A few years ago, I'd found a knife and started carving stray pieces of wood. I would lose myself doing it, letting hours pass by without stopping any travelers. Ama had asked me where the designs came from, but I wouldn't say. I'd wanted to believe the wolf's claw and the various Hebrew letters were just tangled fragments from my imagination. Old shreds of a life that isn't real. But now I have a ring that bears the same symbols.

I twirl my finger around the signet's beveled edges, feeling foolish now that it makes sense. I've been repeating the images on my father's ring all this time? Why? It's eerie enough to hold it, tracing the etchings from a kingdom that no longer exists, staring into the polished gold as if it can hear me. *Where are you?*

It's been eight years since I've heard my father's voice, but I can't pull it back. The last thing he told me is burned into my memory, but even that sounds like something I made up. Something about arrows and Yahweh.

He was holding me against his chest, speaking into my hair while I held onto my little bow behind his back. Maybe I did imagine it. Like the dreams where I wake up muttering to myself. Ziba's always telling me I'm going mad like my grandfather.

I can't let him see the ring, that's for certain. Israel isn't what it was seven years ago. But Saul's markings can only spell trouble in this new nation that's obsessed with the Judean upstart ruling from Hebron.

I study the road again, squinting into the sweltering emptiness. Becorath is one of the few people who knows that I carve. The Amorite dispatch rider had brought me wood after he found me carving into my arm with the tip of my knife. Over the past year, it's become easier to measure Becorath's movements, how long it takes him to ride with his brothers from one town to the next. Where is he?

For the hundredth time, I run through my plan, pulling it into the front of my mind. Today was the day. Lacking any other milestone, I'd determined that my thirteenth birthday would be the last day I would see this place again. I'd even practiced what to say to convince Becorath to help me. I've done it before, hoarding precious coins to coerce him to spy on Ziba. Or steal from him. My way of undermining the man who has my life in his hands. But planning to leave my only shelter behind is another matter.

For a moment, I cling to Ama's image with my eyes shut. She blames herself for my injury, but she's been all I could have ever needed in a mother.

"One day, you'll understand what your father saw in you, and I will rejoice. For now, I'll tell you the truth until you believe it," she had said, her tone taut with steely triumph. But my only chance for seeing myself differently is if I get away from Ziba.

I'd wanted to tell Ama my plan, maybe ask her to leave with me. But she would only try to make me stay. And I'm grown now. I have to start thinking and acting for myself. Maybe one day, I'll find her again and repay her for everything. If I stay, Ziba will hand me over to some man who will keep me begging forever, or worse—hidden away.

The memory still grips me with panic. I remember when the wasteland outside Ramoth looked like a palm spring; it was such an improvement from the caves. All those years, Ziba kept me hidden, dragging me from shelter to shelter while the shepherd-king's men exterminated Saul's, ending with my father's general, and finally my uncle. The only two men who might have remembered me.

Word spread that the Judean king David hadn't sanctioned those deaths. But then, we heard that he'd taken my aunt back from the husband Saul gave her to, claiming she was his wife first. My other aunt Merab had died years ago, leaving hardly anyone left I could turn to.

Ziba had convinced me I'd be killed if I was found, and the terror had strangled me into submission. But now the way is clear, if not welcoming. Enough time has passed, and the nation is occupied with David's efforts to drive our enemies back. Now's my chance to disappear and become something else. Anything besides Jonathan's failed attempt at an heir.

I examine the road, trying to imagine a life at the other end of it in some other city, but it isn't long before Ziba's voice interrupts.

*Go ahead. Try to survive on your own, without me.*

But the ring against my chest speaks to the part of me that disagrees. Maybe Ama was wise to give it to me. At the very least,

I could trade it to someone too stupid to know better. But I have enough money to bargain with now. And I'll use it, just as soon as Becorath shows up.

I study the path of the clouds through the sky, numbly retracing the constants in my life. The sanctuary city of Ramoth-Gilead has never felt like home, though I don't remember much else. It's the longest we've stayed anywhere, but its walls are drab and crumbling, wearing the desert. I'm going to get out of here. I'll shake off the dust and leave Ziba behind.

And if I don't survive, then I won't. All my grandfather's men have died in battle or in exile. And I probably will too.

Ama says I won't. But she can't explain why I'm here, crippled for life. She used to encourage me to pray, but Yahweh doesn't want to hear my voice. Not since my grandfather rejected Him. Better to stay silent and not incur more guilt.

I sit up, hearing hoofbeats rumbling on the town's western hill. Half a dozen riders descend, kicking up a golden-brown cloud that stains the air. Ordinarily, a pack of mounted renegades would spell trouble. Stolen Philistine horses. Curved weapons. No tribal colors. But these Amorites are mercenaries, hired by rich men as messengers or spies. Unburdened by the Law of Moses, Canaanites can be trusted to do things Israelites won't.

Riding out ahead, Becorath reins in next to me while I straighten up, hiding my relief. A year ago, he stopped another beggar from harassing me, slashing the man's chest open with his riding whip. He's kept an eye on me ever since, telling me what he's seen on the road. He knows how tired I am of hiding and begging. Waiting for death. It's time for me to make my own way. And he's my best chance.

Becorath swings himself to the ground, his leathery brow pulling with sweat beneath his turban. "I told my men I had urgent business with the beggar at the gate. Want to know what they said?"

I roll my eyes. "They were there when you said you'd come back." I hold up the bag of coins, and his brows lift.

"Your skill is improving," he concedes, a tight thread of humor winding through his expression. But his hawk eyes wander all over me, looking for something else. Ignoring the whip scar across my chest, he asks, "Who'd you steal that from?"

His scrutiny pulls heat into my cheeks, and I shove the ring away. "It's nothing."

Fortunately, he's satisfied enough not to pry. He picks at the edge of his belt, and I see the glint of the late afternoon sun on the blade hanging there. "I would've thought your owner would be back by now. What do you want me to take from him this time?"

The insult stings my face, unraveling everything I'd planned to say. "He's not my owner," I protest, holding the money out of his reach. I toughen my voice. "I want you to take me instead."

Becorath pauses, turning to adjust the saddle on his horse. "You? What are you talking about?"

I swallow again, still tasting sand. "I want you to take me with you."

"Where?"

I shrug, holding eye contact. "Anywhere."

"Why? So you can fail at begging somewhere else?" He chuckles weakly, looking away for a moment. "If you think anyone else is going to treat you better than Ziba does, then you haven't been out here long enough. You can't live on dreams, boy."

*You don't say?* I roll my eyes again, but insecurity shudders in my chest. I hadn't considered what I would do if he refused.

"I can carve. You said my skill is good. And I've done more for Ziba. I can polish armor, I can mend harnesses, I can do anything you want. Teach me, and I'll do it." I find his eyes again, shaken with sudden intensity. "I know things. When people see me, they think I'm just a beggar, and they don't watch what they say. I can get you information."

Becorath represses another laugh. "Without walking? What kind of information are we talking about? I'm not interested in what new wife David's taking next…"

"I know there are other descendents of Saul still alive."

I have his attention now, but my mouth turns dry saying it. Of course, there's no way he knows that it's me. But, until this moment, I hadn't realized I was so desperate. Am I really willing to dig myself into a hole I might not be able to crawl out of?

Becorath's eyes snap. "Everyone knows that. But I'm after something else. I've been on a very specific assignment for a man from Laish. I don't have time to carry a beggar around. Besides, don't you have a mother or something who will wonder what happened to you? I've seen the street woman who brings you food."

I drop my head. "She's not a street woman. She raised me."

Becorath snorts. "That makes her a street woman. She's pretty, though. What's her name?"

"Naamah," I mumble, wondering why he cares.

"Naamah?" His voice tilts, changing direction. His hands stop fiddling with his weapons. "Naamah bat Ebal? From Gibeah?"

I lift my head, alarm stirring in my stomach. "Yes." The moment I say it, my ears catch the strange way he said *Gibeah*. My grandfather's city, in ruins to the west.

The silence between us is different now, like the slight change in the air before a storm. It drags on, building until I have to look Becorath in the eyes. When I do, my heart misses a beat. How did I miss the greed coiled there, waiting to strike?

With a glance toward the hills, he leans forward, standing over me. His voice drops, turning cold. "You want me to take you? I'll take you."

He pounces before I can react, grasping my collar and hauling me across the ground toward his horse. All of Ziba's threats and warnings claw through me in the instant it takes for my brain to respond. I didn't say who I was, but Naamah's name sparked something for Becorath. I don't understand, but I need to get away.

"Let me go!" Enraged and terrified, I yank at his arm, trying to break his hold, but he just digs in tighter.

"Relax, boy. I know exactly where you belong, and I have a potential buyer who will treat you well."

Becorath has my face in one hand, crushing my jaw while he tries to slip a rope around my neck. And I hear the hoofbeats getting closer. In seconds, his men will be on me.

But then, another voice strikes the air over my head like the heavy crack of a whip.

"Leave him! Let him go!" Ziba shouts, and I cringe, my pleas lodging in my throat as Becorath's grip relaxes.

I stay still where he drops me, not bothering to lift my head. Wishing someone else had come for me. Anyone else.

Because every time I look Ziba in the eyes, I see myself lying at the bottom of a ravine, while he broke the only part of me that was still whole. Telling me my father was dead.

# TWO

## *Mephi*

———————— •• ◆ •• ————————

The way Ziba's looking at me still makes me sweat, pulling my mind back to the caves.

Ama's brother has overseen every bit of pain in my life. He was the one who'd pulled me from the ravine where I'd broken both ankles falling from the cliffs outside Gibeah. Unconscious and submerged in frigid water, I would have died if he hadn't come for me. I'd spent the next month fighting fever, dragged from one cave to another while we tried to avoid the Philistines. Reeling from the pain, the only thing that had kept me quiet was Ziba's promise to leave me behind if I made noise.

Not even a year later, he watched while an Ammonite who claimed to be a physician felt all the crooked bones in my ankles. I remember the man's sour look when Ziba asked him if he could rebreak my legs and reset the bones. "You said he might walk again if you did that."

"There are no certainties in matters like this. In all likelihood, he'll be crippled or limping his whole life. What I can do now won't be simple. And it's not free."

The man was rough, but Ziba's manner terrified me more. He was opening me up with his gaze, trying to decide if I was strong enough. The limits of my strength were always his decision, not mine. He'd finally decided it was worth the risk, and his main concern was whether anyone would hear me scream.

During those months of failed recoveries and blinding pain, Ziba taught me three things: that I owed him everything for my life, that I was cursed by our God, and that if anyone found out who I was, I'd be killed.

All of that crashes into me when I see him.

I huddle in the dust, waiting for my head to stop swimming while Ziba fumes from a distance. It doesn't matter that his anger is temporarily aimed over my head. It'll find me soon enough.

Ziba grips his staff with both hands, and two of his sons move up beside him, teasing the weapons at their belts. Ziba has stolen enough swords to arm his servants and his oldest sons, but Japhia and Shaphat won't use them in my defense unless they have to. Japhia's expression flickers at me, scorn dancing like tiny flames in the corners of his eyes.

My breath lodges in my throat when I hear bowstrings being stretched taut behind me.

"Now you're threatening me?" Ziba thunders, advancing a step. "After you laid hands on *my* charge? I've seen you lurking around these hills, waiting to strike. What were you going to steal from a cripple?"

His arm muscles squeeze, but I also see his throat bobbing up and down. He's ready to fight, but there's a tremor in his anger. I've uncovered something he's been afraid of for years, and I'll suffer for it later.

Becorath waves his men off. "We wouldn't harm him. The boy asked to come with us."

"Do you take me for a fool?" Ziba spits. His staff in Becorath's face forces the man back several paces. The horse sidesteps, snorting nervously, but Becorath's eyes stay locked on Ziba.

"You don't know who he is. Clearly. Otherwise, you wouldn't leave him out here begging."

Ziba's next step kicks dust into the air between them. Ama has joined his sons at the gate, standing frozen with her hand over her mouth.

Her brother's voice is like a blade, cold and sharp. "Don't you ever show your face here again. Ramoth's elders aren't afraid of some petty Ammonite rogues."

Becorath stiffens. "I'm a son of the Amorites."

"On your way. Now." Ziba's false blow strikes too close to Becorath's face. The Amorite hoists himself up onto his horse, and he and his men scramble off toward the hills in the same dust cloud that brought them.

I fold my fingers into fists, both relieved and terrified to see them go. The air clears around Ziba, but his anger isn't evaporating.

"What happened?" Ama asks, her voice small.

Ziba pivots and grabs my collar. "What did you tell that raider? What was he doing here?"

I pull away from him, my hand planted behind me. "Nothing. He…he's not a raider. He's just a dispatch rider—"

Ziba smacks the side of my head. "He's an Amorite! You think he's never been hired to steal or kill? He'd slit your wrists in a second if it would profit him."

"Ziba—" Ama moves closer.

"Don't you defend him!" he yells at her. "Do you know who claimed responsibility for the attacks on Abel last month? Who carried away a dozen women from Endor?" He shakes his head. "I try to give him a little freedom, a chance to be useful, and I find him in the hands of an enemy of Israel!" He shoves me away.

I'd forgotten the bag of coins, but Ziba spots them on the ground next to me. "Probably what the vulture was after." He bends to pick it up, handing it off to his servant. Gimel fixes Ziba with a tight stare as he takes the money, but my eyes hug the ground, refusing to look at him.

Ziba's face is hard enough to strike flint. But somehow, he has the ability to pull sincerity and innocence into his expression at a moment's notice. Something he learned in Saul's court, no doubt. It helps that he usually knows what's going on before anyone else. His goal in every interaction is to come out ahead. And he'll manage it while making you feel like he did you a favor.

For years, he's treated me as though my grandfather's name was branded on my forehead in plain sight. Convincing me I would die if anyone found out who I was. It was easy to believe in the years when David's men were locked in continual combat with Saul's general. But these days, there's no one else for the Judean upstart to fear. It's supposed to be safer now.

Ziba's eyes go deeper, his face cooling. "What is that?" Aghast, he snatches at my collar, finding what he'd overlooked before. His attention shifts to my face, and a layer of restraint drops away from his anger. "Where did you get this?" He lifts the ring, holding it in front of me.

"I gave it to him," Ama says before I can answer.

Ziba turns on her, incredulous. "How could you do that? Look around you, woman! Do you think there's any protection out here for a son of Saul? Or for anyone who harbors him?"

Ama wraps her arms tightly around her elbows. "He's not the son of Saul. He's the son of Jonathan."

Ziba faces her squarely. "Jonathan is dead. Anything of his should have been buried with him. You think you've been the one protecting the boy all these years? It was me." He paces in front of Ama while his sons hide disgusted smiles. "*I* kept him hidden from men who would try to kill him. And what do you do? You give him something more dangerous than his name."

Ama's mouth trembles. "No one's expecting him to have it. But he deserves to. His father saved it for him."

"What a nobleman," Shaphat interjects, joining his brother's laughter. "He and Saul didn't save much else, did they?

Their failure set our people back eight years, making us grovel for our own land."

Ziba chortles agreement, turning back to me. "What did you tell that spy? Have you ever seen him before?"

I clench my fist around the ring, afraid he'll take it. "Yes, but—"

"Did you tell him your name?"

"He didn't ask." No one does.

Ziba bends, his brows lifting. "And if he had, what name would you have given him?"

"Yatom." It sticks in my throat. It's the name he gave me as a cover years ago when we had to stay in hiding. It means *orphan.* I hate it.

Ziba's gaze imprisons mine. "You understand why I called you that?"

"Because I—"

"Because as Mephibosheth, you're helpless against scavengers like that one." He points at the hills, and Japhia snickers.

"Like a lame horse when the wolves come."

Ziba straightens, looking at me like I've been caught in a serious crime. "I've kept you safe all these years with that name. I let you be known as the son of my sister. And now all it will take is one Amorite seeing the marks of Saul around your neck."

"Brother…" Ama placates, her words tumbling with haste. "I'm sure he didn't tell them anything. And no one else knows he's here. All anyone is talking about in the markets is David. They're saying he has enough support now to unite all the tribes. If he can do that, the ravaging will stop. There will be no more bloodshed."

The restraint leaves Ziba's eyes again, uncovering something shaky. "Mark my words, Naamah. You know nothing."

In spite of the heat, a chill bites into me, as though a wolf has closed its jaws around my neck. Ziba has known too much for too long. And he still sees me as a threat to his plans, whatever they are.

Ziba's jaw locks. "The tribes may unite under that shepherd from Bethlehem, but if he rules, the danger will increase, not decrease. Every Canaanite kingdom will rise up, ready to challenge him. And kill anyone in their way." He glares at Ama.

"I have spent a lifetime trying to build a future for my sons after decades wasted under Saul, and I will not see it fall apart now. Not when we're so close."

Glancing at me, he lifts his chin at Gimel. "Get him up. And set two more men to the watch when we get back. The elders will be here after dark, and I want to know the second they arrive."

Gimel barely covers a groan before grasping my shoulders and lifting me up onto the nearest donkey. It's no struggle for the forty-year-old Amorite giant to carry me, but Ziba's servants all know I'm not the same thing as a son. Their contempt is more subtle than their master's, but I can feel it in the way they handle me. Something Ama doesn't always see.

She walks beside me, her face hidden by her veil. Ziba rides ahead with the four sons who are old enough to travel with him.

Years ago, Ziba led the handful of servants who'd escaped from Saul's house after the king's death. While Philistines consumed the land, setting up garrisons, Ziba had gained influence in secret, joining other men of Benjamin on the run. They'd hoped at first that Saul's youngest son would rule, but Ziba was the one who'd predicted his downfall.

Ish-Bosheth had barely been king of the northern tribes for two years before two raiders had killed him, taking his head south to Judah's shepherd-king David. No one had been surprised. Saul's general Abner had been the real strength behind Bosheth's attempts at leadership, but he'd also been killed by David's nephew months before.

Ziba had been almost triumphant when he'd heard of Bosheth's death, confident that he'd been right about the throne completely departing from Saul's grasp. But I'd cried myself to sleep in the dark. I'd lived on the hope that my uncle would look for me. Or that Abner would remember that Jonathan had a son. I didn't want to rule. I just wanted to be found. After that, I stopped repeating the prayers Ama taught me.

*Hear, O Israel, the Lord our God is One.*

Those words won't bring my father back. And if I'm cursed, why would Yahweh want to hear me say them?

I hold my tongue while the donkey carries me up the familiar path. Within the hills that skirt the town, there's a string of shepherd's caves built into the rocky streambed across from a few old cisterns.

Two years ago, when it looked like there would be a truce between Abner and David, Ziba had moved us out of hiding, asking Ramoth's elders if we could settle here. They've left us alone in exchange for the information Ziba obtains from his spies. He takes routine trips now, meeting with the elders when he returns. By nightfall, the cooking fires will be surrounded by men of Benjamin who flock to Ziba hoping for answers.

Ziba's watchmen whistle his arrival, so by the time I ride into the clearing, he's already surrounded. The rest of his sons swarm the center of our camp while Ziba's maid Iscah waits at a distance, holding a water jug. He greets her last, and her satisfied smile quickly fades when she sees me over his shoulder. Her lips tighten, and she whispers something in his ear.

Ziba has outlived two wives, and we all expect him to marry Iscah one of these days. "But not in a cave. Not until we can settle properly in a prominent city in Israel." He's said it hundreds of times. But that's his future, and I'm not expected to share it.

Iscah asks him all the time when he's going to get rid of me. I've never seen her help Ama, and she doesn't now, watching her draw her own water and carry it to the back cave where we sleep. She'll have work for me too, later. Mending sandals. Splitting kindling. Anything I can do with just my hands.

A sharp elbow in my ribs pushes me off the donkey, and I land hard in the pebbly dust while laughter breaks over my head.

"Don't you know how to ride?" Zarethan taunts while I struggle to straighten up, sharp stones pushing into my palms.

A few years older than I, he and Shaalbim are the ones who had dragged me outside the camp, but they've done worse. I'd foolishly tried to fight them once, after they said I would end up hanging from a wall like my father. But Zarethan held me down while Shaalbim dug into my arm with my carving knife. Shocked and humiliated, I'd started cutting myself the next day, continuing the pattern until I felt in control of the torment.

Ziba's other sons follow their example, competing with their brothers for ways to torture me. Iscah and the servants won't stop them.

"Did you miss us?" Shaalbim plants his foot on my sleeve when I try to sit up.

"I didn't." Their brother Azarel shoves between them. "Why don't you try pushing me off a donkey sometime? I dare you."

He glares steadily until Shaalbim and Zarethan saunter off. Once they're far enough away, Azarel offers me a hand, but I don't take it. It's not like I can stand. I keep my eyes down, refusing to stare at the bow slung across his body from his hunt. Ziba's been bragging about his skills for years. But all I had to do was venture to touch a bow, and the mockery started.

"What happened?" Azarel taps his chest, indicating the welt across mine.

"None of your business," I mutter, folding my arms over it. I can't decide why he acts differently from his brothers, and I don't trust it.

"Fair enough." Shrugging, he turns away to join the others.

Hoisting me over his shoulder, Gimel carries me to the strip of blanket at the mouth of the eastern cave. Back from the cistern, Ama shrugs off the heavy pack she carries into the marketplace every day. She does menial work, helping women with odd jobs until harvest, when she gleans in the elders' fields. The hair trailing out from the sides of her veil has been gray for years now. Her nails are dirty from hard labor, and she wears the dust, like me.

Ama pours water over her hands and pushes the jug up against me, but I ignore it. What does it matter? I never eat with Ziba's sons. And I'll just be filthy again tomorrow.

Crouching next to me, Ama unrolls a cloth from her belt. "I brought you food. You had so little this morning. Blessed—"

She's about to pray, but I'm already snatching at the stale bread and sour olives, my gut clenching. The scraps will only sharpen my hunger, but I can't help it. Ziba's sons are supposed to bring me portions from their meal, but I've learned not to count on that.

Ama winces, her expression pinched with sorrow. "Who did this?" she murmurs, fingering the welt on my torso.

I jerk away. "It's fine." the whip had cut right through my robe, but his curses hurt worse.

"I'll ask Iscah for some oil for it," Ama offers.

Pain knits my stomach. I don't want her asking for anything on my behalf. She already deprives herself to help me. As a child, I used to lie awake at night, watching her until my eyes burned with fatigue, afraid that something would happen to the one person who cared if I lived or died. Bent over in the dark, she would cry her eyes out, thinking I was asleep. All I do is cause people pain.

In the clearing, Ziba's sons gather near the center of camp where Iscah's built a stone oven into the base of the hill. The aroma of meat rides the scent of the cooking fires, mingling with the smell of bread. Every mealtime, every feast, I have to listen to Ziba calling each of his sons by name, praising them around the fire. But I've learned better than to wish I was one of them. They've never thought of me that way.

Japhia leaves the group and walks over, carrying a small iron pot which he sets down between two stones. Rotating his staff, he touches my face with the end. "All right, Cripple, let's have it."

"What?" My throat closes.

"I know nobody handed you a whole bag of coins. You think you can steal to get out of begging? Where's the rest of it?"

Fumbling, I hand over a few remaining *shekels* without looking up. Japhia snorts, dropping the coins into the pouch at his belt. "If you think this is all it costs to feed you, you're mistaken."

My eyes blister the ground at his feet while he kicks the pot closer to Ama. "Put some meat on his bones." Half-turning away, he adds, "Don't take long eating, Yatom. You're going to the cistern tonight."

My head comes up, dread crowding hunger from my stomach. "Why?"

His expression tightens, shutting me out. "You know the rules. You stay hidden when the elders come."

"I've never said a word!" I hate pleading with him, but not as much as I hate hiding in the dry well until the men of Ramoth leave. Being left in the dark unfolds every fear that hides in the daylight.

"I'll keep him with me, *Geber*," Ama interjects, gently placating him with the term a servant would use. "He won't interfere."

Japhia scoffs over his shoulder. "His whole life is an interference." He pats the leather pouch of money at his side. "You'd better come up with a better defense, Cripple."

Blocking him with her back, Ama settles beside me, tucking her feet underneath her robe. "I'll talk to Ziba," she promises, keeping her hand on my arm even when I pull away.

She wants to think better of her brother, but he hasn't shown her much kindness either, tarnishing her reputation to keep my identity hidden. Her old employer Palti had slept with her by force before she became my nurse, but my father never made her a concubine. I'm not her son. But Ziba has told everyone that I am by now. The fatherless cripple he has to keep track of because his sister has no man.

The ring thumps my chest again, and my eyes sting. I lift the cord, letting it drop into view. It's bigger than I remember. I vaguely remember Abba wearing it. I felt it when his fingers dug through my hair. When he'd hugged me out in the fields, saying goodbye. But the image is gone before I have to breathe again.

*Your father loved you.*

Ama's earlier words dart back, and I shrink inside. I hate how her insistence digs too deep, fighting with the contempt that's been living there undisturbed. My father isn't here to defend his feelings, whatever they were. I don't see the point in believing something I can't prove.

"Why did you give me this?" I ask Ama, sealing off my voice as soon as it starts to shake.

She stops with her mouth halfway open, considering how to answer. "It's yours, Mephi."

I flinch again, agitated. The name my father gave me is intended for royalty, or at least someone who would carry out the noble mission it implies. Ending idol worship. Defeating our enemies. Expanding into the land of Yahweh's ancient promise. That's the shepherd-king's territory now. Not mine.

Ama's hand rests on my knee. "It's long past time for you to remember who you are."

I squint up at her through my hair. Again, why?

I know what she's whispered to me in the dark, right alongside the verses of Torah that every Israelite knows by heart.

*You're the son of a prince. Warrior blood runs in your veins. Your name speaks of one who will reject all other gods but Yahweh. He has His eye on you, Mephibosheth.*

She always meant it as a comfort, but it never has been. Because what I see in the daylight underscores Ziba's words.

*You're a bastard. A target for the new king's hatred. You're descended from a wicked king who rejected Yahweh, and his sin has cursed you.*

Ama disagrees, but all I have to do is look at myself. I'm not stupid.

I fidget, staring at the ground. "Mephibosheth was Jonathan's heir. And all that died with my father."

Ama moves closer. "That ring was the only thing that wasn't taken by the Philistines after the battle at Gilboa. Your father told me to keep it for you." She gulps back a catch in her voice, grappling with something I share no memory of. She was close to my father. Did she know he wouldn't return when he left us that day?

Her arms wrapped around herself, Ama breathes deeply. "I have done the best I could for you, Mephi. I've taught you everything I know about our people and our God." She pauses, her hand closing around my wrist. "But there comes a time when every man must face the God of Israel for himself."

"We can't look at his face." I shudder, refusing to imagine it. Centuries ago, our people had begged their leader Moses to speak to Yahweh for them, not wanting to approach the mountain where He'd thundered in unrivaled power.

Ama removes her hand. "That's not what I mean. If you have not faced the fact that He made you for a purpose, you have not yet faced Him."

I gulp down the tremors bubbling in my throat, resisting the chills breaking out along my arms. Everything that men of Israel aspire to, everything that makes life worth living, Ziba has. Clan honor. Tribal leadership. Sons. What purpose can I have if all that is out of my reach?

Ama's voice drops, and I have to strain to hear it over the loud chatter around the fires.

"Long ago, Yahweh called to a shepherd from the midst of a burning bush and commanded him to lead our people out of bondage in Egypt. Moses begged the Lord to send someone else, but Yahweh's wrath burned against him, reminding him that He Himself had made the mouth that Moses claimed was too weak to lead. It didn't matter what Moses thought of himself. He had been chosen by Yahweh and had to simply obey. It has been the same for every great man of God since then. Including your father."

I release my breath, not sure why I'm holding it. Why I'm gripping my knees so tightly. These stories are life to our people. We recount them every seven days over *shabbat* meals and in multiple feasts throughout the year. But I don't see any burning bushes around here, so what does this have to do with me?

Ama grips my arm, gaining strength. "Your father stepped forward into many battles he didn't have a clear plan for. He didn't fight because he was always ready and never afraid. He fought in obedience."

And he died. I stare at Ama, hoping she can read the burn in my eyes. "I'm no soldier." I'm not even able-bodied enough to pass for a slave.

"No," Ama agrees, and then I can't look at her. At that stubborn smile that won't let go of hope and won't let me lose it. "But you're a fighter just the same. And that's why I gave you the ring. What you see around you is not the whole of your life. You will not spend the rest of your days begging for handouts or learning the ways of connivers like Ziba. It's not in you."

I wince around the smile that's forcing its way onto my face. "Why not?"

Ama catches her breath before it can slant into a sob. "You're Jonathan's son."

# THREE

*Mephi*

$$\diamond$$

I pull a deep breath into my lungs and release it in a slow exhale, again and again, resisting fear. I hate everything about this cistern. Ziba leaves me here when the elders gather, afraid one of them might see me and start asking questions. Even though they never do.

Drawing my knees to my chest, I push away from the walls, refusing to notice the way the wavering firelight dances over my head, too far away to warm me. Panic wants to reach in and torture the part of me that trembles to be left alone. It's not just the narrow walls and dry depths that frighten me. My legs trap me, as surely as if I were bound. All Ziba would have to do is walk away, leaving me here. And I'd be stranded.

I grip my father's ring with both hands, trying to pull some warmth from the metal. Hating how helpless I feel. I'll struggle against Ziba's grip, resenting his hold over me, but the night shadows bring every ounce of terror back to dance on my nerves until I'd do anything to have him nearby. That night in the ravine had torn through any childhood mirage of safety, leaving each one in shreds all around me. And no amount of Ama's comfort could ever stitch them back together.

*You're a fighter.* Her words are kind lies, barely soothing my mind's tremors.

At my age, my father was already preparing to fight the Philistines who were threatening Israel's borders. And I'm trapped in a cistern, barely winning the war against cold, doubt, and darkness.

Fed by desperation, the words run from my mind without reaching my mouth. *I have nothing to offer anyone. Nothing. Why am I alive?*

Absently, I trace the winding scars trailing my arm. My own answer for the mystery of my existence. I'm getting more deliberate with my knife, turning it on myself when I'm finished carving. Sometimes instead of carving.

I went too deep the last time and had to lie to Ama, saying it was an accident. But it follows the same pattern as before, crooked branches of dried blood crisscrossing the older healing scars on each arm. I'd planned to stop, but then Zarethan said I wasn't really Jonathan's son; I was just a cripple who'd crawled onto his doorstep. The blade couldn't go deep enough to carve that out.

I clasp my arms around myself, listening to every breath as it pulls in and escapes, each one borrowed, offensive.

Ziba says the Judeans' king is a favorite of Adonai. Yahweh's probably waiting for David to find me and end my life publicly in retaliation for Saul's sins. If He were merciful, He would've ended it quickly and let me die in that ravine. Then I wouldn't have to sit here now, fully awake in the middle of my nightmare. Older and wiser about all the ways I can die.

Turning away from the thought, I try to make the most of the cistern's proximity to the men around the fire. Without my knife, their talk is my only distraction.

It isn't the first time they've gathered to discuss Israel's future and our place in it. For as long as they've been talking, I've been listening, hearing about the systematic slaughter of Saul's followers from the depths of this very cistern. I learned far too young that strong men like David take the world by force, while the weak ones have to bow down gracefully or suffer loss. Though, weak isn't exactly the word to describe the sons of Benjamin.

The smallest tribe of Israel is by far one of the fiercest. Our ancestor Jacob, the father of the original twelve clans, called

Benjamin a ravenous wolf, and the men sitting at the fire are no less zealous for tribal honor than our fathers were. But honor doesn't always bind wounds. I can hear it in the bitterness of the voices above me.

"No one else has been beheaded. Praise be." Ahaz's tone pricks my spine, referencing every grisly story I've heard in the past few years.

Benjamin has taken the worst of the losses since Saul's death, first at Gilboa when the Philistines wiped out half the army, then in the fighting with David that followed. We put our hope in Abner and Bosheth, only to watch them soak the ground in blood, losing thousands to David's reputed mighty men before succumbing themselves.

"There's no one left to behead," Jarah mutters, and I hear wine being sloshed into his cup. "David has the rest of Saul's family backed into a corner. Merab's sons won't be able to leave Meholah. Rizpah's children will be watched too. They'll all end up dead."

"At least we know he won't kill Michal." Unsettled agreement rises to meet Bichri's sour comment.

Ama hadn't said much when we got word that David had made Abner return Saul's daughter to him. My aunt Michal had married David when they were young, but after he fled Gibeah, Saul gave her to a man named Palti. Ama had served in their household during that time. Before Palti slept with her, and Michal sent her away. That's when my father hired Ama as my nurse, shortly after my mother's death.

"Michal hasn't had it easy," she'd said when I asked her why David needed another wife. "It's a matter of honor. And power. A king needs to prove that he can hold onto what's his. And Michal was married to David first. Her union with Palti was unlawful."

Another one of the sins staining my grandfather's legacy.

After that, I'd assumed David would be king, even though Bosheth was still alive at the time. I didn't think I would feel so much grief over my uncle's death.

"Well, it's out in the open now. The official word has gone out. The elders have been summoned to Hebron." Gedor, the chief elder of Ramoth, always speaks with authority, confident in his city's good standing with David. "We've sent seven of our own to meet him."

"Jabesh-Gilead has prepared a substantial gift to take with them," Azrikam adds. "At least seven priests wait to bring the Word of the Lord to bear on any decision that arises. Within a fortnight, David ben Jesse will be crowned king of all Israel."

I shift on my knees, listening for Ziba. Usually, the elders question him first about what his spies have learned. But this time, he remains quiet, leaving me wondering what he went after this time.

"The only thing David should be ruling is sheep."

I recognize Shemei's belligerent tone. The only surviving son of Saul's armorbearer Gera has nothing good to say about David.

"That miserable shepherd has been undermining the reign of Saul since his youth. If he was a true servant of the king, he would have died in defense of him on Gilboa. As my father did. Instead, he ran to the Philistines. And now, we're going to hand him control of our northern cities as well as Judah?"

I hear a hissing splash, probably Shemei tossing his drink in the fire.

Gedor raises his voice. "He ran to the Philistines to stay out of Saul's reach. He spent years double-crossing them, wiping out whole raiding parties without their knowledge while claiming to be fighting in the Negeb. It was genius, really. A way to fight for his people while on the run."

"Saul should have killed him in the wilderness," Shemei snarls.

"And then where would we be? Use your head, man," Jarah reproves heavily. "The fact remains, Saul lost a crucial battle, opening the door for the Philistines' involvement here these past several years. He deprived countless Israelites of their sons and their fathers. Like it or not, David is our best chance at uprooting Philistia's poison from our midst once and for all."

Ahaz chortles, "Have you not heard what they used to sing about him? Saul has slain his thousands, and David his tens of thousands."

I cringe as some of the men repeat the song that drove my grandfather mad. David had become legend after defeating a Philistine giant named Goliath. In a jealous rage, Saul had attacked the young warrior, determined to kill him. Instead, half the nation went after the shepherd, hiding out with him in caves all over the Negeb until Saul's death finally gave Judah the opportunity to crown David in Hebron. Seven bloody years ago.

I'm the first generation in a long time to have grown up without fighting. Being trained for war seems preferable to living on the run, never knowing where you'll settle or what belongs to you. Still, the thought of lifting a sword against an attacker turns my blood to ice.

Would I do it if I could walk? Would some wild survival instinct take over, or would I just stare death in the face and take the blade myself? I've dreamed of battle before, but it's always shrouded all around me, reduced to sounds and sensations while I remain trapped on the ground without weapons.

The mood throughout Israel has been lighter these days. For the first time, people believe that we might see the end of Philistine control in the near future. But we have to establish peace between our clans before touching the enemy garrisons.

"And what of our honor?" Shemei continues. "You think that Judean will do credit to all the men who lost their lives?"

"This is why we have gathered, Shemei." Gedor's tense patience coaxes him to understand. "We cannot expect Israel to prosper under a new king unless the tribes are truly united. If we try to resist David's rule, we will only intensify the conflict and weaken the nation." He lowers his voice reverently. "Whatever you believe, it is widely accepted that David does not move on his own. He is commissioned by Yahweh."

"Agreed. Success follows him wherever he goes. We cannot undermine David and expect to defeat the Philistines."

"I'm relieved to hear you say that, Ziba." Gedor leaves his statement open, his tone implying he has more to say.

Ziba laughs lightly. "I don't intend to join any army of David's myself. I only seek a future for my sons. Any one of them would be willing to fight to rid this land of our enemies. I am confident that it could happen within the next ten years if David continues to be favored by Yahweh."

"I'm not speaking of your sons just now." A new sharpness slides into the elder's tone. "There was a rumor for a while that you had taken a surviving child of Saul's from the house of Jonathan."

Gedor's words hang there, taking every sound except the snap of the fire. A fierce burn stings my face, rushing into my ears so that I have to strain for Ziba's answer, which takes far too long.

"There's only my crippled nephew. The bastard son of my sister. I've always provided for him. These hills are no place for an unmarried woman with a useless son."

I expect it to end right there. Where Ziba always ends it. But this time, the elder pushes further.

"That's what you've told us. But we've never seen this boy who's supposedly crippled. And more recently, our spies intercepted a message written in your hand. No telling how long it circled the countryside before it reached us."

I hold my breath as the crackle of an unfolded parchment joins the murmurs around the fire. Azrikam drones the words, but each one adds to the inferno in my chest.

"Abner ben Ner, in response to your inquiry, a son of Jonathan still lives, crippled in both his feet. While not fit to rule, he remains under my protection until you choose to send for him. I only ask for restitution of my father's land, which Saul took from me in payment for his debts."

The elder smears the last words together and stops midsentence, clearly more interested in the beginning. I feel like I'm drowning, but the rush consuming my ears is more fire than water. It was a secret! Ziba had sworn us all to silence, taking my name and inventing a new history to keep me from being found. All the while, he was telling people. Just the ones he deemed necessary.

Sickness twists through me, edging up into my throat. Who else knows? Am I supposed to believe Ziba wasn't planning to use this against me? Of course he was. The question is how and when, not if.

Ziba's tone is hard and defensive. "What is it you want from me? I was honor bound to the first king of Israel and also to my family. What was I to do with a boy that every Philistine raider would have been looking for, to say nothing of David's hothead nephews?" Ziba's voice rises, and Ahaz hastens to conciliate him.

"We're not criticizing your motives or your actions. It is more than probable that the boy would have died without your help. But now, we must keep our eyes on the present. It's no secret that Benjamin and Judah have been at odds over David's rise to power, but the time for putting tribal affinities over the nation's welfare is long past. Only a united Israel will rid us of the Philistines."

Ziba's voice lifts. "I am in agreement. What David is truly made of still remains to be seen. But I agree that no one else has the capacity to rival him."

"And yet, we still haven't seen this boy that you've spoken of."

Ziba's seconds of silence feel like hours. "What is there to see?"

The elder's tone darkens, heavy with accusation. "You sent that message without regard for who might discover it and trace it back here, to us. At a time when the country had never been more divided over the house of Saul." Other men join in, folding one rumbled opinion over the next.

"What are we to make of your secrecy?"

"For years, you hid the boy's identity, claiming he was the son of your sister."

"I had no choice!" Ziba's voice deepens, all the respect gone from it. "As you say, the enemies of Saul are still numerous. How do I know you wouldn't have offered us up to any of them?"

Gedor stands. "Again, your motives are understood. We only want your word that you do not intend to try to make Jonathan's son king, out of zeal for the house of Benjamin."

The elder's suggestion silences every sound at the fire, freezing the beat in my throat. It's as if a door has been thrown open, and I'm wondering whether I'll die if I approach it.

My whole life, my existence has been viewed as a risk. A danger, because of the enemies my grandfather left in the ruins of his kingdom. I've been told I have to go lower, keep hidden to stay alive. Never have I heard an implication that I might rule. The possibility has never entered my mind. And it imprisons every one of my senses.

Until Ziba's scorn shreds the silence.

"The son of Jonathan is no more fit for the throne than a dog would be. He's no threat to David's rule."

"He is crippled, then? Or is that part of your story?"

I flinch, picturing Ziba's reaction to the implication that he would lie. It's not that he wouldn't. He's just a smarter liar than they think. My defenses rise up sharply, anticipating his response.

"Gimel, bring the boy."

It's pointless to huddle against the wall, but I do anyway. I'm horrified that he would do this. After years of making me live under a fist of fear, he's going to expose me just to absolve himself of responsibility! I always assumed that no one would bother to dig deep enough to discover who I am. What will people do when they find out? I no longer believe Ziba will protect me. If I ever did.

"Hurry up, boy," Gimel mutters over the mouth of the cistern, tossing a rope.

I wrap it around my ribcage, winding the ends through my hands for a good grip. The rope yanks, and I fight the cistern's rough edges all the way to the top, where Gimel hauls me over to the fire, dropping me at Ziba's feet.

A dozen darkened faces meet mine over the flames. I won't look at Ziba. He may continue to keep me, but he's not my guardian anymore. The fact that he was willing to expose me now tells me he was already planning to get rid of me. The betrayal is enough to bend my mind in half. My muscles clench, shrinking from danger I can't fight against.

One elder steps forward. "Stand up, boy."

I lose another breath, shocked by his boldness. They really don't believe Ziba. I retreat inside myself, considering it. I've pulled myself up against the cave wall before, digging my fingers deep into grooves I'd carved. And when Zarethan left me outside our camp, I'd forced my legs under me several times. With only the wasteland to hear me, I wasn't ashamed to scream in frustration when my body wouldn't cooperate. But the last time I tried to stand in front of anyone was weeks after the physician had left, and Ziba insisted he had fixed me.

I'd pushed past the pain in my ankles until I was exhausted, but I couldn't make them hold my weight. That's when Ziba decided I was cursed because of Saul's blood. I'd cried in the darkness of the cave where no one but Ama could hear me.

"You're not cursed. They have no right to lay this at Yahweh's door," she'd insisted.

But she couldn't reach inside and remove what had been pressed into me like a brand. She couldn't make me walk.

My fingers grind into the dirt, the slow burn of shame fueling my anger. Leaning into my fists and knees, I plant my bare feet under me and rock back onto them. All I have to do is straighten up, lift to my full height, and defy them all. But I can't.

Tired of waiting, Gimel grasps my collar, hauls me upright, and lets go, allowing my legs to collapse under my weight.

A low chorus of dismayed sounds rumble toward me, pulling fire through my veins. The burn moves into my face, stinging the edges of my eyes. I can't even walk away to escape their scrutiny.

"You see?" Ziba's tone shakes me with the urge to retaliate. But the last time I tried to challenge him, he'd torn a willow branch and left my back so raw I couldn't sleep for days. My fingers itch for my knife. I can always carve my hatred somewhere. I swallow, forcing the poison back down my throat. *Later.*

"I see." The elder's tone is quiet, completely lacking the triumph in Ziba's. He steps closer, bending his head. "Are you the son of Jonathan?"

I want to laugh, but everything hurts too much. The son of Jonathan would have been able to fight any one of them. He would have been trained to command thousands, like David. I don't look up.

"I'm nobody," I mumble. And I've never believed it so much before now. Something shudders in my chest when I say it, shifting the burden of hope that Ama has held me to.

Ziba's arm hangs down, his fingers touching my shoulder. "He doesn't remember the court. He knows nothing of that life. All he knows is that I've helped him survive."

Gedor folds his hands, dragging his tongue over his teeth. "And do you intend to keep him with you? If you're wanting any kind of position under the new king, it might not be wise."

"I have nothing to fear from David," Ziba mutters.

"Of course not," Azrikam rejoins. "But if you intend to resettle in Gibeah eventually, there could be others who do not look kindly on your efforts to spare him. I would distance yourself if you can. Let the house of Saul rest in peace."

Ziba's head comes up. He's tired of their advice. "I'm taking him to Lo Debar. I've had my spies keep an eye on the servants of Saul who are also known to David. Many of them have had their property restored in return for gifts they gave the shepherd while he was in exile. Lo Debar has nothing David wants. He'll leave them alone."

The name of the town closes like a fist around my throat. Lo Debar means *no pasture.* Another empty wasteland east of Israel where I'll be kept like a broken trophy.

"That would be ideal," Gedor agrees quickly. "Leave him with someone who can afford to keep him and won't let anyone ask any questions."

"And if the king decides to search for him?" Zimri questions.

"I will take care of it. The responsibility will be mine." Ziba's flat tone closes the matter.

"Good. Travel as soon as possible while David is occupied in the south. Once the Philistines discover that he wears the crown, they will rise against him, and the roads won't be safe."

"They're not safe even now. There's a contingent of Amorites outside the city. I'd post an extra guard if I were you," Shemei offers.

Arms folded, Ziba nods at Gedor. "Burn the letter."

Gedor hesitates only a second before tossing the parchment into the fire. His eyes touch me briefly before he flicks them away.

"There." Ziba lifts his hands. "He's invisible again."

He lifts his chin at Gimel, and in a few minutes, I'm dumped back in the cave. Ama is awake, waiting to unfold a heavy sheepskin over me.

"I heard," is all she says at first. Her heavy silence tells me she's known about this for a while. "I know you don't want to, but you have to trust Ziba," she finally ventures. "The man he mentioned will treat you well."

I pull my shoulder out of her grasp. Why should he? I'm just unwanted baggage Ziba has to discard before anyone knows he was involved. I'd be a fool to think anyone else would want me. I shudder, everything I couldn't say still trapped under my tongue, defenseless. Even for all my resistance, that's what I am.

"You'll be safe in Lo Debar," Ama insists, but I turn away from her.

Invisible isn't safe. And safe is a lie.

I pull the sheepskin up to my face, but the warmth won't touch the coldest part of me. The part that gapes hollow from Ziba's words. Because he speaks as though I were dead too. As if I had died out on those hills with my father.

# FOUR

## Mephi

---

*When Yahweh is with you, your arrows will fly on the wings of the wind.*

I know I'm dreaming because my father's voice is clearer than I've heard it in years. I don't see anyone, but I'm certain it's him. No one else would say that to me. The relief shaking free in my chest is almost painful, scattering every shred of fear like chaff in the wake of a storm. I look around wildly, trying to see him. Trying to find him. But I'm in an actual storm. The wind's fury is intense, whipping against me, tearing at my clothes.

"Where are you?"

I think I hear him again, and the strength surging through my legs almost makes me sob. I'm definitely dreaming. I feel like I could run to him. But I'm trapped, pinned between two boulders that I can't pry apart. The wind is winding tighter, stealing every other breath.

"Abba!" I shout, but the tempest carries my voice away. Maybe he was expecting me to fight. He said something about arrows.

"Abba, I don't have any weapons. You have to help me!"

Panic erupts in my chest, and I start to see flashes in the wind. Spearpoints. Blades. It's like every other dream, where war is pressing close and I can't fight back.

"Help me!"

Instantly, a man steps out of the storm, as calmly as though he doesn't feel the wind writhing through his purple robe. He bends down, eyes open wide in my direction. "Jonathan?"

I shake my head, trying to decide who he is. Dark, curly hair pulls from beneath a gold band. A long medallion with the face of a lion hangs over his chest. His eyes look deeply into me. But he's a stranger. I don't know him at all.

"I-I'm not Jonathan. I'm..." Why can't I say my name? Urgency screams inside me, but something right behind it tells me to stay silent. *Don't tell him. Don't trust him.*

"Who are you?" The man seems intent on my answer, almost pleading, but I'm hearing something else now. Feeling my shoulder shake.

"Yatom. Wake up."

The wind is gone, and the cave is shrouded in darkness, but Japhia's form looms on the opposite wall, backlit by his torch. He bends over, nudging me. "Wake up."

Grasping the rock shelf just above my head, I pull myself up, fresh fear shaken awake. I'm not sure if I'm still dreaming, but Japhia never comes for me in the night. And never dressed for battle. His leather armor vest is bound around his torso, and his forearms are encased in the greaves Ziba makes me polish. His sword bounces at his side, strapped to his belt.

Ama hovers behind him, wrapped up in her shawl. "What is it?"

"Raiders. Possibly Amalekites." Japhia tosses the words over his shoulder.

Even in the dark, I can see the way Ama's expression turns hollow, fear gaping from her eyes. Then, I hear it. Actual shouts and clashes, the sharp pop and release of arrows. It's as though my dream crawled out of my mind and took up arms outside the cave. Much too close.

"It's a local band. No more than twenty. We'll get rid of them, and if they push too close to the town, the watchmen will call for help." Japhia shoves his torch at Ama, then bends down to grab my collar. "If they see you, they will kill you. Stay hidden at the back of the cave and wait for us. Understand?"

I nod, unable to stop my eyes from widening in alarm. Ziba has enough sons and servants to keep the raiders occupied. They shouldn't push into the caves. But it's been a long time since we've faced a raiding party head-on. The uncertainty of the outcome digs into me, uncovering all the fear that's been sleeping since the roads became safer.

"Japhia, we have no weapons!" Ama's voice cracks after him. But he's already jogging for the cave's mouth.

"I'll send someone. If the raiders get close, ride into town."

Ama's exhale turns into a long, breathless moan. Amalekites killed her parents long ago, and the rapacious remnants my grandfather failed to destroy still ravage the land, even this far into eastern Ammonite territory. But it's been years since we've been directly threatened.

Ama holds her head for a few seconds, then crouches beside me, pulling me against her. I'm chilled by how small she feels. If I were on my feet, I could probably set my chin atop her head by now. But I can't do that. I can't stand up to defend her or to protect myself. And she doesn't expect me to.

My mind pulls away from her arms, wondering if I could find my knife in the darkness of the cave. I've thrown it against the gate before, but my aim isn't very good. Would I be able to use it before it would be used against me?

Ama leans her face into my hair, whispering thickly, "Adonai, grant us *chesed*. Spread your protection over us, and let destruction pass us by."

Focused on the beat of Ama's heart against my ear, I bite my tongue, hoping she can't feel the doubt tensing my body. Had my father prayed before facing death on Gilboa? Every rendition I've heard of that battle centers on Saul's suicide, lumping all his sons together with him as a collective failure. No one ever said my father took his own life. But somehow, the thought of being connected to such despair leaves me frozen. Why was I spared the ravages of the Philistines only to wait for death now?

Ama's grip tightens when pounding footsteps enter the cave, but Gimel doesn't wait for us to ask questions.

"We have to move. Quickly. They're pushing too close." Gimel pulls Ama to her feet. "You need to get into Ramoth. Ziba left a mule for you at the far end. He'll ride to meet us when it's safe."

Ama stumbles over the uneven cave floor. "What about Iscah and the children?"

"There are plenty of servants with Iscah. I'll stay with you."

Gimel wraps his arm around my waist and lifts me over his shoulder. But the hasty concern in his usual gruffness touches an undefined fear at the back of my mind. He's never shown so much alarm where I'm concerned before. Is the fighting that bad? Everything is happening too fast for me to decide. All I can do is let him carry me.

The back of the cave slants up into a narrow opening, and Gimel shoves me through, leaving Ama to scramble up behind us. On the other side of a screen of trees, moonlight spills into the clearing, lighting the path that winds back to Ramoth.

I barely see the mule before Gimel is lifting me onto it. Once I straighten up in the saddle, my eyes lock onto half a dozen dark-bearded strangers on horses. Surrounding me. My heart kicks me in the ribs, but Gimel yanks the mule's halter aside, blocking Ama's way. A man slaps a bag of coins into Gimel's open palm, and the servant hands over the reins, muttering, "Get out of here, quickly."

"What are you doing?" Ama shrieks before Gimel turns on her.

He slams her against the edge of the cave, his other hand gripping the sack of money against her wrist. "Move, and the boy dies."

"Don't touch her!" Panicked rage has my body in a fiery grip, and my fingers are biting into the saddle horn. The animal is sidestepping now, jerking its head away from the raider's attempts to grab him. "Just stop! Leave her alone!"

"She'll live. If you come with us." One of the raiders leers at me from the ground. His eyes are like two shining pieces of basalt within the cavern of his turban.

"No!" Ama screams. She's throwing her whole weight against Gimel, but she won't budge him. Her wild eyes meet mine over his shoulder. "Go! Mephi, go!"

I gasp, the shallow air barely hitting my lungs. Jagged shards of panic dig into my thoughts, scattering them. But Ama's scream ignites some instinct in my body, and I shove my heels into the mule's sides.

I hold on as the animal darts through the line of waiting warriors and scrambles up the nearest hill. Rocks crumble beneath us, and I grasp for the reins, yanking sideways until the mule clears the trees, reaching a semblance of flat ground.

Now, he's running under me, heading for the plain at the west end of Ramoth. We're still not close enough to attract the guards, but if I make it to the gate, the watchmen will see me. Shouts ride the wind, and the chaotic rumble of hoofbeats chases after me as the others gain ground. I've never ridden this fast, and the wildness is taking my breath, unraveling any clear thought and flinging it behind me into the night.

The darkness has spun the landscape into something unrecognizable. Or maybe it's the terror twisting my vision. I just have to get away. I have to get help for Ama. The shock of leaving her behind with a traitor scorches my senses, making it hard to hold on. How long was Gimel planning this?

The mule rears up sharply as another rider angles in too close, darting out ahead of us. Grabbing a handful of mane, I manage to hang on when the animal plunges back to all fours. But I can't control him anymore. He's bucking, spinning from side to side as we're hemmed in by other riders. They slide into a tight circle, and I see six armored shapes on all sides. Five bows sighted at me.

"Get down, boy." One man dismounts, moving toward me with measured steps, like a hunter. The other men tighten the circle while my mule shakes its head, stamping nervously.

The pulse of fear drives back and forth between my ribs. I can't get off without showing them I'm crippled. Amalekites or not, these scavengers take captives for one purpose—slavery. If they see that I can't walk, I'm as good as dead.

Cold sweat claws my body, turning my fingers slick against the saddle horn, but I can't move. The man reaches up and grabs the mule's halter. Once he has it, another raider springs to his side and yanks my wrist.

Unable to catch myself, I hit the ground hard and frantically pull myself away, hoping to deceive them for a moment longer.

"Stand up!" The raider drags me up onto my feet, but when my legs buckle, the coldness of his laugh paralyzes me. "That explains why you weren't fighting."

"Please—" I gasp, edging away, but I can't get anything else past the tightness in my throat. It's all attacking me from the inside. If Gimel handed me over, does that mean Ziba won't come after me?

The men press closer, and my eyes dart wildly from one to another. The crescent emblem of the Amorites hangs over one man's chest. They're not Amalekites. But does it matter?

"Don't damage him too much. He's broken already."

The raider's smirk is like a burn on my skin, and he lets me feel it fully before he unsheathes his sword, turns the hilt, and knocks me out.

# FIVE

## *David*

---

My first waking breath scatters my dreams, and a slice of sunlight winks at me through the tent canvas. After so long in Hebron, it doesn't take me long anymore to get my bearings. I turn onto my back and let the trill of early birdsong tug me awake.

I haven't dreamed of Jonathan in years. Actually, that's not true. If I kept a record of my dreams, I'd find my old friend more times than I could count. He's a part of this journey that's brought me here. But my visions have taken on new life these days.

I stay still for a moment, letting the images fold up behind my eyes. I no longer try to make sense of them myself. Yahweh will weave them together and reveal what I need to know. For now, it's more important to listen. In the quiet, I still hear the echoes of the voices from the glade in Hebron.

*We are your bone and your flesh. Even when Saul ruled, it was you who led Israel in her battles. It was the Lord Himself who named you a prince over our people.*

I remember the prophet Nathan's eyes glowing like embers. "Shepherd them, David. Yahweh has raised you up."

The burn reignites in my eyes. I cry so much easier now than I did as a youth. Not only for all the death I've seen, but also for the life that's opening before me. Every promise Yahweh has made coming into view.

I stare through my tears at the woven ceiling over my head. "Who am I, Adonai, that you have brought me this far?"

The answer folds around my whisper even before it leaves me.

*You are Mine.*

My heart swells, expanding to take it in. The God who formed the universe I love, with all its stars and hills and rivers—the Chief Shepherd of Israel has chosen to pour His love into me like anointing oil filling a cup. He has been my strength and my song, guiding me every step of the way down this stormy path from my father's pastures to the throne of Israel. As He promised.

As Jonathan said He would.

I stand up and let the wool coverings fall to the floor, stepping out into the clearing beyond my tent. Over Hebron's green hills, the morning stars sing in the pale dawn, and I breathe deeply to let their music in. As badly as I want to sleep out here, I know why I don't.

All I have to do is stand in the forest in the middle of the night, and I'm back in Saul's war camp, plucking my harp strings before the fire while Jonathan lounges on the other side, waiting for my voice to crack or for me to trip over a fingering. His teasing never hurt, always tempered by the force of his love. He was my brother.

I fold my arms over the ache in my chest. In those early days after his death, I'd wake up lunging for my sword, only to stab a wall or a tent peg instead of the Philistine who'd killed him. Joab had removed my weapons and posted more guards after that, quipping that I'd need my own harp player now that I'm king.

Distracted, I look out over Hebron's valley, fascinated by the way the pale moonlight fills up Jacob's ancient well in the fields beyond my camp. Fires across the landscape illuminate the tents of the faithful followers who've journeyed here to crown me. After seven bloody years, the elders of the other tribes have finally united with Judah under me. But right now, I'm seeing another forest, a different time.

Back in Horesh, on the run from King Saul, I'd been burdened beyond my strength, unable to see beyond the walls of the cavern I was hiding in. I had cried out to God so many times that I feared the cave would start echoing back.

"Bring my soul out of this prison, and I will give thanks to your Name!"

I was drawn to the promises that made my heart bleed, aching for fulfillment I feared might never come. Because Saul still lived, and I wasn't going to kill him in order to achieve my kingship.

And then Jonathan came.

Saul's son hadn't forgotten me, and for some reason that helped me believe that Yahweh hadn't either. The faith Jonathan revived in my heart has refused to weaken again, even when I realized he wasn't coming back. But my faithful Shepherd has tended my wounds, and I'm finally able to sleep. I've been able to let go of Abner and Bosheth, knowing their deaths weren't at my hand. My men rest easier. And in the silence, I hear Israel calling.

Yahweh's presence has grown closer, heavier. Songs pour from me in the daylight, filling cups of praise that I've stored away from nights dreaming with Him. It's happening—what

Jonathan and I talked about so many years ago. Building Israel. With Yahweh as the foundation. Walking out that dream makes me feel as though my brother is still alive.

But tonight, I saw him younger. He appeared in my dream with the same tangled raven hair, the same dark eyes that could overflow one minute and hold you in a death grip the next. But he was much younger this time, without the graying beard and the extra creases around his eyes. Without the arrow wounds and the royal robes. He was huddled on the ground, half of him hidden by massive rocks.

I grip the medallion around my neck, my fingers tracing the shape of the lion's face on its surface. "It's his son, isn't it, Adonai? I still haven't found him."

Agitation winds back through me. Seven years ago, I dreamed of a boy trapped under rock and understood it was Jonathan's lost son. Seven years! He could be dead by now. I walk over to the pool where I was crowned, shunning the possibility.

"I promised Jonathan I would look after his family. I didn't want to fail him in that, Adonai. What am I missing? What can I do?"

*Wait.*

Sensing the distinct breath of the *Ruach,* I pause, recognizing the staff of the Shepherd guiding me away from the edge. I've gone off it before, losing my peace to the pull of man's opinions and expectations.

The past months have been chaotic—reclaiming Michal, losing Abner and Bosheth, quenching the tumult of Joab's vengeance after Asahel's death. But every time I've sought Yahweh's instruction, I've emerged victorious. I close my eyes and feel the crashing settle. When it does, truth soothes my mind like oil closing a wound.

The God who built strength into Jonathan cares more about his son than I ever could. He will guide me until I find him. In the meantime, there's so much to do. There's a city to be conquered, a kingdom to be established.

There's life in Yahweh's path. And God help me, I will walk it until the day I die. Barely moving my lips, I alter the question, shifting my focus.

"What now, Adonai?"

And the answer reverberates in my bones, winding fresh cords into my heart.

*Zion.*

# SIX

## *Mephi*

———◆◆◆———

Pain hums in the back of my head, prodding me awake.

Feeling the unsteadiness of the animal's gait beneath me, I catch myself abruptly, certain I'm about to pitch to the ground. But rough hands hold me up. Other legs squeeze mine on either side. My vision blurs, smearing light and landscape together. Terror stabs behind them, forcing me to focus. *You're not safe.*

Blinking furiously, I look around, but I don't recognize a thing. Why should I? The last time I traveled, it was in a cart, under cover of darkness. Ever since then, I've been staring at the gate of Ramoth-Gilead. But the town has disappeared. I don't see any trees. This is just another empty wilderness path, leading to some hidden camp in the eastern Arabah. What matters more is the men who surround me.

More than twenty ride at a steady pace all around. I'm riding one of their stolen Philistine horses, with a raider up against me. Ziba's mule follows, tied behind another mount.

Their relaxed trot tells me the men aren't afraid of being followed. At least not yet.

Tension shoots pain through my eyes again. Even if I could walk, I'd never make it anywhere before they shot me. They're not Amalekites. They're Amorites, like Gimel. I'd never paid attention to his heritage before, but now it makes sense. How long has he carried that plan, waiting for a chance to betray me? And why did they take me alive?

Then, I see Becorath riding just ahead of me to the right, and my stomach clenches. His deep-set features look foreign now. It doesn't matter that we spent a year talking at the gate. He's not of Israel, and he wants something from me. Perhaps he always has. Still, I'd allowed myself to believe he cared about me a little. Not quite a friend, but...

The memory still makes my cheeks sting. A year into begging at Ramoth, I'd dozed under the hot sun, only to wake up with three beggars at my throat. Even on the streets, survival was only for the strong, and no one was above exploiting my weakness. One of them held my own knife at my throat, while the other two searched my clothes for money.

I still don't know why Becorath stopped. He'd slashed his riding whip against the ground as a warning and then cut open one beggar's back when he didn't listen. Once they'd crawled away, he'd returned my knife to me, frowning at the blood on the blade.

"They cut you?"

"No." I'd snatched it back, desperately defiant. "I carve."

"You have skill," he'd whistled, his eyes moving from my bleeding wrist to the scraps of wood lying nearby. "If you don't die of infection, you could probably make some money at it."

Becorath glances back at me now, but he's probably not thinking about that. In the end, the raider lust won out. As Ziba always warned.

I study the landscape again, fresh desperation searing my lungs. I'm done sitting around waiting for everyone else to protect me. They don't. Unless it will profit them. My heart's rhythm rising, I try to think of the most desperate thing I could do.

I glance down at the items bouncing against my leg on the saddle. One of them is a long, leather-bound knife. If I were a warrior, I could snatch it and bury it in the gut of the man behind me, maybe threaten the others until they let me go. But twenty of them, armed with bows? I'm not a fool.

Still, my fingers inch toward the knife, almost on their own. Before I can reach it, the raider's hand shoots up to my wrist and yanks my arm backwards. Metallic breath puffs in my ear. "You want to fight me, Cripple?"

Burying his elbow in my ribs, he shoves me off the horse, and I hit the ground hard enough to empty my lungs. Dazed, I cough into the dirt while the men laugh, turning their horses to surround me.

"Go ahead, boy. Fight!" The raider tosses the knife down at me, and I grab it without thinking, hurling it over my head the way I've practiced. It's a reckless shot, but it flips through the air with surprising accuracy, only to be snatched mid-spin. The raider tosses it to his other hand, and Becorath pushes into the group.

"I told you he wasn't to be harmed. Now, get him back up! We don't have all day."

His servant dismounts, manhandling me back onto the horse. "You're sure Palti will want a damaged son? Ziba didn't have much use for him."

"Ziba has fifteen sons of his own. Palti was left with no heir. All he requested was that we find one that could have been his."

I don't expect an explanation, but Becorath offers one anyway, reading the utter confusion on my face.

"After his wife Michal was taken from him by the shepherd-king's men, Palti hired a few of us to assassinate David. But that proved more difficult than stealing a jeweled crest from the neck of a *Nephilim.* One man was captured, and he revealed the whole plan to David's nephew Joab."

Abner's killer. Coldness stings the back of my neck.

"After that, Palti had to go into hiding. He's kept in touch with us, sending us in search of any heir he might have overlooked."

I frown. What does any of this have to do with me?

"His maidservant Naamah might have given him a son." Becorath glances sideways. "It is more than possible that she did."

And they think I'm that son? I close my mouth. So, they *don't* know who I am. But they will, just as soon as they figure out I look nothing like this man. Unless Palti doesn't care and decides to keep me anyway. Ama says Michal was my father's favorite sister once, but I never met her or her second husband.

Becorath aims false comfort in my direction. "So, you see? All this time, you had a father. Ziba could've gotten rid of you a long time ago."

I keep quiet on the horse, feeling my father's ring pushing up toward my collar. For a second, I allow myself to imagine it. Maybe my whole life is a lie. Maybe I am just Ama's bastard son by her old master. But she wouldn't have lied to me. I'm certain of that. Emotion carves into my face when I remember her screams. I don't know what I'll do if Gimel hurt her.

Being surrounded by hostile strangers makes me realize how much Ziba's protection has supported my life, making me think it could continue, even in obscurity. He's misused me, but he's kept me alive. Something no one else owes me. The feeling of exposure yawns around me like the mouth of a grave.

We don't stop until the sun slips behind us and the ground slopes into a hillside. A brushy, sun-scorched thicket conceals a modest camp with a handful of tents and carefully- banked cooking fires. A shrill whistle announces our arrival, and several men and boys of various ages jog over to meet us. A few women look up from the fires, wearing the symbols of the goddess Asherah around their necks.

I had no idea so many Canaanite tribes still roamed the land, but I suppose the lack of leadership since Saul's death has made it easy. No one's after them to clear out of the territory. Their biggest stronghold is in Zion, south of Gibeah, where the Jebusites have built a city.

Becorath's men shadow me closely until we reach the largest tent at the far end. The sprawling structure resembles a king's dwelling on the move. I adjust my grip on the saddle horn, my fists aching from clenching so hard. Palti was supposed to be wealthy, but now he's on the run. Do I want to be tied to a man who's guilty of threatening the new king? I still have the benefit of anonymity. But Palti is someone Joab's cohorts are definitely looking for.

The servant at the door ducks inside the tent, and a middle-aged man emerges in his place. His hair is graying, but his beard is still dark. His robes are rumpled and creased. And his eyes are slanted and calculating, betraying little emotion. It's a strange instinct, but as soon as it takes hold, I believe it. He's no one's father.

"Well?" He runs a cloth through his hands and flings it aside.

Becorath dismounts, stiff with confidence. "My lord, we found Naamah in Ramoth-Gilead with her brother Ziba. And this boy."

The rider behind me climbs to the ground, dragging me with him. He holds me on my feet for a few seconds before awkwardly releasing his grip, letting me stumble to my knees.

"He can't walk?" Palti questions immediately.

Becorath doesn't answer, because it's obvious, but I already dislike this man. Every minute I look at him, he disgusts me more, assessing me like a slave they dragged over.

Palti turns his head side to side, squinting. "He doesn't look a thing like me—or Naamah. She was beautiful." He pulls a sneer through his teeth, and I want to punch him. "You should have sent a message first before snatching a cripple right out of the dust."

Becorath clears his throat. "He said Naamah was his mother."

"No, I didn't." Embarrassed, I blurt it out without thinking. "She's been with me since I was a child, but I'm not her son. I'm just Jonathan's."

Palti's craning his neck as though it hurts, but when I say Abba's name, his head snaps straight. "Which Jonathan?" A thousand thoughts toss behind his eyes.

Becorath leans around me. "The Hassar? The oldest son of Saul?"

I'm frozen, suddenly unable to say more. My father's name hangs between us in the humidity of the air. Then, Becorath's hand darts to my neck. My collar has slipped open, completely exposing my chest.

Becorath turns the ring over, his eyes changing color. He swallows twice, breathing heavily. His gaze goes all the way to my heartbeat, tripping it up.

"Do you want him, then?" One of his men addresses Palti, whose shrug feels deliberately cruel.

"Why? He's not my son, as he told you."

Becorath's jaw twitches. "Weren't you married to Jonathan's sister? Has she told David about the boy?"

He's hit a nerve. Palti turns to stone, tightening his arms in a death grip around each other. He sounds like a dead man talking, his voice hoarse and hollow.

"Michal had no use for Jonathan. He opposed our marriage and committed treason, defecting to David because of an old friendship. And he had the nerve to threaten me for touching

Naamah." His mouth twists. "Then, I had to watch them take my wife back to the Judean shepherd, leaving me with no heir. David can watch the boy die for all I care."

I feel like he's slammed a door in my face. Palti blinks, finally seeing Becorath instead of whatever memories torment him. "Your people have claims on him, don't they?"

"Yes."

One word, but it's like a fist in my stomach.

"Take him, then." Palti shrugs.

He turns away, and Becorath's grip on me clenches. I can hear his breathing, hissing in and out through shut teeth, his temper rising like mounting flames.

From behind us, one of his men clears his throat. "Brother—"

Becorath turns sharply. "Get him up. We'll ride to the next outpost and find Kemuel."

"For Gibeon?"

Becorath looks over my head. "Yes. For Gibeon."

Gibeon? My mind rushes, chilling my insides with everything I know about that clan. Saul nearly drove the Gibeonites to extinction during his reign. Of course Becorath belongs to that tribe. And the Canaanites' bloody pagan traditions are nearly as numerous as the laws of Israel. If sacrificing their own children is commonplace, why should they spare me?

Two of his men grab hold of me, throwing me over the horse again. They yank my arms straight and twist rope around my wrists, binding my hands to the saddle. Becorath climbs up behind me, kicking the animal until it lurches into rhythm, scrambling for grip on the desert trail.

I grasp the saddle horn, trying to hold onto hope as it dies inside me. I've learned to read people by the way they touch me. They're not handling me the same. I was valuable before, somebody's son. Now, I'm bound and dragged. Not spoken to.

Like a lamb hauled away for sacrifice.

# SEVEN

## *Mephi*

———————◆————————

Becorath's fingers twist around the reins, clamped tight over my wrists.

After another full day of riding, my forehead is scorched from the direct aim of the sun, but the fresh glare of danger burns worse. I've had hours to consider what they might do to me, but I still can't decide how to plead with them. It would be one thing to convince an Israelite to show mercy, at least out of fear. A man like Ziba has clan honor to think about, and the Law of Moses to govern his actions. But these men aren't of Israel. They're Amorites, descended from the one clan that hates Saul the most.

The sight of the larger camp we're approaching adds fuel to my fear.

This one looks more permanent than the last. Dozens of tents are built unevenly against the hillside, along with lines of animal pens and a half dozen ramshackle market stalls. Women sit cross-legged, weaving cloth over crude frames or heating bread over hot stones. The sight shoots pain through my stomach.

It's the second day I've gone without food, and my skin is so scorched, I don't remember the cupful of water at dawn.

Becorath's brother rides up closer, keeping his voice low. "Kemuel might not agree. You know what happened to the sons of Rimmon after they killed Bosheth. This is not the time to tempt David's wrath."

Becorath tenses behind me. "He's one cripple, not the king of Israel's northern tribes. Kemuel's own father was murdered by Saul's men. Right beside ours. Whose blood do you think will matter more to him?"

His brother glances right at me then. His expression reminds me of Ziba's the night he watched the physician rebreak my ankles. Aware of the pain. Unwilling to stop it. The truth hangs like a millstone over my chest. After years of struggling to survive, all it took was one servant's betrayal, one mention of my father's name to undo any chance I had.

My breaths coming short, I lock eyes with the Amorite. "Please, take me home." My mouth is so parched, it's a struggle to form words, and my own thirst terrifies me. Why offer water to someone you're just going to kill?

Becorath scoffs. "Ramoth wasn't your home. It didn't look like you had any."

My shoulders drop. How many times have I thought that over the years? But it was enough that Ama was there. She'd treated me like her own son, something Palti wasn't willing to do. Fresh anger pierces my stomach when I remember the careless look on his face.

As shameful as it was, I had protection before, a wall of invisibility around my father's name and my broken body. Now, both have been exposed. Sharpness prods at my eyes. What if Ziba doesn't come? I can't picture Ama resting quiet if he refuses to rescue me. But what if he convinces her I'm dead? What if she's dead, unable to tell him what happened?

Becorath bends over me, the muscles twisting in his forearms. Freeing my hands from the saddle horn, he dismounts, his eyes refusing to lift. "You should've kept quiet."

Dragging me off the horse, he snaps his fingers at two scowling servants. I can tell the men are getting tired of having to carry me everywhere. One of them just yanks the rope, letting me skid along behind him.

Growing impatient, Becorath seizes the back of my collar and catches me up under his arm. Striding ahead of the others, he carries me through the door of a large tent and throws me down in front of a heavy woven screen separating the space into two rooms. The hide and cloth walls are heavily stained with incense and spices.

Becorath snaps at the bearded servant in the corner. "Jabin, we need to speak to Kemuel, now!"

Someone's hand pushes my head down toward my knees. "Don't speak."

Bent over, I press my face into the floor and wait, wondering if they'll ever let me straighten up again.

Behind the screen, Jabin speaks to a handful of others, and an older voice answers. Something in the man's tone encourages me. It's steady, lacking the hostility I've been hearing.

The tapestry lifts, and sandaled feet step heavily in front of me. "Becorath! Tubal!" The men clasp hands over my head. Then, I feel their attention shift. "What's this?"

Becorath's voice is as tight and dry as the ropes around my hands. "He's the son of Jonathan, the son of Saul, the king of Israel."

"David is the king of Israel," the elder murmurs.

I tense on my knees, sensing him moving closer. When his hand slips under my chin and lifts my head, I nearly cry out, but he's just looking. For a few painful breaths, I stare into the elder's wrinkle-rimmed eyes, trying to find something inside them. Anything I can cling to. He's lost men because of my grandfather. But he's older and wiser than Becorath. Maybe he'll see past his own pain and realize he has a chance to stop mine.

Kemuel sighs. "Why have you brought him here?"

"Why do you think?" Becorath snaps. "You were there the day Saul broke faith with us. And the day we swore that blood would answer for blood. You said it yourself, over my father's body."

"I remember." Whatever hides beneath Kemuel's words is carefully controlled. "Why did you do this now? If you had waited, we could have spoken to the king."

"The king will not give us justice, and you know it," one of the elders says from behind. "David once lived in Saul's house like one of his sons. He will not hesitate to put his private covenants above our need for restitution."

Kemuel frowns. "But didn't Saul cast him out? David spent years trying to escape death."

Tubal steps forward. "Yes, but even from exile, David refused to retaliate. He was even willing to negotiate with Saul's general."

Jabin nods agreement. "David has other things on his mind just now, and revenge of any sort is not one of them. He intends to ride west from Hebron and take Zion from the Jebusites. If he succeeds, he'll have the Philistines on him in a matter of weeks. Tribal affairs outside of Israel will not be a priority for some time."

Kemuel sighs and holds up his hands. "Then, we are left to determine this on our own."

Becorath's arms tighten within one another. "We have always been on our own in this. I don't see why one Israelite king should care about a vow another one broke. If it was nothing to Saul, it will be nothing to David."

Kemuel fixes a cold stare on him. "Then why did he bury Abner and Bosheth? Why did he punish the men who killed them?"

"He's young." Becorath spits it like an insult. "Despite all he suffered, he's still soft. He's only interested in winning the hearts of the people."

"And you don't think he will discover what we've done?" Kemuel leans forward, his face creasing. "Haven't you heard what they say? That David was bound to this boy's father with the hand of their God? I will not see more of us die for one presumptive action. David may be occupied now, but he will certainly have an opinion about what you are suggesting."

He turns his head sternly. "We may have a right to restitution, but taking this boy's life is outside of our jurisdiction. If we do, we send a message of defiance to David and can only expect retaliation. Even now, we risk the anger of whomever you stole him from."

"He was begging outside Ramoth. He means nothing to anyone." Becorath's statement stings my skin like a hot ember.

"What is the alternative?" Tubal asks over his brother's angry breathing.

Kemuel releases a long, frustrated sigh. "Hold him until we can send word to David. Then, we can present our case to the king himself and ask for the lives we do not have authority to take."

"Are we debating this?" Becorath flashes.

"No. I'm deciding this." Kemuel steps forward, a full inch taller than both the younger men. "You have acted rashly, and we can only hope we don't suffer for it. Again."

"It was not our actions that caused our suffering the last time. It was the bloodlust of his grandfather!" Becorath points vehemently.

"His grandfather." Kemuel assesses me again before addressing his servant. "Jabin, you knew Saul and his sons. Is it certain that this boy is their blood?"

"Unmistakable." Jabin's answer surprises me, since I've never really been told that I look like my father. Coldness winds up into my dry throat again.

Tubal lifts my chin with his fist, exposing my chest. "This is Jonathan's seal ring. Only the sons of Saul wore these."

The contempt in his eyes stiffens my spine. I sit up, emboldened by a sudden shred of strength. "My grandfather was a great man. He saved Israel from the Ammonites and killed thousands of Philistines. He—"

I'm still talking when the back of Becorath's hand cuts me off. The slap throws me back against the floor, and my defenses curl away, folded up tight inside me while the Amorite spews venom over my head.

"Your grandfather was a *murderer!* With no word from your God, he ambushed our people and slaughtered them like animals! We hadn't taken up arms. We trusted him." Unruly pain shakes free in his voice, and he grinds his teeth over it. "An eye for an eye. Isn't that what your Law teaches?"

"It also says that vengeance belongs to Yahweh," Kemuel barely whispers, but the words pluck chills along my arms. Is he afraid of our God? I glance at him through the powerful sting that's consuming my whole face.

Wild breathing shoves Becorath's chest up and down, and he leans forward, pointing at me. "Saul did *not* follow Yahweh. He turned his back on Israel's God and invited His curse." His eyes move down. "Look what He's done to the boy."

My muscles jerk, shrinking back in shock. Somehow, he found a way to strike the inside of me, and it hurts infinitely worse than my face. I feel utterly exposed, as though someone's thrown back a heavy cloak I've been hiding under for years. Ziba's pushed in before, attacking me where I'm vulnerable. And my usual response was to take refuge in private anger. Cut myself. Think of little ways to get back at him. But anger is useless now. I can't fight this.

Becorath seethes, his resentment smoldering. "He should have been the son of some harlot. It would've been better for him. But the house of Saul deserves to crumble until there's nothing left."

A deep pain awakens in the center of my gut, winding sharp branches up through my chest.

Kemuel glances down at me, and his tone sharpens. "Get him out of here. Feed him. Unless you want to present a carcass to David."

Tubal yanks me up against him, and his brother turns to storm out of the tent. But Kemuel's voice grabs them at the door.

"Becorath. Tubal. I stood with you when your father died. We joined forces to fight together. If you act without me, you act alone, and our partnership is finished."

His words are heavy and unflinching, but only Tubal seems to feel them. Becorath shoves past me, heading for the outer edge of the tents where his men are waiting. "Tubal, follow!" he bellows, as the others fall behind. "Let Jabin take him."

Tubal drops me in the dust, and Kemuel's servant yanks the rope until he can grab my arm. The spot near my elbow is bruised from their grip, and the sides of my legs are rubbed raw from being dragged. My garment has frayed open at the seam, exposing my ribs.

Hauling me over to the animal pens, Jabin opens the pack on one of the horses, pulls out a chunk of bread, and drops it in my lap. I'm starving enough to eat past the tremors churning in my sides.

Jabin waits for me to swallow, then lifts my wrists to tie them off. "I wouldn't have your cursed blood for all your grandfather's gold."

"How much do you want for him?"

Ziba's voice rips into my panic, pulling a frantic gasp from my lungs. In the second Jabin's not watching, I stare up into a face that's half-hidden by a dark Canaanite cloak. But it's him.

Ziba's eyes snap a wordless warning into mine before he looks away. Clenching my fists, I refuse to move, pinning my gaze to the ground so I don't reveal anything. Just beyond Ziba, Japhia and Shaphat saunter back and forth, their aimless manner playing with the cords of hope holding me together.

"Who?" Startled, Jabin squints, taking Ziba in up and down.

"The boy." My heart punches my ribs while Ziba's gaze drifts over me with mock interest. He's probably been following me for a while, but couldn't approach before. Becorath would've recognized him from Ramoth.

"Why would you want a cripple?" Jabin's hardly paying attention, pulling the length of my rope through his hands.

"Have you seen them beg?"

Shame scalds my cheeks, but Jabin doesn't take his eyes off the rope until it's wound securely around the side of the pen. "Unless you have enough for a prince's ransom, he's not for sale."

"He doesn't look like a prince to me," Ziba mutters, unconvinced.

Jabin looks at him once, reaches in the front of my tunic, and lifts the ring.

Ziba pretends to inspect it, snorting, "He could've stolen that off of anyone, picked it up after someone dropped it. You're really going to let one trinket determine…"

"Jabin!"

At Becorath's voice, Ziba turns his back sharply, and his sons follow suit, spreading out to avoid attracting attention.

Becorath approaches with Tubal at his side. He lifts his chin at Ziba's retreating form. "What was that about?"

"Someone mistook the boy for a slave," Jabin shrugs.

Tubal rolls his eyes. "A slave would be easier to dispose of."

"There's nothing difficult about disposing of him," Becorath snaps. "Not if you learn from Saul."

Ziba turns to the side, listening.

Tubal faces his brother. "So, you're going against Kemuel?"

Becorath leans closer, snarling. "If Kemuel has forgotten what it felt like to hold his own father's dead body in his arms, then so be it. I have not. Have you?"

Tubal's expression closes. "No."

"Then keep quiet. Put the boy in your tent and guard him closely. When I give you orders, obey. That's all."

I can't see. Panic is pushing back into my vision, immersing everything in a strange white fog. I scan the crowd frantically for Ziba. After hearing such an obvious threat, I expect him to fling aside his cloak and turn on the men. He wouldn't have come here without surrounding himself with plenty of armed servants in disguise. He came knowing he would have to defend me.

But when I finally find him, he's moving away, angling through the crowd to the edge of the market. My eyes grab hold of him as fiercely as I might do with my hands, but his manner shrugs me off, forcing me to watch in silence while he walks away, leaving me to the scavengers.

Without even looking back.

# EIGHT

## Mephi

— ◆ —

I won't sleep.

Every hour, my fear sharpens with the night shadows until it's almost a visible being crouched in front of me. Breathing with me.

I've been left alone in Tubal's tent, but when the desert wind shifts the walls, a spearpoint of moonlight pushes in through the door, gleaming off the edge of a guard's armored shoulders. I might not escape this. Becorath won't wait for David.

Hour after hour, Ziba still doesn't come, and the fear that he won't bends my mind until the slightest thought is a struggle. My body aches from the tension holding me taut, and my eyes burn with sleepless tears. If I do see them again, his sons will never let me forget the way I huddled against the horse pen like a frightened sheep. My best chance for escape had been on that mule outside Ramoth, but I couldn't even make it to the gate.

If my father could see this, he would look at me exactly like Palti had, with shame and disgust. I'm no fighter. I'm a beggar. All I can do is plead for my life. And no one will listen. Because it's easier to throw money at me than to be saddled with the responsibility of my life. No one wants that. Not Ziba, not that unknown man in Lo Debar. Certainly not David.

My mind shudders around the clearest thought I've had all day. Why should I survive this? Utterly paralyzed, I stare down the question, trying to decide how to breathe around it. If I can't make a life for myself, if I can't be anything that my father hoped, or bring honor to Israel, then why should I keep breathing?

I almost scream, biting back the bitter defiance rising up. I may not have much of a future, but I don't want to end my life impaled on a Gibeonite spear. I still want to live. Can I expect to when I haven't even spoken Yahweh's Name since my capture? Can I expect mercy?

Footsteps close in on the tent, nearly soundless on the sand, and my heart freezes. I feel the heavy shapes in the dark—too weighty to be shadows. And then they pounce.

Throwing aside the tent door, thick arms grab me up, lifting me off my knees and slamming me into an armored chest. Other hands seize me from behind and yank my head back, impeding any reaction.

The distinct smirk on one of the faces pulls chills across my body. Someone clamps a heavy hand over my mouth, but I struggle anyway, trying to tear myself out of the strongest grip I've ever felt.

"We don't have all night!" a voice growls, and the men sweep me up onto a mule outside, throwing me across its back like baggage. They tie my ankles, interlinking the ropes so that I hang at an awkward angle but won't fall. Lastly, a thick cloth is tied over my head, with the rope through my teeth so I can't make a sound.

Someone slaps the mule's hide, and hooves gallop away through the dust under me, crashing into underbrush with others close behind. I cough, gasping for air and gagging on my own fear. In spite of Ziba's warnings, it's been many years since I've had to contemplate actual death. I'd always expected there to be more of a struggle. Instead, I'm just choking muffled pleas for mercy to Yahweh. Only He knows what sort of death is only steps away.

The mule stops, and my head spins when someone tears the cloth from my face.

"Over there!" a man orders, and the hands force me off to the side, slamming my back into a tree. A rope digs into my throat, holding me there, voiceless while the men wind more cords around my body, tying me to the tree so I can stand there without using my legs.

A half-breath escapes me when one of them pulls a knife and cuts into my tunic, but he stops with the cloth, slicing my robe down the middle to expose my chest. His blade lifts my father's ring into the faint bit of moonlight sifting through the branches overhead. I make the mistake of looking into his eyes, and the hatred gleaming there stops my heart.

Another man holds a parchment in front of his face and starts to read, but it takes several seconds before the words make it through the wildness of my heartbeat.

"Saul, to Malchi and the thousand at the garrison of Beeroth. The Gibeonites shall die, to purge Israel of any further Amorite influence. No one is to be spared. Show zeal for your king, and plunder their possessions for the throne." The man stops reading, and his eyes lift from the paper before he stabs it into the tree above my head.

Between the ropes crushing my windpipe and the hatred seething toward me, I can't catch a breath, let alone form a lucid thought. I don't see Becorath, but I'm certain he's one of the angry figures in the dark. The man grabs another knife and aims the tip at me, speaking to the figures in the trees.

"Two decades ago, it was our people who were bound at Saul's feet. Defenseless, while he slaughtered them one by one. Our sons. Our women." He leans close to me and shudders explode in my chest. "All the blood in your body couldn't atone for what was shed in Gibeon. But you won't be the only one to die for it."

Horrified, my deepest self pulls away, running far and fast—the way that I can't. The rest of me, the part that will suffer, is trapped against the tree gasping in the fog of terror that's dragging useless adrenaline through my limbs.

"Please—" I say it for no reason. I won't be heard. They've already made up their minds about me. To eliminate any doubts, the man slides the flat of his blade down my ribcage. "You're going to bleed to death. Slowly. Like your father."

A wave of pointless anger grips me, but there's nothing I can do with it. His hatred rushes in my ears, filling my head, but a single word drifts through the choking fog.

*Chesed.* Mercy. Lovingkindness. Unmerited favor. Every bit of meaning it carries screams against what's about to happen. There's no mercy here. What good would it do to beg for it?

*Yahweh?*

My mind grabs onto His Name like a branch in a raging river. To this day, I've never touched the side of Him that might care. I've always seen the God of my people as a distant, raging Being of fire, brooding on a mountain, waiting to take vengeance on His enemies. He flattens cities with sulfur and blinds arrogant enemy kings. But if Ama's stories are accurate, His kindness is the strongest thing about Him.

I'm grasping for it now, so fiercely that the pursuit is blocking out the terror hissing in my ears. He's my only hope. But is He listening? I've barely spoken His Name.

*Yahweh!*

I flinch when a sudden slice of moonlight parts the branches, touching me before the knife can. Then something sharper enters the air to my left.

There's a hissing whine, the heavy sound of wood slamming into bone—and Becorath cries out in the trees. Followed by his brother. A third man stumbles back, an arrow through his eye. The man with the knife looks around wildly, locks eyes with me, and slashes my side right before an arrow takes him down. The wound isn't as deep as he wanted, but it still shocks me. My body clenches, encased in ice even as I feel the hot trickle over my ribs.

Armed figures tear through the underbrush, and a familiar voice shouts orders. The sharp sound of knives cutting rope slices my nerves, and when the fibers give way, I fall flat on my face. Hands turn me over, and I stare straight into Ziba's eyes. His expression is fixed and unmoving, but it speaks more forcefully than he ever could aloud.

He was right, and he knows it. He barely gets his arms under me before the terror pushes too deep, and I can't see or feel anything.

The next time I open my eyes, there's a stinging ache pushing through my body. My hoarse cry breaks halfway out, and it takes far too long for the faces around me to take shape. My sight is spinning darkness, and my head rolls against rough bark.

Japhia and Shaphat are standing a few feet off, watching the tree line while two of Ziba's servants bend over me. One dips a cloth in a bowl, cooling my cheeks and my lips before moving to the raw skin around my wrists. Another holds a bloody cloth against my side.

"You're safe now." Ziba holds a waterskin close to me. "Drink."

My heart is still stuttering, my mind shaken to pieces, but my thirst is maddening. I gulp water until it sloshes down my chest.

Ziba pulls his belt knife and grasps a figure lying on the ground. Yanking him close, he cuts through the man's woolen cloak. Becorath's empty face falls to one side, an arrow buried in his heart.

Revolted, I flop to the side of the tree, gripped with sudden nausea, but Ziba just shoves his arms around me, binding my ribs with the cloth he cut. "Be a man for once in your life. He would have killed you if I didn't take him down."

I push back from him, my voice ripping like ragged cloth being torn down the middle. "I saw you back there in the camp. I saw you. You left me!"

Shaking enough to make my side throb, I bury my knuckles in my eyes. With my head bent, I'm unprepared for Ziba's attack.

"I *left* you?" he hisses, then grabs my chin, forcing eye contact. "Your *father* left you! He knew that he was going to his death, and he went anyway, leaving you to the Philistines. To men like that." He points at Becorath's body. "Once again, through no merit of your own, you've been given a chance to live.

Now, will you go to Lo Debar and be grateful for your life back? Or would you rather I open that cut a bit wider?"

I gape at him, unable to respond.

Ziba stands up, addressing his sons. "Let's move. The others won't be far behind us."

The sting at my side chews through my ribs when they lift me. The ring thumps against my chest, and I yank at the strand of twine, but my trembling fingers can't snap it.

Why do I still have this? It's brought me nothing but trouble. Becorath was right. I should've been born to a street woman. Or died on the night I fell. It's useless to be Jonathan's son.

I pull wildly at the ring, hating how it's bound me to a hope that isn't real, a future that died at Gilboa. Ziba's right. My father ran to a doomed battle, leaving me to the vultures that wanted to see Saul's line extinguished. He abandoned me to be hunted and hated, all because of my grandfather's sin.

Heat shoves through my veins, rising each time I try to breathe.

*I hate you. I hate you.*

My vision starts to swim, and I grip the ring harder, wishing I could fling it over the next hill and be done with it. But I won't. Because it's the only thing in my life that isn't broken. It would feel like I was tossing myself over with it.

# NINE

## *David*

———————— ••◆•• ————————

Oil lamps glow in the room behind me, but out on the battlements, my lungs are full of the sweet-scented evening air.

My new antechamber overlooks the south wall of my fortress, the stronghold of Zion, and I can see the farthest from here. Behind us, the southern mountains brood over the valley that embraced our fighting men. It's soon enough after the battle that my ears are still filled with the clash of iron and bronze, the rush of a thousand feet in full pursuit of our destiny.

The pride of the Jebusites has been leveled, their stragglers melting into the scraggly forest past the Kidron Valley. The hills beyond lump together in the inky night, looking like giants bent over on their knees.

It's the first moment of rest I've had in days, but my pulse still hums with anticipation. I feel Yahweh's smile on this place, as though my anointing lives in these walls. The powerful pleasure that poured over me with the prophet's oil has covered Zion with the scent of purpose. Israel's future will endure from this place.

The victory over Jerusalem was also the homecoming I've yearned for all these years, and my heart is full of it. But tonight, my mind is elsewhere, temporarily imprisoned in the parchment folded tight in my fist.

A northern dispatch rider brought it to me, and it's maddeningly short. Written by a spy from Benjamin's territory.

*My lord king, live forever. I believe you desire information about a son of the fallen prince Jonathan. Though I do not have the message in my possession, I have witnessed a letter sent by an unknown servant to Abner ben Ner, briefly mentioning the son you're seeking. But Abner was dead before it reached him, so I cannot say if the boy still lives. I only thought you should know.*

Concern battles with my gratitude, and I clench the paper. I've already memorized the contents, but it's still not enough. I shift my weight, my sandals scuffing the stone pavement in a gentle pace. How can the child of a prince just disappear? But even my own questions are stale at this point. I've given up voicing them because they haven't turned up any satisfying answers. Just the same ones I've been fighting since Jonathan died.

They're all dead. Everyone connected to Saul, except a few concubines and their children. Most of the servants who escaped deny working for Saul's family, and none of my spies have found any trace of Jonathan's son.

A brief, horrible thought pulls apart from the others and drifts past me like a piece of ash lifting from a fire. I fold my arms, bracing while I let it touch me. He could be a captive somewhere. But if that were the case, our enemies would've used him by now. They wouldn't hold onto a valuable hostage this long.

Gratefully, I slam the door on that possibility. Mephi's either dead too or being purposely hidden. Perhaps he doesn't even know who he is. He was a little child when he disappeared, and no close relatives remained to raise him.

I sigh heavily, picturing the unknown servant trying to contact Saul's general. If Abner had lived, I might've found Mephi by now.

"Feel like home yet?"

Abishai joins me, and the satisfaction in his face silences my questioning. Sliding the paper under my robe, I reach over and clasp my nephew's shoulder. "Once again, Yahweh has provided."

The lamplight gleams in Abishai's eyes, revealing a vulnerable awe in his aging face. He folds his arms over his iron-clad chest. "He said so little when you were anointed as a boy. Only that you were chosen for your heart. Sometimes, it all felt like a dream. Back then, did you think we would end up here?"

I want to say yes, but my mind floods with a hundred different dark memories of nights spent flinging broken songs at cave walls. I shake my head. "I knew Yahweh would be faithful. That's about it."

And now I'm witnessing levels of abundance and kindness that I never imagined I would see. It's staggering.

Yahweh has sheltered and guided me every step of the way, through every stifling year with Saul's armies, then on the run throughout Israel and into Philistia. He's brought me here and crowned me, given me the Zion fortress.

Now, new visions fill my heart—plans to bring the Ark of the Covenant to the city from its temporary home in a tent. After years of wandering in circles around these dreams, waiting for fulfillment, the rush of activation is dizzying. We have so much to do, but it's finally happening. Yahweh's Name will dwell here.

Inside the fortress, doors open and close. Abishai looks behind us. "They're starting to gather, my lord."

Returning his smile, I follow him inside.

My council gathers in twos and threes until the room is filled with warriors. I meet their eyes, letting my gratitude touch each one as they gather around the table. These men knelt beside me when a cave was our only fortress. They'd joined themselves to my future when we were fugitives, daring to believe Yahweh's Word in spite of the king who pursued us. Everyone here has earned his place and my respect.

Each man's title is a testimony to the skills they've been lending to my cause for years without recognition. My heart pulls when I see the sons of Abiathar, the priest, ready to serve in their father's footsteps. The legacy of Ahimelech, who died at Saul's hand for helping me, will be honored in his namesake, and Zadok.

Jehoshaphat and Seraiah hold pens over parchment, ready to record my words and compile them in the scrolls that are already taking up two rooms at the base of the fortress. Benaiah, the chief of the laborers, hunches over the end of the table, his massive shoulders dwarfing those beside him, even Joab.

My oldest nephew wears more scars than most. Our relationship has held all the fury of a hailstorm, and yet he's never left my side. Bold and fierce as a lion, Joab was the natural leader of my army before it functioned as such. Our establishment as a recognized force in the region has made him all the more dangerous.

More than ever, my heart yearns after Yahweh's instruction. His Word has guided me personally for years, but now that I'm king, his judgments will spell the difference between victory and defeat.

From the head of the long cedar table, I declare the *Shema*, the prayer of Israel over the men, speaking into the zeal on each face. "Hear O Israel, the Lord our God is One."

The passion wound up in the sacred words grips me with reverent fear. If I do not walk in the counsel of the Lord, how will they?

Joab lifts his chin, his dark eyes full of news, but Abiathar's smile sparks my remembrance. As long as we seek Him, Yahweh will be honored in this place, in us.

I sit down, addressing Benaiah first. "Are the laborers fully established in their duties?"

"Yes, my lord," Benaiah rumbles. "I've organized the builders to repair the south wall. Once that's finished, we can continue building up the rest of the surrounding ones, from the

Millo inward. Your wives and children have been installed safely in the north palace, and there are more than enough servants to answer their needs."

"So much for the blind and the lame keeping you out," Joab mutters. Low laughter circles the table. Our enemies' earlier threats sound ridiculous now.

The defeat of the Jebusites has worked like a spell over the neighboring inhabitants, sending foreign armies cringing out of their strongholds to pledge their loyalty to me. Hiram, the king of Tyre, has sent a generous abundance of cedar trees, along with carpenters and masons to build up my house within the city. But our work is far from finished, and I have a feeling our next order of business will take us away.

"Speak, Joab."

My general leans forward. One hand is braced against the table, while the other never leaves his sword. "The news of our success has reached Achish. Already we've received word that the Philistines are mobilizing, preparing to march in full force on the Valley of Rephaim."

The valley of the giants. Fitting.

Goliath's kinsmen will be among them. Achish's seeds of vengeance have been bearing bitter fruit, and now he has evidence that I have fully turned against him. In spite of my years hiding amongst his people as a covert mercenary, I never was and never will be his ally. Which means war.

Joab's eyes glitter. "We have reignited the fire."

I drum my fingers lightly on the table, letting my thoughts enter my mind and pull away, one by one. I've fought Achish's men for years, and there's only ever one winning strategy. I nod toward the priests.

Zadok and Ahimelech hasten to their feet, unfolding the holy *ephod* and placing their hands over it in prayer. The memory of each battle washes up against me as they murmur petitions for wisdom. Finally, Zadok's eyes glow, filling with Yahweh's answer. He looks at me, speaking for the Lord.

"Go up to the valley, for I will certainly give the Philistines into your hand."

"We are to go to Baal-Perazim," Ahimelech adds. "There, the Lord will burst through your enemies like an uncontainable flood."

"So be it." I breathe silent thanks, ignoring the sharp quickening in my chest.

This isn't the time to search for Jonathan's endangered son. This isn't the time to expose someone so vulnerable. If he's alive, he's no doubt heard of the deaths of Saul's kinsmen and doesn't want to be found. The knowledge comes with pain. I've never held back from battle. But I'm not used to delaying over something this important. Something I promised.

*We had a covenant, Adonai.*

I draw in a breath, letting resolve settle into me. He knows. He sees Mephi the same way He saw me when I huddled in a cave asking again and again if He meant for me to be king. For now, my prayers will reach out and touch Jonathan's son, if nothing else can. I close my eyes briefly, touching the space under my robe where the message is concealed.

*Go after Him, Adonai. I believe you have your eyes on him, and Your wings are swifter than mine. Make your presence unmistakable around him. Unmistakable and unforgettable.*

# TEN

*Mephi*

———◆◆◆——

I jolt out of sleep, expecting the pull of the ropes, but instead, my hands touch ground on either side of me, my fingers folding into dusty grass. I'm used to catching myself awake, clawing at the disappearing edge of a cliff that isn't there. Sometimes, I could swear my mind is still stuck out on those hills near Gibeah. Still falling.

In reality, I've just slumped over onto the ground, too exhausted to shiver anymore. It takes too much energy, and the cold is too deep for that. It's trapped in my bones, more from my inner pain than the whining night wind.

A few feet away, Ama weeps, bent over on her knees with her face covered. She's been crying since Ziba brought me back to the camp where the others were traveling, barely a day behind him. Actually, she's been crying since the night I fell, when we lost my father. The depth of her sadness tears into me, waking me up to everything else that hurts.

Rope burns circle my wrists, and bruises bloom along my arms. The deep knife wound is hot and throbbing under the bandage Ziba wrapped over it. I shift my weight off of my side, and Ama's head comes up. She crawls over and pulls me close, pain warbling her voice.

"I thought I had lost you. I thought we were going to find you somewhere or hear that you had been…" Her sob catches, lengthening into a deeper cry, which she buries in my hair. "Yahweh has spared you."

I barely resist pushing away from her. Yahweh hates me. I'm the grandson of a murderer who killed priests, and broke promises, and hunted his own warriors. Even if I close my eyes, I can't unsee the hatred in Becorath's face. My capture by the Gibeonites should have been the end. Why am I alive?

Ama squeezes my arm, avoiding the bruises. Her other hand strokes my hair. "Just sleep, all right? You're safe now."

But I'm not. *We're* not.

Pain shoves into my face, stabbing my eyes. My father ruined her life when he gave her charge of me. She's devastated by the truth that she never wanted me to know. But I felt it in the raiders' hands, in the hatred that cut into my side. I can't forget how they looked at me with empty animal eyes. I wasn't human to them. My grandfather had shed the blood of their people, and so they wanted mine.

How can I live knowing that could happen again? Am I supposed to believe that this man in Lo Debar will choose my life over his own?

Remembering, I glance across the camp, my stomach clenching. "Where's Gimel?" I haven't seen him since Ziba brought me back. But the fear that the servant would have hurt Ama is still churning in my mind, even now that she's close by again.

"Abba killed him when he found him with his hands on Naamah," Zarethan announces sourly, stalking past. "She told him everything."

Ama's arms tighten around me. "I still can't believe he betrayed us."

"Well, he's dead," Ziba mutters from the other side of the fire. "And with so many of their scavengers lost, the Amorites shouldn't come after us. If we can get to Lo Debar without being followed, the real test begins."

I know what he means. I heard it from the Amorites. David's army will be on the move by now, taking Zion from Jebus, angering the Philistines who have had their claws in the region for eight years. Our old enemy is fueled by an ancient fire that's easily reignited. Once they're stirred up, they'll swarm the land like bees released from a hive, and only time will tell if David's mighty men are strong enough to stop them.

But it doesn't matter. Ziba will be far away from me by the time armies clash again. The calculation in his eyes tells me he's already imagining it. He's eager to distance himself, and once he leaves me in Lo Debar, whether I live or die won't be his concern.

No one says a word to me as we ride southwest through the same brushy plains I traveled with the raiders. I've never felt more hunted, waking every night covered in sweat, my heart clawing through my chest. All I can see is the Amorite faces, their hatred cold enough to freeze my blood. The bruises from their fingertips are still swollen, and every night, Ama holds a damp cloth against my eye where it's turning purple from Becorath's slap.

"You shouldn't waste water until we reach the Jordan," Iscah reproves, guiding Ziba's nine-year-old twins along. But Ama ignores her.

She isn't saying much, but she's worried. She knows how dangerous a deep knife wound can be. I can feel it pulling under my clothes, the ache deepening with the mule's steady trot. But there's not much we can do about it. When Ziba rode after me, the rest of them had to pack hastily and follow. There wasn't time to collect oils or medicine from Ramoth. All we have is water, and precious little until we cross the river.

I haven't spoken since Ziba brought me back. I ride along in silence, watching the landscape change around me, the cracked, arid trail slowly giving way to sun-scorched green slopes. More date palms grow toward the water. I sit up against one while Ziba's servants make camp.

Sweat trails my face like tears, and my robe is still torn. When no one's looking, I press my hands against my side and find the skin purple and cracking under the bandage. With the slightest pressure, the slice pulls apart, starting a slow, dark trickle. I fold the cloth back over it, my pulse unsteady. All it would have taken was a few more inches, a deeper upthrust into my heart instead of across my torso.

The thought is poisonous, dragging terrible heat through my veins. What am I supposed to do now? Live with the threat of death reviving itself every time I close my eyes?

My skin prickles as the strangest feeling rushes over me. I'm seeing it all over again—the moon burning through the trees, and the word that entered my head beside Yahweh's Name. *Chesed.* Am I supposed to believe that's what I received? A bitter rescue by a man who despises me so that I can hide in a ditch for the rest of my life? Adonai should have let me die.

Ama bends down next to me with a waterskin. "Here."

Her face is out of focus. I turn my head away, and an irritated edge slips into her voice. "Mephi, you have to drink." Her eyes drop to my side. "Let me see it."

"Why don't you let Azarel look at it?" Ziba suggests, settling down by the fire to sharpen his sword. "He's a hunter. He knows wounds."

Azarel rolls his eyes, sets his bow aside, and comes over to me. I pull away, but Ziba's voice hardens. "Let him see it."

I keep my eyes lowered while Azarel lifts my arm and peels back the bandage. He winces, whistling softly. "It's deep. You'll need beeswax or something to seal it when we get to Lo Debar."

As if the land of no pasture is going to have a physician who's waiting to treat Saul's cast-off grandson. I fold my arms over the wound.

Ama sits forward onto her knees. "You know your father was captured by Philistines as a youth. They found him in the forest and tried to take him for ransom. He fought them off, but he was badly wounded by the time Abner got to him. There's no shame in it."

I close my eyes, blinded by the anguish eating up my insides. Does she even understand what happened? There was no honor in this wound. I didn't fight anyone off. I didn't live because I was a brave warrior like my father. I lived because, for some reason, I couldn't die.

A few feet away, Shaalbim scoffs, shoving to his feet. "What's one more wound after what he's already done to himself?"

Ama whirls around. "Shaal!"

Ziba sighs. "Come now, Naamah. You've never noticed what he does while he's pretending to carve? Cutting into his own flesh like a madman?" He eyes her darkly. "You're unclean just by touching him."

Ama gapes, horrified, but Shaalbim just shrugs. "It's true. Tell her, Cripple."

"Be quiet," Azarel snaps at him. Still bent over me, he tries to retie the bandage where he opened it, but I recoil, pushing his arm away.

151

"Don't bother," I mutter. "I don't need your help."

He leans back, his manner tightening. "It's not my fault you are the way you are. Or that my brothers are fools. But if you want me to hate you, I will. God knows, it would be easy."

I almost feel relief as he stalks away. I've never been able to trust any of them. Why should he be an exception?

Ama inhales deeply, trapping emotion under her folded arms. "Don't do this again, Mephi," she whispers sharply. "You can't keep disappearing somewhere I can't find you."

She's referencing the years I stayed quiet, traumatized by my first brush with death. When I finally started talking again, Ama was the only one I could look in the eyes. The only one who never threatened to leave me.

She touches my scarred wrist. "They could have killed you, but they didn't. I've always said it. Yahweh has His eye on you."

I stay silent, unable to explain how that terrifies me. I was there. Something came through those trees and rescued me. But what I can't figure out is why.

Hours pass, and I can't sleep. The strangest feeling sits on me like a cloud, refusing to lift. Whatever saved me hasn't left.

Somehow, I'm not alone. I'm still being watched. But for what purpose, I can't tell. Afraid to wonder, I turn on my right side, hugging Ama's cloak around my wound. It's biting now, and I can feel the heat through my clothes. I shut my eyes, but Ama's words are waiting right behind them.

*He has His eye on you, Mephi.*

The moment I think it, a chill strokes my arms and a strange wind steals over me, shutting out sound. I fold my arms tighter, trying to adjust my shoulder against the ground. Trying to believe I'm not feeling this. I'd cried out to Yahweh because I was scared. But now, I'm sure I made a mistake. I'm unclean, like Ziba said.

Still, there's a distinct question in the silence, a heavy invitation, and I shudder, afraid to open my eyes. *You don't want me. Not really. Leave me alone.*

When I sit up the next morning, I know something's changed. For the worse. The sharp tightness in my side is climbing my throat, and my eyes ache around the slightest bit of light. Unless I focus hard on it, Ama's voice is distorted, as though she's speaking through water. Or maybe, I'm just hearing the water.

The narrow pass of the Jordan carves through the land in front of us, sloping down to water the sand-choked territory to the south. The river used to be a gateway for our people, the final crossing into the land Yahweh promised us. Now, it's more like a barrier. The wilderness towns scattered beyond it have grown up out of necessity, whenever the Philistines pushed too close, and our people had to run and hide. It's not a place to live. It's a place to avoid death.

We cross at the lowest depth, but the water still swirls around my ankles, sending a chill up my legs. The rush on either side of me spins dizziness through my body, and I grip the saddle, trying not to fall.

By the time we ride into Lo Debar, I'm resisting chills, nearly breaking my teeth in an effort to keep them from knocking together. I can feel the sheen of sweat on my forehead, beneath my hair.

A stick gate opens to us on the south side of the town. Off to the side, a collection of stonemasons are layering boulders for a wall, but it's clearly not going to be finished anytime soon. We're not stopped by anyone, but I notice the expressions changing as people count Ziba's sons, and then finally notice me. By the time we've reached the crumbling well and the aging winepress in the center of the marketplace, we're being stared at with open pity.

Two men with short spears and tarnished armor point Ziba uphill when he asks for the home of Machir ben Ammiel. The house we approach is one of the largest around, but still modest, mimicking the other stone structures along the street. Outside the area where the wall is being built, there's another cistern and a collection of tents and cooking fires.

Iscah's eyes spark angrily when Ziba sends her with the others to camp on the outskirts for the night. But Ama stays beside me. I sway on the mule, struggling to hold myself up.

A man's voice speaks from the door, but I don't bother to look up. I don't want to see whatever's in his eyes, whether pity or annoyance. I wish I could close my ears too, and not hear Ziba trying to feign politeness. I've dreaded this moment for years, when he would wash his hands of me. I'd been foolish enough to think I could avoid it by escaping on my own. But now, every semblance of a plan has been muted, silenced by the pain in my side.

Ziba turns around and lifts me into his arms, and another man steps closer.

"Good God," he whispers, touching me briefly. "Bring him inside."

Ziba carries me through the narrow doorway into a long room. From the corner where he leaves me, I can see into a side chamber where two older women are tending a fire. A younger one enters from a back room and tilts her jar into a pot over the flames. She straightens up when the older man enters.

"Kezi, bring water."

She nods brightly and obeys, approaching Ziba first. He's already seated around a low table in the center of the room. Ama steps politely out of the way, but once more servants appear, the girl named Kezi pulls away toward her.

"Are you Naamah? Come with me," she says, and they disappear into another room.

Given the ramshackle look of the town, I'm surprised by how clean and well-dressed the servants are. The old man must be an elder of sorts. His robes are a deep russet color, which means he can afford dyed cloth. Glancing at him when his back is turned, I decide he can't be that ancient. Perhaps fifty or sixty. He turns around too quickly for me to look away, bending down to see into my eyes.

"You're safe now," he says softly, his hands brushing my forearms.

My pulse shoves into my throat. It's unsettling how he looks at me deeply, like he knows me. But he can't. I don't know him.

He lowers himself to the cushion at the table's head, lifting his chin at Ziba. "The woman who went with my niece. That's your sister?"

"Yes, *adon*." Ziba bows his head. I've never seen him show so much deference. Something he can summon from his days in Saul's service, I suppose.

Ziba sighs heavily. "She used to serve in the court of Saul, as I did. Until we lost him. I wish I could have done more for them both, but in any case, I've had my own fifteen sons to provide for."

The man who must be Machir laughs graciously. "You have as many sons as a warrior has arrows." He angles his eyes over to me, then back at Ziba. "He can come closer."

Painful surprise blooms in my cheeks when I realize he wants me to join them at the table. I turn my head so I don't have to see Ziba's fake sorrow. "He's been like that since the Amorites took him. He isn't used to any of this."

*Any of what?* I wonder, scoffing inwardly. *Kindness? A roof over my head?*

"Thank Adonai you recovered him." Machir's tone implies that he knows more than he'll reveal. But he won't show me anything except the same honest smile. "It's all right." He beckons to me.

I wait for Ziba to explain that I can't walk, but I don't hear anything. Whatever's on the table is smearing together, and an anvil pounds in my head each time I blink. I lean into the wall, but nothing will stay still. Heat climbs in my body, but I can't stop shaking. I move my hand and realize it's sticking to my side. With blood.

Machir gets up from the table and crouches in front of me.

My muscles clenched, I jerk back against the wall. "Don't—"

Overhearing, Ama hurries to my side. "Easy, Mephi; he's going to help you."

I don't care. I don't want him touching me. He thinks I'm just an unfortunate refugee, a servant's son. But he'll find out the truth, and then his pity will disappear.

"Caleb, help me," Machir directs a servant, lifting me into his arms. "Naamah, follow us back."

After they carry me into another room, I expect to be left alone, but Machir stays, lighting an oil lamp near me while Ama cradles my head in her lap.

Her voice tilts, shaken with worry. "He was wounded seven days ago. We didn't have anything to clean it with."

Machir touches my face. "He's burning."

Gripped with fear, I can't stop shaking. "Please don't touch me...please..."

"No one's going to hurt you," he murmurs.

"Stop lying to me!" My voice breaks into a cry, and Machir's hand closes around my wrist.

"*I* won't hurt you, Mephibosheth," he amends, but his sincerity is lost on me. All I hear is my name. I look at him, my eyes filling. He knows who I am?

Machir turns to the servants at the door. "Get fresh linen. Kezi, have Miriam heat more water. And bring me the jars in the storeroom."

"Yes, Uncle," the girl says in a small voice before disappearing.

The two servants join their master on the floor, and one starts easing my arm out of my sleeve. The threadbare material slips easily off my shoulder, exposing my whole side. Machir winces, the lines around his eyes deepening. His fingers press on either side of the wound, and I feel teeth edging up into my ribs.

"It's healing over infection. See that?" He shows Ama the thin dark lines sliding under the skin. They mimic the ones climbing my arms. He traces the old cuts on my wrist with one finger, but says nothing.

A servant kneels beside him with a basin, and Machir wrings out one clean white cloth after another, joining the others in wiping the sweat and grime from around the wound. He doesn't stop with my side, washing all the way up my arms and down my legs, and I cringe, tolerating it with my eyes tightly closed. I've only ever bathed in snatches in the cave. I'm not used to servants. And I'm willing to bet they've never washed the feet of a beggar before.

Kezi returns with a steaming kettle and a wooden box containing several clay jars. Machir fills a cup with water, adding herbs and something from a tiny vial. "Drink this."

It's almost too hot to swallow, but I take it anyway, feeling honey slide down my throat before the sharp herbal taste burns my tongue. Machir takes a leather roll from the wooden box and unwraps a thick knife, handing it to one of the servants. "Heat this in the fire, Caleb."

I flinch, turning my face against Ama's arm. I remember when the healer had come from Ramoth the night Ziba's servant was wounded after a wolf attack. He'd said he needed to cut into the wound to clean it of infection, or he would lose his leg. Even from the back cave, I'd heard the man screaming.

"Steady." Machir's hand is heavy on my chest. "It'll bleed, but hopefully the poison will leave with it and you'll be free of the fever." His fingers find the ring at my breastbone, and he and Ama share an unreadable expression over my head. "It's been a long time since I've seen one of these," he whispers.

Caleb returns with the knife before Ama can answer. I cringe again, teeth gritted. "Please…"

Machir grasps my shoulder. Like his grip, his tone is commanding, but somehow gentle. "Listen to me, boy. I've been a healer since my youth. I've seen war wounds much worse than this. I promise, you will be all right."

I don't know why, but I'm suddenly desperate to believe him. Somehow, his gaze reaches deep and stirs a shred of wounded strength. I'm tired of running from trouble. It always finds me. And if more pain is going to get rid of the poison in my side, then so be it.

The girl is back at her uncle's shoulder. When she hands a piece of leather over his arm, I refuse to think. Without hesitating, I fit the leather between my teeth and bite down, forcing deep breaths over it. I'm ready.

A smile lifts Machir's silver-flecked beard. "Good boy."

Ama reaches over me to grab his wrist. I can feel her shaking. "Thank you. For helping him."

Machir pats her hand, placing it back onto me. Sudden youthfulness dances across his face. "He's not going to die. He's going to live, and get stronger, and cause all kinds of trouble. Like his father would have wanted."

My fingers are folded tightly around Ama's wrists, bracing me. But when Machir says that, I relax my grip, bewildered. Who is he? How does he know my father? Or my real name?

But instead of an answer, the knife cuts into my side, and a popping white light fills my head until I can't see anything.

# ELEVEN

*Mephi*

———————◆———————

I know I'm not awake, but I keep blinking, waiting for the walls and the floor to stop switching places, twisting every time I move my head. My senses writhe in a heated fog, but I'm in no hurry to feel anything. I'm barely able to register the strange luxury of being enclosed in warm walls rather than a dank cavern.

I'm lying on a soft cot, covered with a fresh blanket, and someone has combed through my hair, removing the knots and tangles. Now that I've been washed, the scars on my arms are more visible.

"He'll live. I've closed the wound. Once the fever lifts, his strength will return."

Machir's voice folds into the warm scents of honey and herbs in the room, but then Ziba's cuts in, turning everything cold.

"He shouldn't cause you any trouble. He'll be grateful enough for your silence." He pauses. "I paid a substantial ransom to free him from the Amorites." The false emotion in his tone stirs nausea in my gut.

*Liar.*

Machir's answer holds a layer of iron I didn't hear before. "You've done enough. It's time you think of your family."

I blink again, and suddenly the room slides into focus. In the doorway, Machir hands Ziba a long leather purse. Ziba bows, carefully covering his satisfaction. "May Yahweh bless you for your kindness." I tense when he turns to me. "I trust the boy will come to be grateful for it."

Then he's gone without another glance, finally rid of me after eight years. I wait to feel relieved, forsaken…something. But there's nothing. Just the stubborn pulse in my chest and the gentle groan of my side.

Machir stares after him, soundless thoughts crossing his brow. When he looks at me, his forehead smooths out. "Thirsty?"

He takes a waterskin from a hook on the wall and fills a cup, holding my head so I can drink.

"Ama?" I ask, and Machir tilts his head.

"Sleeping. She'll stay with my servants. I doubt anything could make that woman leave you." He kneels beside me and covers my forehead with his hand. "Fever's going down. That was a nasty wound, but it should heal now."

I drop my eyes, not wanting him to see the rest of it, buried too deep for him to reach with his knife.

"Naamah told me what happened with the sons of Gibeon," he says.

Biting down hard, I turn my head away, refusing to lose control. But fighting the wildness feels like holding back the Jordan when it overflows its banks. All I can see is the look the raider gave me before opening my side. This town without walls won't protect me from that.

"Will they come here?" I finally manage.

"They have no reason to. Even if they did, they're not taking anyone who belongs to me."

That's right. He practically paid for me. Why, I can't say.

Machir chuckles a little. "I know who you are, Mephi. Even if Ziba hadn't told me, it's obvious. You look just like him."

When I hear what he's saying, I can't help scoffing to myself. Because I don't look like my father. Ziba says I look like my uncle, Bosheth. Or Saul, except skinnier. I clasp my arms around myself while Machir settles back on his heels, his smile full of everything he's seen.

"My father, Ammiel, was Saul's physician. He removed a couple of arrows from your father once."

His face softens, and my heart starts pounding harder, pushing pain through the linen bound at my side.

"He was a beloved warrior, your father. Always putting Israel before his own safety or comfort. He sacrificed everything for this land."

Everything including me. How could his duty to Saul have been worth more than what his presence would've meant to me? It's something I'd rather not think about. Ever.

Machir chews his lip, his eyes slanting sadly. "I didn't want to believe the messengers when they brought the news. It didn't seem possible...Jonathan."

His pity is making my skin crawl. It doesn't matter what my father was. No amount of virtue on Abba's part could save us from Saul's curse.

"Many of us wondered what happened to you. We assumed..." He doesn't finish, but he doesn't have to. They all thought I was dead. He clears his throat. "Naamah tells me your legs were broken on the night you fled Gibeah."

I nod, searching his face again. He has to know that I won't be very useful as a servant. Why would he agree to take me?

Bending over me, Machir feels down my legs, tracing the crooked slant of each ankle. He shakes his head, inhaling slightly as he pulls back. "Decent breaks. Right at the top of both joints. I could try to straighten them if they were freshly broken. But they've healed wrong for too many years. I won't risk it." He pauses. "I'm sorry."

I shrug. I've been living with it for years.

His eyes move up my arms. "Did the Amorites do that too?"

I shake my head, pulling the sheepskin up over my scars. "The people here—who do they think I am?"

Machir settles back against the wall. "I've dropped some hints about an orphaned cousin of mine. That's all anyone will need to know. Most of the people here are related to displaced servants from Gibeah. My own niece Keziah was brought here after her parents' death, and no one asked any questions."

His kindness reaches out to me, but his next words reignite my defenses.

"If we have any trouble, we can always send word to David. Your father—"

I push myself up, ignoring the pain digging through my side. "No! David will kill me." The words burn on my tongue, and the tremors are back, climbing my throat.

Machir blinks. "He would not. He was good friends with your father. He—"

"His men killed my uncle," I interrupt him, my vision spinning. "They would watch for any opportunity to get rid of me." My words break and tumble like unsteady waves over rock, but I have to make him understand. He doesn't know what it was like to face death tied to a tree. "Please. Swear you won't tell him!"

Machir's calm expression doesn't move. "All right. If that's how you want it. We'll be left in peace here. When my father died, David sent enough money for me to settle wherever I chose. But I requested to stay here, out of the way, where I could help the ones who would rather not draw the attention of the sons of Zeruiah."

Thinking of David's bloodthirsty nephews turns my heart cold, and I grip my knees, trying to stop shaking.

A thousand thoughts fill Machir's eyes before he adds, "You're going to live, Mephibosheth."

"Why?" How can he be sure?

He leans forward. "Because Yahweh wants you to. One day you'll actually see that."

* * *

The next day, I wake up without fire in my side. The pain is still there, but a smoldering ache has replaced the raging chaos that had consumed my whole body. The full light of morning is pouring in through the small window cut into the wall over my head.

I fidget, dragging myself off the cot. I'm not used to sleeping into the daylight. Ziba's servants always came for me at sunrise, before the city gates opened.

Still stripped to the waist, I can clearly see the patterns of the scars tracing my forearms. A thick, dark finger edges up from underneath the oil-scented linen Machir bound around my ribs.

I touch it, and the ache deepens, but the wound isn't gaping anymore. Whatever Machir sealed it with will hold.

I can see clearly now, and the fog has unwound itself from my senses. I'm not feverish anymore. I'm going to recover. Then what?

I draw myself up against the wall and listen to the sounds of the village coming to life on the other side. Mules braying, gentle chatter, the occasional clank of metal, and the crackle of fire. The warm scent of bread prods my hunger awake, and heat fills my face. What am I going to have to do to earn my food here?

I wonder how long it will take for people to start asking questions once they see me begging outside Machir's house. I can't think of anything else he would do with me, though this town doesn't seem like much of a crossroads. If I remember right, we're not too far from Mahanaim, one of my uncle's many hiding places for the two years he reigned as a puppet king.

Abner had thought they'd be safe. But raiders had still found them, traveling all the way here to carry my uncle's head south to David.

I shudder, pulling my knees into my chest.

Sandals scuff the floor, and I look up, expecting Ama. But it's the girl. Kezi.

It's the first time I've really seen her, without the haze of sickness in the way. She's smaller than I am, but again, you can't tell because I can't stand up next to her. A simple tunic covers her slight frame, her thick, dark hair is bound over her shoulder with a veil, and she's carrying a water jug. But she has sunlight in her face. I can't remember the last time anyone smiled at me like that. I wonder what she has to be so happy about.

"Shalom."

There's a greeting I rarely hear, if ever. And the girl practically sings it.

She pours water from her jar into a bowl against the wall, her smiling eyes edging to the opposite corner. "Aren't you going to wear that?"

I hadn't noticed the clean tunic folded neatly on the floor. Beside it there's a pair of sandals, along with a belt and overgarment. The colors of Benjamin streak the material in a simple striped pattern. "They're not mine," I venture.

Kezi's rippling chuckle scatters my wits for a moment, but there's no trace of derision in her laugh. "Of course they're yours," she says gently. "My uncle had Naamah lay them out for you."

Not a word about the filthy, ragged tunic I had been wearing, with holes right through it. She definitely pities me, but it isn't that maddening, patronizing look that I've seen so often from people in Ramoth. I study the clothes again, feeling like I'm back at the gate. How childish to be so bewildered by any sort of kindness.

"Should I send someone to help you, *adon*?"

A flush climbs my cheeks, pushing pleasure aside. "I'm no lord," I mutter. "I'm just Mephi."

"I know." Kezi nods. Her brightness makes me squint. "And I'm just Keziah. Machir is my uncle."

I fidget, wondering how many *shekels* had changed hands. In spite of his kindness, I'm sure Machir's planning to toss me out as soon as I've recovered. What kind of rich man keeps a cripple at his table? Unless it's all a ruse, and he's keeping me for something worse. That's still a possibility.

I look up sharply, feeling the burn of Kezi's curiosity in her eyes. "I can't walk," I summarize.

"I know." She gives up searching for words, her cheeks red. "Your nurse told us what happened. What you faced. The servants say you're either braver than most or favored by Yahweh."

*Ha.* I settle the angry laughter inside before attempting a reply. "Both wrong. Ziba pulled me out of the ravine. He killed the Amorites and brought me here." My eyes flare with tears that won't fall. "I had nothing before, and I have nothing now."

A frown pulls at the skin between her eyes. "You have your life. And that woman who's like your mother. Most of the people here have lost something. Land. Family. But my uncle said he always knew you were meant to survive."

I swallow, my throat hard. "He doesn't know me."

"He knew Jonathan." She lifts the jar onto her hip and leaves without another word.

Unwound, I rub my face, angrily shoving my hair out of my eyes. So, that's it. They admired my father, and they think that I'm the same. Well, that won't last. They'll figure out soon enough that wearing his seal ring doesn't make me his heir. And it's been hanging in plain sight long enough.

Crawling across the room, I yank the tunic and robe over my head, afraid some servant will appear to try and help me. The sandals are unnecessary. I toss them aside, my mind playing with the unanswered questions Ziba left scattered behind him.

Ama's brother doesn't care about me, but he's not haphazard. He left me here for a reason. What is it? My stomach curls tight under the fresh leather belt. Machir might not keep me in a cistern, but he doesn't need to. My legs chain me to the ground wherever I am. I have to figure out what Machir wants with me. Otherwise, whatever he's planning will unfold behind my back until it's too late for me to escape. Like with Ziba.

I don't have much time to think before Ama steps into the doorway. She looks more rested than I've ever seen her, wearing a clean dress and green veil. Her smile widens when she notices my clothes.

"We're going to be safe here, Mephi." She beams, her voice thick with thankfulness. "Ammiel was a faithful servant to Saul, and Machir is just as honorable. Yahweh has brought us to a good place." She bends down and kisses my cheek. "You look better. How do you feel?" I shrug, but she just adds, "You should eat."

She tugs my arm, pointing at the low table in the front room. The long linen cloth is spread with fresh bread, fruit, dates, and nuts, but I hold back, hesitancy warring with my hunger. I'm not going to take a chance at being reproved for helping myself.

"Where's Ziba?" I ask, searching the room cautiously.

Ama's lips tighten. "He's still camped outside the gate with his family. They won't be staying too much longer. I can't believe he finally used that letter from your father after all this time."

My stomach turns cold, but before I can ask her to explain, a light tap at the outer door interrupts me. The servant named Caleb opens it, and I'm startled to see a wizened old man leaning on a cane with a cloth wrapped around his eyes. A middle-aged woman gently supports him, holding a basket in her other hand.

Machir appears, his hand outstretched. "Shalom Isaac, Elspeth."

A smile cracks the blind man's expression, and he grasps Machir's hand.

"Here, Caleb." Kezi enters from the kitchen and hands him a basket covered with a cloth. Caleb gives it to the woman in exchange for the one she's holding.

Flushed and smiling, the woman bows her head. "Thank you. I will be back later with the weavings."

"Thank you, Elspeth. Keep your father out of trouble, eh?" Machir nods teasingly at the blind man.

Isaac chuckles, angling his head at the woman. "Always."

Ama whispers into my shoulder. "Hundreds were displaced when the Philistines took Gibeah, but I didn't realize Machir supported so many. Apparently, Elspeth is a widow who looks after her father. They help with weaving in exchange for food."

Machir sweeps his hand over the table. "Come in here and eat something, Mephi. You're too skinny for thirteen."

I inch closer, my cheeks painfully warm. Obviously, a crippled orphan isn't such an anomaly here. Ziba took one look at this town of beggars and blind men and decided it was a perfect place to dispose of me. Machir smiles and pushes a chunk of bread against my hand. "Come on."

I take it slowly, but the moment I sink my teeth in, it's a struggle to control myself. I turn away slightly, facing the wall. I have to at least try to avoid looking like a ravenous beggar. Fortunately, Machir is distracted.

The next knock at the door is more insistent, and Caleb opens it to a six-foot-tall dispatch rider in an armor vest. Again, Machir clasps hands with him. "Abinadab—you returned faster than I anticipated, my friend."

"With all the attention in the south, the roads are easier. For now." The man flashes a grin of cracked teeth and sits down while the servants bring water. He nods at Ama and winks at Kezi.

"Did you manage to get everything sharpened?" Machir asks him.

Abinadab nods, smirking. "Ox goads, axe heads, even the sickles. The Philistines at the forge were completely distracted by the news about David."

I look up, the bread turning to sawdust in my mouth.

Machir's brows lift with interest. "So, it's true? He will take Zion?"

Abinadab slams his hand down on the table. "Took it already! Thrust the Jebusites through, and sent the rest fleeing for the coast. Of course, they'll run straight into the Philistines. Achish's cohorts won't leave David in peace for long."

Kezi laughs, and the servants start whispering like it's news they've been waiting for. But one battle doesn't restore the region. This one merely gave David a place to build a palace. I look down at the bread in my hand. How long before the Philistines start rampaging again?

Machir's eyes gleam. "The Jebusites have had control of that region for as long as I can remember. I thought they would hold out for a few months at least. How did he manage to take it so quickly?"

"God is with him, Uncle. You've always said that." Kezi's simple declaration startles me. Of course, they're friends with the shepherd-king. A strange pain works its way into my stomach as Abinadab continues.

"All the land knows it. The king of Tyre has already sent David a gift of cedar trees to build up the stronghold. Word is, he wants to bring the Ark of the Covenant down there, build a house for God in Jerusalem. But he'll have to deal with the Philistines first."

"Will he have the capacity after taking Zion?"

Abinadab chuckles. "That didn't expend any energy. The Jebusites are eating their words. They threatened him, saying that the blind and the lame would keep him out. But David had his men climb up the water shaft and infiltrate the city before the Jebusites had even rallied for battle. Needless to say, they grossly underestimated him."

"Many do," Machir comments thoughtfully.

"Not anymore. With Tyre building his house and every other noble in the region offering his daughter as a concubine, David will take the heart and soul of the land before he's been king five years. He threw siege mounds against Jerusalem, and before the first day was ended, Joab had sent messages throughout the whole city that the blind and the lame they spoke of would never enter David's house." Abinadab's tone darkens. "Our neighbors will think twice before insulting him."

I swallow. That settles it. If the blind and the lame are hated by David, I'll have to stay clear. Somehow, it doesn't comfort me that I was right.

Abinadab's focus shifts across the room. He lifts a finger at me. "Who's this?"

Machir doesn't hesitate. "An orphaned cousin of mine from Gibeah. When I found out he was staying in Ramoth, I sent for him."

Abinadab reaches for more bread. "He's a fortunate young man. Those who survived Saul's mismanagement will have a chance to see Israel rise again under David. Maybe even fight alongside him. What do you think about that, boy?"

My face stings, and I look down. Evidently, he doesn't realize I can't walk. Or that I'm Saul's grandson.

"I-I'm no fighter," I mumble.

He shrugs, undeterred. "You'd better learn then. Taking back our land from the Philistines will require another miracle like Elah."

I keep my face turned away, hoping Abinadab will stop talking. I've heard the stories. Elah was the valley where David killed the Philistine giant Goliath. And Saul had tried to kill him later, jealous of how the young warrior's success highlighted his failure.

My mind darts back to my dream of the man with the lion medallion. Was that David, the king of the lion tribe? Is he planning to search me out once he's done with the Philistines? Why else would he have been Machir's first suggestion?

Unable to eat more, I fold a piece of bread in my fist and shove it under my cloak. How is Machir really connected to David? Did the king make him promise to turn me over?

I jump when Ama touches my arm. "You could learn to fight, you know." She keeps her voice low. "Your father was an expert archer. I saw you pick up Azarel's bow more than once."

*And I was beaten for it.*

I pull my shoulder away, resentful. It's bad enough that I used to want to fight. I can't forget how I would fall asleep with my little bow as a child. But that was when I had use for it. When I would climb that tree in my father's garden and jump from it without fear. I was a different person then.

Fortunately, no one talks to me again. As the room empties, I shove another chunk of bread under my robe and edge away from the table, pulling myself toward the back door where the servants keep disappearing. Kezi jumps, nearly tripping over me. "What are you doing?"

While I'm deciding how to explain, Machir appears. "You don't need to hide anything, Mephi. You won't starve in my house."

I glance up through my hair, wishing I could believe it. How do I explain that stealing is the only life I know? Stealing and begging. Which reminds me. He must be wondering how I'm going to earn my keep.

"I can work," I begin, but Machir doesn't let me finish.

"Naamah said you can carve. She said you've developed a unique skill over the years."

Flustered, I don't answer. No one ever showed much interest in that before, except Becorath. Thinking of him still stirs helpless rage in my stomach. That should have been the last time I ever trusted anyone, but here I am having to trust Machir because I have no choice. His attention slides beneath the surface, searching me. "Come with me."

Machir's servants must be waiting around every corner because they appear instantly to help me outside. They lift me up to ride behind Machir on his mule, but we only ride a short distance through the town to a carpenter's shed.

Inside, an older man with wood shavings folded into his beard bends over a table. He slides a long, flat blade with two handles up the surface of a freshly-cut plank, and the wood curls up like parchment in flames. The man drags the tool all the way to the end of the plank before looking up.

"Mephi, this is Ebenezer. He's built almost everything in this town." Machir's servants help me down off the mule, settling me on a bench in the corner.

Ebenezer looks much older than he probably is. His squinting eyes are sunken down into wrinkles, and his hands are gnarled and calloused, but his movements are smooth and precise. Dusting his hands on his leather apron, he lifts his eyes. "Another stray?"

"A cousin's orphan from Gibeah." Machir's hand hasn't left my shoulder. "He hasn't been able to walk since he was five."

Ebenezer's mouth screws tight. "Doubly unfortunate, eh?" He reaches behind me for two long pieces of wood, each the length and width of a shepherd's staff. He holds them up in front of himself, giving them the same measured look he gave me. "Stand him up."

Machir's servants lift me onto my feet, letting Ebenezer hold the wood up against my side. Running his hand down my arms, he touches the tips of my fingers and marks the wood with a chunk of coal. My stomach drops. Feeling my full height isn't something I'm used to.

Machir explains, "Ebenezer's father lost a leg to infection years ago, so he learned how to make crutches to help him walk. As well as a few canes for men like Isaac."

Seated once again, I fiddle with a chunk of pine while Ebenezer finishes marking up the wood. Picking up a thick knife, he chops into it, trimming the length.

"The boy carves," Machir offers. "Perhaps he could be of use here."

The carpenter glances up, then tosses me a smaller knife without comment. The blade is thin and sharp, easily concealed. Ebenezer's eyes lift briefly from his work as my hands start to move.

"Was it your father's trade?"

"His father was an archer," Machir says quietly for me.

"For Saul?" Ebenezer's tone sharpens.

Machir doesn't answer. I keep my eyes on the wood, guiding the knife to cut away anything that doesn't look like the head of a wolf I've carved over and over.

"We have some bows here," Ebenezer says over his own work. "A few warriors have come and gone over the years, men who used to serve in Saul's army. The remnants of families that have been cut apart." His lips press together. When he breathes again, a piece of sawdust lifts from his beard and drops to the ground. "Those who stay need a means of protection. Swords have become…rare."

Like they were in the days of my father's youth. When Saul had become king, Israel had only two swords. My grandfather's kingship had put a sizeable dent in the Philistine army, but you wouldn't know it now, with the garrisons outside Benjamin's cities controlling trade and most of Israel's power concentrated in the south. With David.

"I'll be back." Machir touches my shoulder and walks away, trailed by his servants.

Left alone with Ebenezer, I watch the old man blow dust off a thick wedge of wood, fitting it sideways into a groove in the walking stick. Several cut pieces already line the crude shelves nailed into the stone wall around the fire. A dusty sleeping mat is rolled up next to it. He must live here in the stone hovel among his tools. Strange that he doesn't have anyone to help him.

But then I remember what he said. This town is populated by Israel's missing pieces, and from the number of canes and walking sticks leaning against the wall, it seems that many of them are maimed in some way. Again, I grapple with Ziba's reasons for bringing me here. Did he imagine I would simply join the other cast-offs wasting away? But it seems like Machir intends for me to be some sort of apprentice for Ebenezer.

The thought isn't unwelcome. My hands are busy, and it's the calmest I've felt in weeks. But that doesn't mean I'll be able to carry wood, or chop trees, or lift heavy burdens of stone into place. I swallow that down, scraping the tip of my knife against the slant of the wolf's jaw while the low crackle of the dying fire eats up the silence.

My eyes skirt the walls again, locking onto what looks like the frame of a bow propped over the bedroll. Distracted, I cut too deep, nicking my finger. I rub away the bead of blood and keep chipping wood shavings onto my feet.

"Did you make that bow on the wall?" I ask.

"I did," he answers simply, holding up the two staves to measure them against each other.

"Do you still?" It's been so long since I've been close to a bow. I let myself imagine picking it up, maybe testing it to see if my hands remember.

Ebenezer squints sideways. "I make weapons for the watchmen, though we haven't been attacked in years. David has kept the Philistines fairly occupied, and if he succeeds in driving them out, then maybe we'll have a chance to rebuild." Tension flickers in the veins of his neck.

"Did you fight for Saul?" Again, I'm not sure why I want to know. Begging at Ramoth's gate, it hadn't mattered who came or went. But if I'm going to live among these people, I want to know if I'm surrounded by enemies or friends. So that I can gauge how they'll react when they find out who I am. Which they will. I've learned that no story keeps for long.

"I was a craftsman in Gibeah." Ebenezer clears the rattle from his throat. "The bows here belonged to my sons. They went after David."

"Why?"

His shoulders lift, but for the first time I see the heaviness on them. "For the same reason everyone does. God is with him."

My hands turn cold around the knife, a pit opening in my stomach. Not everyone left Saul because he drove them out. Some men followed David because they saw his success and wanted a better future for Israel. One that required the throne to depart from Saul's house.

"Why didn't you go with them?" I ask.

"I'm a woodworker, not a soldier," he answers tightly. "But my sons would have been forced to follow Saul to Gilboa. At least, following David, I can assume they lived."

The coldness deepens in my stomach. Evidently, he hasn't received word, one way or another.

Ebenezer stands up next to me, the two crutches under his arm. He studies the crude shape in my hand. "It's good. The wolf of Benjamin. And with only the knife." He picks it up and turns it, rubbing his thumb up under the wolf's teeth. "I have tools that will help you be more precise. In time, you might be of some use to me here."

I doubt it, but I won't argue. I suppose I should be grateful that someone wants to teach me a trade instead of tossing me in the streets. Ama's right. I'm not meant to survive the way a beggar does. Nevertheless, it'll be a fight to find my way. And I haven't decided if I have the strength.

Ebenezer sets the crutches upright against the floor. "Stand up and put your weight—" he stops himself. "I suppose you can't do that. Here."

Propping the crutches against the wall, he puts his hands under my arms. I grip his sleeves while he struggles to push the wood into position. He drapes my arms over each crutch, bracing my hands against the handles halfway down each one. I lean heavily, the frames pressing deep under my arms when Ebenezer lets me go.

No one's ever set me upright on crutches before. Afraid to stumble, I grip harder, my pride clenched tight against the awkwardness.

Ebenezer stands back, studying me. "The length looks good. In time, I can add some places for your feet to brace, since you can't use either one."

I can't take my eyes off my feet, hugging the ground at a strange angle, refusing to straighten, unable to hold me. I can't imagine ever walking like this. Is it better to hobble a few steps and fall on my face than to crawl as I've always done?

"You'll get used to it." Ebenezer shifts awkwardly, running his hands over his apron.

Fire churns up into my throat. Machir shouldn't have said anything about archers. After everything my father was, after all he wanted me to be, I can barely stand up supported by wood. My father gave his life to protect this land from the Philistines, and now it's all David's. And I'm here, unable to fight for anything.

I move one muscle and lose my balance, one crutch slipping. Ebenezer grabs me, repositioning his hands under my arms.

"I'm sorry," I mumble hastily.

"It's all right."

I'm grateful that he eases me back onto the workbench rather than trying to force the crutches back under me. I can't explain how much it hurts to have my own weakness unravel every effort. I'm thirteen, and Ebenezer is an old man. I should be getting up to help him.

"You'll get used to it," he says again. He absorbs my frustration for a few moments then nervously looks up the road. "I'll find Caleb to bring you home."

My heart clenches around the word. My home was in Gibeah, like Machir said. Back when I had a father who would have trained me to defend Israel. Lo Debar is merely a camp of exile.

My fingers clench around the knife, and my eyes wander, looking for a distraction. I can't cut myself here. There are too many people around. Only a few feet away, half a dozen men are untying horses from a makeshift corral, preparing to leave. Because everyone does, except for the widows and blind men who have nowhere else to go. Like me.

I'm surprised I haven't seen any of Ziba's sons. No doubt they're trying to leave as soon as possible. They'll need to get south before the Philistines start moving. Only a few years ago, men of Benjamin would have been viewed with suspicion in Judah, but if I know Ziba, he'll probably move as close to David as possible. A man with that many sons won't be overlooked. And Ziba will reveal just enough about his past skills to make himself indispensable. It's his way.

He'll regain the property he lost to Saul. Somehow. But what kind of inheritance waits for me? Something wounded aches in my gut, besides the gash that's already there.

Pushing off the workbench, I ease onto my hands and knees and crawl to the opposite corner. Where the bow is. It's simply made, but larger than I'd thought. I lift it, rising up onto my knees until its full length is in my hands. Gripping the shaft, my fingers find the curled symbols carved into the edges, and I pluck the loosened twine like a harp string. Instantly, my eyes start stinging, like I'm staring into fire.

My father is gone and so is my ability to fight. But holding the bow, I know I can't cut either from my mind. I can't ignore the images shoving into view. Abba's face twisting, his arms grabbing me up when I asked why he was sad. His hands cupping my face, telling me something he wanted me to remember.

The impulse screams at me, and I stretch the bow, arching it up as though I've fitted an arrow to shoot. It's made for a man, so I can't draw it fully. But even shaking and straining, my arms settle into the motion, imagining that I can. Relaxing into the sensation. Until a strange sound reaches my ears. Something like a sneer.

I relax the bow abruptly, and my vision focuses into the yard beyond where Ziba's son Azarel is standing in the corral. Watching me.

# TWELVE

## *Mephi*

———◆◆◆———

The evening meal in Machir's house is even more chaotic than the morning.

Since he's one of the few men in Lo Debar with any significant means, his home is continually frequented by the destitute in town. Only a few are actually bound to him, working off debts they couldn't pay. I don't ask where Machir gets his money because I remember. David.

Throughout the day, I've pieced together more information from the servants. Machir's father, Ammiel, knew David when the Judean was a young soldier in Saul's army. Apparently, David respected him enough to restore to Machir everything that his father worked for.

Watching Machir rise to greet guest after guest, his door continually open, I can't resist the sliver of admiration sliding through my pride like a splinter. Whatever he's getting from the new king, he deserves it. He lives more openly than any rich man

I've ever seen, distributing food to those outside the door and welcoming more than a dozen neighbors to his table.

To my disgust, Ziba is one of them. He barely glances at me when he enters, but his five oldest sons make it clear what they think of me sitting at the table. Japhia and Shaphat lift their eyebrows, but Shaalbim and Zarethan are more obvious, elbowing each other and whispering. Azarel's eyes are full of words, accusing me silently across the table.

Fortunately, the deafening chatter keeps the attention away from me. I force food down, trying to be grateful. I've never had this many full meals in my life, and it's strange not to be hungry. I try to focus on that while the men take turns praising Machir for his generosity.

"May all Israel be as prosperous as you one day!" Ziba lifts his cup, and I wince. He'll find a way to prosper no matter what king sits on the throne.

"The land will prosper now that we are free from Saul." Abinadab's words pull heat into my face. Looking over my shoulder to hide it, my eyes catch Kezi's. Her mouth spreads in a careful smile.

"Now that David is king over all Israel, his influence will bless every tribe, not only Judah," Machir comments.

"The sooner the better," Japhia mutters, chewing. "We've lived under Philistine control for too long."

"It shouldn't have been like this." Shaphat's voice tightens. "Israel's king was meant to ensure lasting peace for our people. Enough to give us a chance to enjoy what we've worked for. Instead, it's just like before. All these rogue tribes harassing our borders. The Philistines grabbing control of the forges…"

"That will not continue," Abinadab reminds him. "Under David, they will be driven back and kept behind their own borders. The giant-killer will remind them of their place," he grins.

"And establish us in ours." Zarethan straightens. "I'm joining his army as soon as we can safely settle outside Jerusalem."

Machir's brows lift in Ziba's direction. "You're traveling to the city of David?"

Ziba sets his cup down. "Of course. We will provide him with loyal soldiers to expand his kingdom, for all our sakes." The pride lighting his face works through my chest like a needle.

"You aren't worried that David's nephews will look askance at a former servant of Saul?" Abinadab probes.

Ziba returns his smirk, but I can sense the extra tautness in his tone. "I was merely a servant to the captain of the guard. No one they would remember. David himself was an armorbearer of Saul's, before driving him mad with his success."

He laughs roughly, lifting his chin in Ama's direction. "Remember, sister? It started with a few spears lobbed at the boy in the dark while David was playing his harp. Then, Saul finally ordered his death before all the councilmen. His hatred was like oil on fire, always spreading, never quenched."

Ama sits in rigid silence, some dark memory edging her face. She's rarely spoken of my grandfather's sins. But I forget that she served in Saul's fortress long before she became my nurse.

Ziba's eyes glitter across the table at her. "Saul was relentless in his pursuit of David's death. But could he obliterate the Amalekites who slaughtered our parents? Of course not. Even Yahweh's command wasn't enough for him."

He takes a long drink, letting his eyes touch mine over the rim of his cup. His gaze winds into my gut like a clenched fist.

Abinadab leans in Ziba's direction. "That's why Yahweh removed the kingdom from his grasp and gave it to David. That man's heart has been pure toward our God since he was a boy making songs to sheep."

"His songs were to Yahweh," Machir rejoins, awe filling his face. "The praises he writes contain more intimacy than the words of a priest. My father used to say that David was Yahweh's warrior first. Back in Saul's court, he didn't just sing during feasts, but before battle. His songs stirred the men to fight for our God."

"That's why he is so favored," one of the elders adds. "Melek Israel was meant to follow closely in the statutes of our God, leading our people in obedience before Him. Only men who do that can expect the success that follows David."

"Men like you, Machir," Ziba declares warmly, nodding across the table. "Your father was wise to align himself with David, and now you reap the benefits of it. You share freely with those who have nothing, as the Law commands, and our God will surely reward you for that."

I stare at him, both amazed and disgusted by the way he can cloak his manner with enough respect to appear like a different man before anyone he chooses. For a moment, I wonder what Yahweh thinks of his duplicity.

Machir swallows, taking the compliment as graciously as though it was sincere. "The Law is clear about our treatment of the poor—the widow, the fatherless, the sojourner."

He doesn't look at me, but an inner fire is consuming my whole neck and face.

"You've done a bit more than simply not putting a stumbling block before the blind," Ziba continues. He's smiling directly at Machir, but his words pull toward me. "Most of the town depends on you for sustenance."

I slide my hand under my cloak, gripping the handle of Ebenezer's knife. It's rich of Ziba to mention the command against abusing the blind and the lame when his sons have spent the past eight years knocking me down.

"Doesn't the Law also say that a young man should stand in the presence of his elders?" Shaalbim's muttered tone burns with poison, and I feel the sting across the table.

Machir fixes a cold stare on him, absorbing his derision before talking over it. "Ziba, when do you intend to travel?"

"After *shabbat*." Two days.

The mention of our day of rest makes me sick with shame. As a beggar, I hardly kept track of the days, one afternoon in the sun rolling into the next bitter night. I've let Ama worry about which traditions I maintain and which ones I ignore. What kind of son of Israel am I? After all that I've become, I'm not even sure I'd be accepted at a *shabbat* meal.

Ziba continues, "After killing their champion and double-crossing their king's armies, David is Achish's greatest enemy. The

Philistines will attack David far from here, try to draw him to their borders. If we split into two camps for safety, we should be able to avoid any of their scouts. David's men won't refuse travelers during a time of war."

"I would imagine not. Even Saul kept Gibeah's gates open for refuge during the springtime battles." Abinadab's tone is even, but his gaze is searching for something Ziba isn't saying. My chest tightens when I realize he's staring at me.

"What is it?" Machir asks.

Abinadab inhales, then shakes his head. "Nothing, he just—with the Benjaminite robe, he looked almost like…"

"You're not the first," Ziba interjects. "Many men have said he looks like Saul. Just the tribal resemblance."

Abinadab frowns at Machir. "You're of Manasseh. You have a Benjaminite cousin?"

My heartbeat is frozen, insecurity crowding in around it. All I can do is lower my head and hope Machir intervenes. Which he does.

"The boy's parents knew my father. He's dependent on me now." He changes the subject. "Talk to my servants before you leave, Ziba. They'll make sure you have everything you need."

Mercifully, most of the men start to disperse. In the commotion of getting half of them out the door, I'm forgotten again. I jump when Ama touches my arm. "Relax. No one knows anything. Machir has no reason to tell them."

I don't answer. I'd believed that about Ziba for eight years.

I wait for the house to empty before crawling away. The others don't know that I can't walk, and I'm not in the mood for more scrutiny. With Ama in the kitchen helping the servants, I press my shoulder against the side door and pull myself out onto the low slab of rock that serves as a porch.

The night air cools my skin, and I close my eyes, waiting for the tension to lift. But the distraction merely displaces it. For all Ama's reassurances and Machir's honor, what would the men of this town do if they discovered me? All Ziba's efforts to make me into something other than Jonathan's son haven't touched the reality.

I feel it every time someone speaks against Saul—the blood in my veins shrinking from their accusations. A few stories about Abba's skills with a bow won't change the guilt that's trapped under my skin. Why shouldn't Machir betray me to David, get a bigger reward from the giant-killer? My hand finds the knife while the thought wanders through my mind.

I press the flat of the blade against my wrist, sucking in deep. *Don't. Don't do it. It doesn't change anything.*

But Saul's death evidently wasn't enough to atone for his sins. He not only failed, but he went down in rebellion, defying Yahweh by consulting a witch before going to his death. That's why disaster follows his descendents, as surely as favor follows David. It chased me down, broke half of me. When will the rest of the curse be sealed?

"What are you doing out here?"

My churning thoughts are loud enough to drown the sounds of the few people still milling about. But somehow, I know the words are for me.

Leading their mules, Shaalbim and Zarethan saunter over to the back of Machir's house. Azarel is close behind, his eyes cold with warning.

Zarethan looks down with mock surprise. "Only the knife? You didn't steal the bow too?"

My throat closes. Of course Azarel told them all about that.

Shaalbim's mouth twists. "Good thing your father, the archer, didn't see that attempt."

Fury explodes in my chest, and I straighten up, muscles tensing. It's almost welcoming to feel the heat of anger spreading over the cold deadness.

"Leave me alone. I'm not your father's problem anymore."

A storm rumbles in Zarethan's eyes, and for a second, I wonder if this is what it's like to face an enemy in battle. Before I can take a breath, he smashes his fist into my face. His brother kicks me over, planting his foot on my shoulder.

"Our father risked his life to keep you alive. But you're still the same ungrateful little parasite, angry at him because you can't be king."

I gape, all the fight sucked out of me. "That's not—"

"As if the throne was ever going to be yours. Yahweh took it from Saul before Jonathan even ruled," Shaalbim snorts.

"Stop." I twist one muscle, and Zarethan digs in deeper, pushing my face into the ground.

"What were you going to do with the knife? Kill yourself before Machir turns you over to David?" Shaalbim snarls, scraping his sandaled foot across my face. "You know that's what he'll do with you, right?"

"He won't!" Struggling fiercely, I manage to lift my head and shoulders from the ground. They fight so dirty. "Just let me go!"

"It's in the letter from your own father." Azarel steps up beside them, his stare freezing the beat in my chest. "Jonathan instructed Machir to give you to David. What else would he do with you?"

"At least Jonathan was strong enough to face death. You might be a cripple, but you've spent your whole life running." Zarethan bends over me, and I shake in his grip, deep coldness stealing all the warmth from my body.

"Our father isn't the reason you're cursed. And we will no longer be associated with it." Zarethan's eyes drop, and he snatches the knife from my belt. "Let us help you with this."

Grasping my arm, he yanks my sleeve up and slices into my wrist.

# THIRTEEN

## *Mephi*

———◆◆◆———

I huddle on the step, my arm bent against my side. Blood appears on the edges of my robe, leaking from the fresh cut. The crutches lie across the threshold behind me, but I can move faster without them.

Machir's house is built at the edge of a hill, and I crawl toward it, releasing dirt and pebbles as I scramble downward. The slope isn't steep. I reach the bottom easily and then crouch there, cold to the bone in spite of the warm breath off the desert.

My mind rushes with the fury of a sandstorm, leaving me choking in the dust. Exactly like being caught in a desert wind, I can't hide from what's chased me down. Machir lied to me. My father left me to David, the same way he left me to the Philistines.

Ziba's sons are right. Just like their father was right. And the elders in Ramoth. And every other man who's ever called me an orphan or a stray or a dead dog. I bend over, my hands clasping my elbows while the insults bounce around in my chest with nothing to stop them. Each one widens the gap between me and the future that was discussed around Machir's table.

David's kingdom has no place for me, except as a prisoner. Or a public execution.

I angle the tip of my knife against the blood that's already moving down my arm. My father and I have one thing in common. We both know what it's like to have death overtake us. Except I'd felt the curve of its teeth and survived. Maybe my punishment is different. Spending my life with myself, knowing I'm a coward who can't face an enemy's hatred. Why should I put myself through that? Why not end it like Shaalbim said?

I might have Jonathan's blood, but I'm hardly his heir. I'm worthless to David and offensive to Yahweh. It's against the Law for a lame man to serve before Adonai in the temple anyway, so what does our God think of me? How can I expect to approach Him, even from a distance with a sacrifice?

Because there's something else tainting my blood. Something Saul knew well. Rage. Anger so fierce and ravenous that it's tearing through my thoughts, poisoning each one. My mind feels like a burning structure filling with smoke. If I so much as lift my head in the tumult, it'll choke me.

I'm gasping around the hatred, my breaths short and twisted. I hate David and everyone who followed him, praying for Saul's demise. I hate Ziba and his sons. I hate being like this.

I press the knife down, waiting for fresh blood to appear before streaking a line across my forearm. And a shorter one beside it. Focusing on the bloody branches lets my breathing settle. I'm gripping harder than I need to, cutting too deep. But it's useless to stop. Not until I cut through the memories, sever whatever cord still binds me to Saul.

With each slice, I feel the tug on my heart, the grip of hatred trying to release. Even as I know it won't. Each time, I have to go deeper to find relief.

"Mephi!" Kezi's wild footsteps sliding over the rocks is a different knife, cutting open what I'm hiding in. She's about to shout, but when she sees me, she pauses, gasping, "Mephi, what's wrong?"

I feel small in that moment, but I don't even bother to pull my sleeves down. The blood will push through at this point. Kezi takes two steps toward me, then runs back up toward the sound of more footsteps.

Machir descends the slope next, exhaling when he sees me. When he notices the rest, he just stands there, letting the torchlight twist a dozen emotions across his face. The silence darts back and forth between us, leaving me without any clues of what he's thinking.

I wince when I hear Ama, her voice reaching over the top of the hill. But Machir calls up to her, "He's here; he's all right!" Lowering his voice, he orders Caleb, who's closer, "Bring my mule down here."

Machir hands over the torch and comes to kneel beside me. "Let me see."

His voice is impossibly gentle, but I pull back before he can touch me. "You'll be unclean…" Only a day before *shabbat* too. I choke on a broken breath, wondering how I'll explain this. Maybe some evil spirit is tormenting me, like Ziba used to say. Maybe I am going mad.

I look up, wincing, but there's no accusation in Machir's eyes. Just a deep sadness. He folds his hands around mine, releasing the knife. "My boy, you know the Law forbids cutting ourselves on behalf of the dead."

"It's not for the dead." I sniff, pulling a hand away to clear my eyes.

"I think it is."

I open my mouth to argue, to try to explain what I've never fully justified to myself. But all that comes out is a weak, "I know."

Tension snarls around me, trying to push in again, but Machir's steady tone is like the door of a sheepfold, holding back the wolves.

"You're not going to die, Mephi," he says again. "You're going to live."

"Why should I?" My words break, stumbling over a desperation I've been afraid to touch since the Amorites took me. I press my fists into the ground. "Everyone says Yahweh spared me, but they don't know what it's been like—to be spared. How do they know He's not waiting for another chance? I have nothing to offer our God. I couldn't bring honor to a father if I had one. He's forsaken me for Saul's sin."

Machir moves his hands to my shoulders, pulling me closer so our knees are touching. "Mephi, why did Yahweh command us not to eat meat with blood in it?"

I pause, letting Ama's instruction in Torah wind back through my mind. "The life is in the blood. Blood is for... atonement."

"Yes. Life is a gift from Yahweh. That is why we cannot approach Him after shedding the blood of another. The blood of each man is precious and sacred. It is not to be esteemed lightly. Even in our own eyes."

His eyes go deep, uncovering the self-loathing I've tried to keep hidden. I shake my head, my chest jumping as I remember to breathe. I want to believe it. But my faith is bruised after years of being told the opposite.

I shrug. "So, He wants me to live. That doesn't mean He isn't ashamed of me. My grandfather failed Him as king, and I—"

I wasn't given a chance to fail as a prince. But I have anyway. I fall silent, and a tear escapes down my face.

"Come with me." Machir stands up, lifting me onto his mule before climbing up behind me. Gripping the reins, he guides the animal downfield toward the setting sun. He stops when we can see the Jabbock fjord, where I crossed the Jordan several days ago. By the time we reach it, the sun is a slate color, melting into the water, drained of its radiance.

Machir points over the river. "Not far from here is the town of Mahanaim. The place of two camps."

One for men and one for angels. I know the stories. But Machir's going to tell me anyway. It's an instinct with elders.

"Our ancestor Jacob, the father of all our tribes, came to that camp with his whole family on the night he wrestled with Adonai's angel. Do you remember what he was doing there?"

I grip the saddle, resisting the sting in my wrists. "He was fleeing."

"He feared for his life and for his children. He had wronged his brother, and he thought Esau meant to kill him. Jacob was a trickster who had stolen the birthright that belonged to the oldest son. But that night, he wrestled with the angel of God and prevailed. And though he went back to his camp limping, he had received a new name—Israel, prince of the Lord. Adonai's royal blessing covered him from that night on."

Machir's hands leave the reins to cup my shoulders. "Mephi, the princes of other nations believe that royalty is something you simply step into by birth. But Israel had to fight for his blessing. As we have had to fight to take possession of the land our God promised us. Canaan was our inheritance, but we still had to contend for it. Some princes wrestle. But they will receive what they seek if they refuse to let go."

His chest lifts, touching my back. "Don't let Him go, Mephi. Yahweh has never failed to turn our deserts into springs of water. He will heal every one of these scars if you let Him."

My heart squeezes, the ache rising and falling behind my ribs. The revelation feels infinitely over my head. But I'm tearless, and the pounding in my veins has subsided. I actually feel tired, the promise of rest working its way through my body. "How do you know?"

A smile warms Machir's voice. "I'm much older and a fair bit wiser than you, Mephi. The Law of Moses says that if we repent of our sins and walk in obedience, Yahweh will receive us back as His sons. That is where every Israelite belongs. In His embrace. Your father lived there, even when Saul wouldn't. That is your inheritance."

I stay quiet, unsure how to respond. As present as He is in our nation's stories, Yahweh still feels like a distant King, sending messages from a foreign country. Even if He saved me, I have no idea what He wants, or how to begin to approach Him. Maybe less resistance is enough of a start.

I close my eyes, and the strangest phrase lifts from my mind. *I'm done running. Will you teach me to walk?*

I feel someone's smile, but there's no way Machir heard me.

"Come." He dismounts and reaches up to me. "I'll help you wash, and tomorrow you can present an offering."

My first time ever doing that on my own behalf. But then, I am thirteen. Insecurity teases my stomach, but the nervous energy is not unwelcome. It's an open path in place of the pit I lived in before. The simplicity makes me wonder if it was there all along.

Machir carries me down to the river and sets me in the shallows. I usually hate it when people touch me, but with each handful of water cupped over my blood-streaked limbs, it becomes easier.

I get through the experience without flinching, and before midnight, I'm stretched out on a sheepskin, bandages encircling my arms. An oil lamp breathes silently next to my head, and I drift toward sleep, staring at the flame.

Machir had promised again not to turn me over to David, and strangely, the seal on my heart that kept me from believing him has weakened. Whatever my father intended, why should I believe Ziba's sons over the first man who's shown me kindness in decades? I know I'll never forget the way Machir looked at me at the bottom of the hill. How was he able to see past the blood and choose to help me?

I turn onto my side, ignoring the sting in my wrists.

It's still not my home, but for the first time, I'm able to feel the warmth of the walls that let me in. I'm able to rest. Instead of dreaming of the Amorites, I think of the brooding presence I'd felt on the road, the merciful moonlight that parted the branches and touched me before the Amorites could.

For the first time, Adonai's hand doesn't feel sinister. Maybe it was a rescue after all. And maybe that's all my father's God wants. One step at a time. Even on crutches.

When I sit up the next morning, something else made of wood is lying at my feet.

It's a bow.

# FOURTEEN

## *Mephi*

———◆———

*A month later*

I'm gripping too hard.

I can tell by the strain in my hands that the arrow will hit crooked. And it does. Even a mere twenty paces off. After weeks of awkward practice, I don't know which is more humiliating—the weak slant of my aim or the ache that crawls my neck and arms after a day of shooting.

Even with a smaller bow, it's still a challenge to hold the weapon steady. Readjusting my knees around the awkward posture I've had to get used to on the ground, I flex my arm muscles, wishing I didn't have to see every one of my lopsided attempts scarring the splintered target. Wishing no one else would see.

I refuse to pay attention to the half-dozen onlookers, but there's more every day, stopping on their way home to watch

215

me. The tangle of unkempt olive trees behind Ebenezer's hut shouldn't attract much attention, and I'm not the only person in Lo Debar who can't walk. Just the only one with a bow.

"There. I told you." Abinadab's attention pulls heat into my face.

"Who is he?" another man asks, his voice lowered.

"He's a Gilboa orphan. Bound to Machir."

"I thought he was crippled."

"He is." Abinadab points at the target. "And yet, look at that."

"No warrior stays in Lo Debar," his friend mutters. "Why does a cripple need to fight?"

Machir turns. "You can speak to him, you know. He's of age."

The men fall silent, but my throat pinches. They don't know how long I've wanted to do this, how many years Ziba's sons wouldn't let me touch their weapons.

Abinadab chortles, looking past me. "Is the boy planning to train with the watchmen next, Ebenezer?"

Ebenezer clears wood shavings from his workbench, pretending not to hear.

Machir blocks the men with his back. "You're not bad," he assures me, his hand on my arm. "You need time."

I sigh heavily, resisting the pull of impatience. "My father—"

"Saul's warriors were doing this since they were children," Machir interrupts loudly, and I turn red while he explains to the others, "His father fought among Saul's sons."

"Be grateful you don't have the motivation they lived with," Abinadab grumbles.

I adjust my hands again, my stomach tense. Ama had told me that Saul was a harsh father, especially hard on Jonathan. I'm almost grateful that I don't remember meeting my grandfather.

I narrow my eyes at the olive trees, bringing the short distance into sharper focus. Sweat clings to my lip and rides my eyebrows. And my leg muscles ache from the awkward way I have to brace myself in order to aim the bow. But I'll sit here until I do better. It's my life now—that, and working for Ebenezer.

Machir had brought me back to him the day after my first *shabbat* here, once I was clean from all the blood, my scars carefully covered. "I can help you," I'd mumbled, waiting for him to scoff and ask how. But the carpenter had merely pulled up a stool for me and spent the rest of the morning guiding my hands

217

around one of the thin saws. Now, I sit there every day and cut whatever he tells me.

I sharpen his tools before he uses them and chop wood with a small hatchet. Ebenezer doesn't utter a word of complaint over anything I can't do. While he splits branches in the poplar grove, I bind the smaller ones with leather straps and drag them back to town. On my hands and knees. The struggle doesn't matter. It's a relief to have my knees and knuckles scraped raw for a good reason.

Most of Ebenezer's work involves repairing damaged wagons or structures, and building everyday items for people in town, though he's sent a few tables and benches to Mahanaim, a mile west. Watching him closely throughout the day and imitating his use of the tools, it's easier to ignore my legs. But the crutches are always propped close by, waiting for me to be brave enough to try them again.

For now, I practice in the dark, when no one's looking. But the weakness in my ankles prevents me from gaining more than a step or two before stumbling. The most I've gotten out of the experience is the sight of my shadow standing straight against the wall. That's something. My elbows and forearms are perpetually bruised and scratched from crawling. But I refuse to be carried everywhere. And I won't beg ever again.

I flex the bow a few times, testing the tremor in my muscles. Maybe instead of practicing with the crutches, I should plant my hands against the floor and push up off it. Over and over, to strengthen my upper body. I use my bandaged wrist to wipe sweat from my forehead. The deep cuts are finally healing under the linen.

"You'll get better," Machir assures me. "Your arms are already strong from compensating for your legs. But your muscles aren't used to the bow yet. I said you would have to work at it, remember?"

I sigh again, equally annoyed and grateful. Machir's quiet kindness still seems unreal, offered too freely to be genuine.

Weeks ago, he'd taken me to make an offering at Lo Debar's makeshift altar. I'd sat with him afterwards and watched the flames char the sacrifice, wondering how certain I could be that it was enough. I'd presented what the Law requires for cutting into my own flesh, but would Yahweh really accept me because of one offering?

Hearing my unspoken questions, Machir had turned to me and asked his own. "Do you believe Adonai gave you your life back, Mephi?"

The silence had caught fire, burning in my face until I managed to shrug. "I don't know why. I don't know what He wants."

Machir had just smiled. "What do you want? What would you do if you could walk?"

A month ago, I would've thought something dark. Find the nearest cliff. Jump off. But now it's more accurate to say that I'm at a loss. Unwilling to die, but unsure what to do now that I have to live.

"I want to be strong," I'd admitted, completely shocked with myself. "I want to learn a trade. I want to fight."

It was the first time I'd ever voiced that to anyone, but Machir hadn't mocked me. He'd simply asked Ebenezer if I could use one of the smaller bows he's kept from his sons. "We both know you're equal to the task," he had told me, leaving me all the more determined to master it. I don't need to be a soldier to fight.

The carpenter hasn't said much about my efforts, but I haven't missed the long, thin shafts of wood he's been sanding down and stacking in neat piles, ready for fletching. He's begun teaching me how to attach the flecked feathers to the ends of the arrows, securing them with pine pitch and twine. I have no idea why I trust either of these men, but I can't deny that I do. And it's a welcome feeling, however foreign.

I fit another arrow and draw the bowstring back, tightening my arms against movement. I close my right eye, my left darting for the target.

Machir's hand warms my shoulder. "Patience. Saul's general used to say, no tension, just zeal."

As if battle advice is going to help me with mere target practice. I twist my face into a scowl. "What is that supposed to mean?"

Humor tugs at Machir's mouth. "Figure it out."

I pause a moment, feeling how my stomach is tied up in knots and my muscles writhe with frustration. Positioning my hands, I stretch the bow taut again and drag a deep breath over everything, slowly letting it out as the side of my hand touches my face. My eyes pull the target into focus, and my arms adjust to the weight. The tightness eases from my stomach, and I wait to feel the warmth of the late sun on my shoulders before releasing.

The twine snaps through my fingers, and the arrow hits the mark on the tree just off-center in the time it takes me to blink.

Machir laughs once, and my smile comes out of nowhere, filling my face with warmth. A quiet pride beats in my chest, and I can feel the straightness of my shoulders, refusing to bend forward.

I should have done this years ago. Every time I take the bow in my hands, something drops into place inside me like a key finding a lock. It doesn't matter that I'll never be taken seriously as a warrior. I know I'll be doing this for the rest of my life.

I've spent too long without purpose or occupation. It's time to start exploring what I can do. My mind jumps back to the crutches, and my fingers tighten around the bow. I'll master those too. If Ziba ever comes back here, he'll find me on my feet with my arrows in this tree.

But he won't come back. We've received word from Mahanaim that David has engaged the Philistines in the Giants' Valley. His success has rallied plenty of new recruits to his side, and when he returns to Jerusalem, Ziba's sons will likely join them. I'd rather not think about Azarel and the others. But I still wonder what it would be like to be among them, training to face our enemies in combat.

I settle the thought, lifting another arrow into place, looking for a farther tree to shoot at. It's not likely that I'll ever fight. And even if I start to earn money with Ebenezer one day, there's no guarantee I'll collect enough to pay Machir back. But I can start somewhere. These daily challenges will work the weakness out of me. Then, who knows?

My next arrow hits right before Kezi steps into view.

Machir's niece seems like everyone's favorite daughter, flitting from house to house helping the widows with washing and mending, or looking after their children. But she's always willing to talk to me, and she's at my side without fail as soon as the sky reddens in the west. Ama walks alongside her, wearing a clean gown and a real smile.

But I'm not ready to shoot in front of them yet.

Kezi lowers her basket and shades her eyes at the trees. "Well done," she says brightly. Her cheeks are flushed, and a rose of Sharon hangs askew in her hair. "My uncle let me shoot once. A long time ago." She chuckles thoughtfully. "I was too nervous to imagine ever using it in defense. Even though many of the women here can fight."

"They can?" Picturing gentle Elspeth, it's hard to imagine.

Kezi shrugs, blushing. "Not like warriors, but they've had to hold their own before. The Amalekite who blinded Isaac would have killed them if Elspeth hadn't dropped a millstone on him from the roof." Something heavy fills her eyes, pulling them toward the ground.

My stomach curls around the thought. I hate picturing someone like Elspeth so desperate, but it's not the first time I've been invited to consider how the people of Lo Debar live. I'd misjudged Machir, assuming he was a tightfisted rich man like Palti. Or a cold opportunist like Ziba. But most of the people here have fought through the dust to stay alive, like me.

"Instinct takes over if you have to protect someone you love." Ama's face softens, and I wonder at the smoothness in her brow. It's like all the painful memories she's worn have been untangled and removed from her eyes.

Kezi touches one of the arrows. "Why do you do this? Is it because of your father?"

My chest winds tight against her efforts to pluck at any errant heartstrings. I refuse to look at the men beyond her waiting for my answer.

"I just have to. I won't wait for someone else to fight for me."

Machir considers me, his eyes easing into the distance. "I trained with your father for a while, back when Saul needed every man to fight. I saw him confront weakness at every turn. Every man does, whether he can walk or not. The strength of your body will never match what you have here." He places a fist against my chest, where the seal ring is hidden. "And here." He taps my forehead. "Tame that, and you will be equipped to govern your body."

I absorb everything in baffled silence, unsure what to do with it all. No man has ever given me so much counsel in one breath. I've been used to pity or mockery, but an honest assessment of my weakness without shaming me for it? That's all new.

"You've mentioned his father before," Abinadab presses Machir. "Was he close to Saul?"

Ice climbs my throat, but Ebenezer's bitter comment silences further discussion. "Everyone close to Saul is dead. How much more do you need to know?"

My face flames, but the men finally start to scatter, leaving us alone.

Ebenezer brings me the fresh arrows he's made, staring at the bow for a long moment. "There will always be enemies. Every man needs to learn defense. But you should be glad that no king will demand your service." He drops the arrows at my side and stalks away.

Ama moves up beside me. "He blames Saul for the loss of his sons?"

Machir sighs. "They fled Gilboa only to run into Philistines pouring in from the south. Ebenezer won't say, but they likely died trying to reach David."

I pick at the arrows, feeling the emptiness again. Even this place remembers Saul with resentment. Is it wise to keep them in the dark about me? Ama gives me a pained smile, likely wondering the same.

"I have an idea." Machir motions to his servants and Caleb jogs over, leading his master's mule. Machir stands back with his arms folded. "Have you ever ridden before, Mephi?"

"Yes." It's how I get everywhere.

He shakes his head. "I don't mean sitting on a mule while it carries you somewhere. Have you ever *ridden* before?"

The night I'd fled Ramoth pursued by raiders chases me down, giving my stomach a weightless feeling.

Machir lifts me up into the saddle and points west. "Go down around the hills and skirt the cedar grove on the north side. You can practice shooting the bow from up there. Then, follow the trees and wind your way back."

"Alone?" I'm sure there's still a threat of raiders this close to Ammonite territory.

"I'll go with him." Kezi pulls herself up behind me before anyone can say anything. My heart jumps into my throat, but her uncle doesn't stop her.

Machir pushes the reins into my hand with an enigmatic smile, and Kezi's arms encircle me, clasping her fingers over mine. Thickness swells in my throat. I have no choice now.

"Just make sure you come back." Machir grins up at us.

Kezi's voice at my shoulder pulls heat into my neck. "We will."

The mule hardly needs any encouragement, springing into rhythm with the slightest nudge of my feet. My stomach leaps, and Kezi's arms squeeze around me as we approach a low pile of dead branches. "Lean forward," she urges me, and the mule responds, sailing easily up and over the wood, its hooves hitting the ground on the other side.

Kezi laughs, spreading her hands once and catching a shriek when we lurch forward. With each lift in the saddle, the ground pushes up closer, and my body braces for collision with it. I can't count the number of times I've been pushed off an animal's back. But every moment I don't fall lifts my attention a few more inches over the mule's head. With my focus on the glint of the river, our pace feels more like flying.

Only the pounding of the mule's hooves and the strain of his muscles keeps me bound to the earth. The momentum of our speed lifts my stomach, cooling the rushing air and pushing the scent of the river into my mouth. Kezi's hands at my waist keep a strange pain pulsing behind my ribs. One that's never been more welcome.

Even as we pull up slightly to hug the river, I can't shake the sensation that I could jump from the saddle and land on my feet. Stirred to my core, I lift my head and pull the feeling all the way into my lungs.

Maybe Yahweh is answering my prayer after all.

For the first time in years, it feels like I can walk.

# FIFTEEN

## *Mephi*

———————— ••◆•• ————————

The rocky plain stretching toward the Jordan embraces the tumult of my thoughts, and my breathing settles into something steadier than I've felt in years. Only a month ago, this wilderness had seemed like a tomb, ready to shut me out from the world. Now, I'm more focused on the way the sunlight wavers in the current, the way my body surges with life from the ride.

Kezi reaches around me and tugs at the reins. "There." She points to a collection of cedars thirty paces beyond us. "Shoot that. I'll move."

She swings herself to the ground, up to her waist in the tall grass, the wind filling her veil. "What are you waiting for?"

I blink, snapping my attention back to the trees. Fumbling for an arrow, I arch the bow, breathe, and spear one of the distant branches with my shot. My stomach drops when Kezi praises me, returning to the saddle. Maybe having her around is good.

"Where's Abinadab to see that?" she chuckles, turning the mule a few paces toward the river. "Our watchmen don't train as much anymore. You'll be the best shot around in a few years."

My face warm, I slip the quiver back over my shoulder in silence. I'm not sure if I believe her, but I can't deny that I want to.

Kezi looks around. "I've been here since I was four, and I've still never been this far outside the gates. You've traveled all over, haven't you?"

I swallow. "I wasn't paying attention. I didn't care where I was."

"Do you care now?"

I shrug, almost laughing. I have absolutely no idea how to answer, but I have to admit, it's the first time I've actually wanted to stay somewhere. Instead of a cave where I'll starve or count stolen coins, I have actual walls and a full meal waiting for me. A bow I'm learning to use. A man who doesn't mind if I work by his side however I can.

The hint of pleasure spilling into my spirit surfaces in a boldness that's ready to kick the mule into a canter and charge for the gate.

But Kezi's hands at my waist stop me. "What's that?"

Across the valley, other hoofbeats thunder into view, riding a dust cloud. I make out one single rider, and the colors of Benjamin across his shoulders relax my defenses. He's not a raider. Still, I fold the reins tighter, my hands suddenly sweating. The mule stamps in place, resisting the extra squeeze of my legs against his sides.

The rider reins in next to us, kicking up the rock debris at the foot of the hill. "I've come to warn the elders—" He doubles over for a breath. Sweat and dirt crease his forehead beneath the rim of his helmet. His horse prances, ready to charge up the rise. "The Philistines are on the move again!"

"They're pushing north?" I nearly shout over Kezi's sharp inhale. Instantly, I think of Ziba's family traveling toward Jerusalem. Are they about to walk right into enemy soldiers?

"I thought David defeated Achish's army," Kezi says over my shoulder.

The man squints into the sun. "They've returned to the valley with double the troops. Mahanaim is arming themselves. I must speak to the elders."

He shoves his horse into a gallop toward Lo Debar's back gate, and I breathe over the fresh dagger in my side. *Not again.*

It doesn't take long for the darkness of my early years to come racing back like dozens of black warhorses, their charging hoofbeats eating up the ground I've covered since then. I see myself huddled in utter darkness, gulping back the pain chewing through my ankles. Or hiding under piles of blankets in a cart while we escaped to yet another city disguised as merchants.

I'd learned to breathe through the suffocating succession of running and hiding, but thinking of returning to that life makes me want to buck and run like a captured stallion. Still, the weeks of aiming the bow aren't completely lost on me. I grit my teeth, summoning back the sense of fight that builds in my chest when the weapon is in my hand.

I urge the mule back up the hill, refusing to think of how vulnerable Lo Debar looks in the empty landscape. How vulnerable I am. I'm past believing I'll simply hide in a cave until the disaster passes by. But how logical is it to imagine myself sighting a single arrow at a cloud of Philistine locusts?

On the other side of Lo Debar's gate, the smoky scent of panic is charging the air. A crowd is clustered around the elder's house in the center of town, obscuring the well and pushing into the fields. Everyone chatters nervously, unsure whether to talk or listen. The widows are the only ones who hang back. Elspeth clutches her father's shoulder, while Isaac sits at her feet, his face carefully blank.

Kezi slides to the ground and elbows through the women, but I stay on the mule, riding closer to hear.

Ebenezer moves up beside me, his hands tucked under his arms. "They've regrouped. After David sent the first battalion running, Achish doubled back and sent twice as many troops after him."

The sharp edge of fear cuts back into my stomach, filling me with resentment I've never been able to answer. The Philistine king decimated our northern tribes, and now the rage that wasn't satisfied at Gilboa is turning on David.

Machir holds up his hands in the elder's direction. "Hold on. Why would we plan to leave if they're not marching this way? They're amassing in Rephaim now. David will answer this threat as he did the last one."

The messenger pants, his helmet clenched under one arm. "David has barely returned to Jerusalem from the first battle. If he doesn't surprise Philistia with an even greater show of strength, who knows what direction they'll take?"

Like floodwaters picking up debris, a dozen voices join in the tumult.

"We are too small to face an attack! We have too few fighters."

"The Philistines have no use for Lo Debar; they'd just wipe us out."

"We should go to Mahanaim. Take refuge in a town with proper walls."

His forehead creased with concern, the town elder Gad tries to talk over the chaos. "When will we know if they intend to come here?"

The messenger is already turning his horse toward the gate. "The way they're moving these days, I'd say within a fortnight. I would arm yourselves if you can, but at least take the weak ones to Mahanaim."

The tight crowd barely parts to let him through, and once he's gone, the murmurs start growing to a fever pitch. Lo Debar's population is mostly weak ones—indigent craftsmen and aimless refugees. Subsistence farmers. And the potential threat is unraveling everyone.

"Steady!" Gad's brother lifts his hands. "We will count the fighting men and consider what weapons we have stored up here. Then we will make a decision."

"Should we not inquire of the Lord?" Amram, the priest steps forward, but he's barely heard.

Lo Debar isn't exactly known for being visited by special words from God. The people here have enough to scrape by, keep the basic laws in simple measure. But there's no official temple. No prophet. Any priest who knows anything on a national level is with David.

Gad waves his arms for silence. "We'll send the women and children to Mahanaim. Our able-bodied men will gather their weapons and return to me. We'll wait to see if the Philistines are actually heading this way."

Machir moves to the edge of the crowd, and I follow him on the mule. It's been a long time since any of us have had to consider a Philistine attack. But the dread is tangible, weighting the air like humidity.

Ama and Kezi join us, a question in their eyes. Machir paces by the well, his chin in his hand. "Kezi, go and pack," he says. "Tell the maids they will accompany you to Mahanaim until we receive word that it's safe."

Kezi and Ama hurry toward the house, but I tense in the saddle. "I'm staying here."

Machir turns around. "What?"

"I almost died running the last time. I'd rather die fighting." I say it through the tremors taking hold of my body.

The warmth in Machir's eyes burns through the shock on his face. He knows I'm serious. But he doesn't agree. "I don't think that's a risk we should be planning for." He exhales, touching my knee. "You're not a warrior, Mephi."

My breath winds tight in my chest. I know he's right. As much as my arms ache to draw the bow, it would only be a matter of minutes before a Philistine sword would cut it from my hands.

"So...we're just going to hide like sheep and let the wolves come?" The words taste bitter. I've spent too many nights shaking in the shadows, waiting for rescue.

Machir shakes his head, his arms crossed. "We should trust the one Yahweh anointed."

The fierceness in his tone makes me lift my head. He's troubled but adamant.

"There's a reason David's survived every battle he's been thrust into. Even when he was a boy, he shocked everyone with how he would jump into the fray, continually dancing on the edge of death, and somehow emerge victorious. Many believed it was only youthful zeal, but he duplicated that success as a commander. Even as a fugitive, armies grew around him. When a man can lead others into the favor of God that he himself enjoys—that's a true king."

Machir's face smooths out, his manner growing pensive. "David was anointed king many years ago, and he has only begun to step into the fullness of that role. He was raised up for Israel's sake. Adonai will not abandon His chosen."

My chest fills and drops, the edge of unruly emotion rolling through me like a tide. "Who's His chosen? David or Israel?"

"They both are." Machir lifts his eyes to mine. "David isn't your enemy, Mephi. He and your father were *neshama sheli*. One soul. His favor was always meant to protect you."

I twist the reins, considering. It's the first time I haven't flinched hearing the shepherd-king's name. He's never done anything against me, but it's been hard not to resent how Saul's rebellion made David's anointing necessary in the first place. I've always looked at David's favor as something unattainable, something to marvel at from a distance while remaining empty myself.

But now, without meaning to, I'm seeing him the way I did in my dream, wearing the lion medallion. Reaching out to me in the storm. I've never met him. Never seen him personally defend me. But according to Machir, the anointing David carries was meant to bless our people.

Whether he's right about my father or not, the fact remains. David's favor is Israel's. The knowledge is like the smooth, colorful lines of a tangled tapestry, revealing a cohesive image on the other side.

I glance into the clearing behind us where the men are collecting farm tools, a few bows and spears. Amram stands apart from the others, nervously wringing his hands. It's the first time I've viewed David's success as a benefit to those around me. But in this case, it will save us all.

"We should pray then," I say quietly, not sounding like myself. "We should ask Adonai to help David defeat them." It sounds too simple. But it's absolutely what we need to do.

Machir's face settles. "Come with me."

He pushes toward the elders, and I ride up behind him, my chest burning. Resenting David won't save us from another Philistine rampage. Only an army led by the anointing of God will. I know that much from the stories of my grandfather's failures and David's wins.

I intend to listen from a distance, but Machir shouts for silence and gestures at me. "Gad, the boy has something to say."

When the men look at me, my mouth goes completely dry. Breathless, I have to force the shreds of my voice to form words.

"We don't have to run. We ran before. But that was when… Saul ruled. David is king now. We should stand strong, and trust his armies to be successful." I swallow, avoiding the elder's eyes. "We've faced plenty of trouble, but we don't need to abandon our position when we have a king who carries God's honor."

Gentle awe eclipses the men's faces like a sunset changing the color of the land. But what's more insistent is how the words are reaching inside and changing me, as if someone else was speaking them. A chill envelops me, riveting every sense to the reality I've ignored.

Ama's stories run back through my mind, shaking off the slumber of years of ignorance. I'd passed over them, assuming that the genealogies and battles of our past had little to do with me. My life was about survival. Getting to a place where I wouldn't be killed.

I hadn't cared about David's battles, believing they were more to do with him seizing control of what had belonged to my grandfather. But now, it's all pulling together. It's like the bow in my hand, tugging a string I didn't realize bound me to this land, to a future I didn't know was mine. My father's legacy is very much alive. And it's not a light thing.

The strength of my legs doesn't matter. I'm an Israelite. David's battles are mine. The awe of it widens my heart like tent pegs being stretched to expand a dwelling. Like a sunrise lighting more and more of a landscape, chasing away the dark.

My heart thumps in my throat. It does matter what I think of David. I can't ignore him anymore, even if I'll never meet him or fight for him. He's our king. If he's victorious, so are we.

"The boy's right," Amram agrees, his timeworn voice quieting what's left of the crowd. "War has driven us across the Jordan, but we must not think we are forgotten of Israel. We should stand with our brothers, as we can."

"And we will," Gad declares, lifting his hands. "Tell the families to wait. At sundown, we will petition Adonai to have mercy on us. We will fast and proclaim that His promises to David will stand."

Hearty agreement swells through the crowd, and the ache doubles in my chest. This is what I've missed, so long held at length from any kind of family or tribe. I never would have guessed I'd find either in Lo Debar. But now, I'm in the midst of men who will boldly face whatever comes, because they trust Adonai. And they aren't afraid to count me among them.

"They still don't know who I am," I mutter under my breath.

Machir smiles. "You're a son of Israel who's survived his scars to grasp a bow and bring Yahweh's own promises before Him. That's all that matters for now."

My stomach tightens, churning with anticipation. Could that really be enough? I'd always imagined Yahweh ready to demand something from me, some sort of restitution for my lineage. But is it possible that He really spared me, and now all He's looking for is an acknowledgement of His power, a willingness to give Him my life?

As evening clouds fold in over the sunset, I crouch up against the olive tree I've splintered, and listen to the elders' prayers lifting in response to the priest's petitions.

"Adonai, you have been faithful to raise up the son of Jesse for this hour. Deliver us from the Philistines by his hand, that Israel your firstborn son may glorify you! Remember your promises to David. Remember your vows to Abraham, Isaac, and Jacob."

I pull my knees closer, my fingers locked around my bow, but nervous energy still strokes my skin. The air is changing around me, the way it did on the road, when I was hoping to hide from Yahweh. As the prayers rise, each man folding his words into a collective moan, the sensation grows around me like a storm building. The crackle of lightning cuts the haze over my head, forking across the valley, giving my tension visible shape.

But it's not a feeling of danger. The more I sit with it, the more I want to get closer. It's a presence that invites nearness, like a father's form in the dark. But it's also commanding, as if I'm at the end of a rope, being pulled toward a future I don't understand and can't see.

I rub my thumb over the side of the bow, trying to grasp at an edge of what I'm feeling. It's a faint memory, so brittle that if I think about it too hard, it might disintegrate.

Ama had told me about David's battle with Goliath, the Philistine giant who'd threatened our people decades ago. I always sneered privately at the story, picturing a shepherd boy showing off in order to gain favor with my grandfather. But I remember something else Ama told me. Something my father used to say.

*Nothing prevents the Lord from saving, by many or by few.*

It's gone in less than a breath, but for some reason, a veil has parted tonight, and I'm able to see in closer. David wasn't alone in that valley. What the army saw was a shepherd with a sling, but he wasn't *only* a shepherd.

He was Adonai's anointed back then.

I wonder why I never realized that before. If anyone mentioned it, I hadn't put things together. It never caught fire inside me.

But now, it's no longer just a story. It's burning hotter with each breath, and I have to answer it. Adonai wants me to. Maybe that's why He's been after me since my brush with death. For some reason, He wants to know what I'll do with David.

"Yahweh—" I whisper, and my lungs explode. I'm in Lo Debar, not up against the holy mountain of Sinai, where Moses received our Law. But the God of that mountain has come down. I know it. For the first time in my life, I feel truly seen. And I'm afraid to open my eyes. I bend over on my knees.

"Adonai Yahweh, I'm not worthy to ask anything. But I know you're here."

Maybe that's enough. I did tell Him I was done running. I set the bow aside and open my hands, refusing to imagine Yahweh's eyes taking in my scars. The ones I put there. "You see how your enemies have come out against us. For Israel's sake, go before your servant David and save us by his hand."

Just like that, I can breathe again. The rushing sensation recedes like a wave pulling back out to sea. I no longer feel set apart on the hill, isolated from the others. What has opened in my mind is so simple, and yet it's tugged me over some invisible line where a different future is possible.

I can't clearly define it until I'm back in Machir's house, drifting toward sleep. Then I understand.

It's the first time I've ever spoken Yahweh's name in a direct prayer for David, picturing him as a friend instead of an enemy. It's the first time I've believed our God wasn't waiting to send his new king to crush me.

And somehow, it's the closest I've ever felt to my father.

# SIXTEEN

## *David*

--------◆◆◆◆--------

I drum my hands against the hilt of my sword, imitating the persistent hum building inside me. My thoughts burn hot, filling the camp with smoke while I wait for movement. His before ours.

For this battle, I have the strangest directive yet—to wait for Yahweh's armies to enter the trees and begin marching. But my thousands have been assembled since sundown, refusing to sleep. And the forest above Rephaim is more silent than a tomb.

The blood and dust of the last battle had barely been washed from our shields before the message came that the Philistines had returned to the Giants' Valley. After my years of dancing just out of his reach, I'm not surprised Achish isn't finished with me yet.

But the news had reached us too late, giving us barely enough time to prepare a counterassault. I glance across the camp at Joab, breathing through the regret pinching my eyes.

We both still feel how strange it is to march into battle without his youngest brother.

No messenger has come close to replacing Asahel in speed and accuracy. It's been more than two years since his death, but I still can't forget the way Joab raged through his own tears, describing what his brother looked like with Abner's spear all the way through him. I should have known then that Joab wouldn't rest until Abner joined Asa in death.

I close my eyes, and the image shifts. I wish I could be done losing men. There's a host of warriors that I would have by my side now if not for the wars that took them. But it's the dream of Yahweh to free Israel. And He chose me for that task years ago, even before I'd set foot in Saul's court. If it's a fight to achieve that, so be it.

I push a long, slow breath through my lips. Yahweh's instructions repeat in my head, stronger than the whine of exhaustion in my ears.

*Bring your troops around to the rear of the Philistine army and wait for Me there. When you hear the sound of marching in the tops of the balsam trees, then rouse yourself, for the Lord has gone out before you to strike down the Philistines. From Geba to Gezer, you shall strike them down.*

The words wind into my heartbeat and set it dancing. I breathe silent thanksgiving through my smile, imagining it. Whether by many or by few, Adonai will keep His promises to us, even if He has to march through the trees Himself.

And so, we wait. We won't move until He does. Adonai kept His promise to come like a mighty flood and burst our enemies apart at Baal-Perazim. Now, we need Him to do it again.

My fingers find my sword again, grounding me.

Goliath's sword.

Since the day I nearly broke my arm using it to sever the giant's head, it's been more than a weapon to me. It's been a symbol of Yahweh's faithfulness in every battle fought. Adonai was my deliverance in the valley of Elah when I'd reached for a sling instead of Saul's armor. And He was my refuge when I lost Goliath's sword to Achish when he'd captured me at Gath.

I set my teeth, resisting the anger cutting through my veins. The Philistine king hasn't changed. He's still the same cowardly murderer, mocking us from behind giants and using my own losses against me. His latest message tangles around Yahweh's words, digging through my mind. *Are you ready to join your brother in death, shepherd-king?*

Still raging from my betrayal of his trust years ago, he's lashing out, hoping I'll react rashly and throw my tired forces against his multitudes in a disorganized counterassault.

In seconds, it all comes rushing back like evil floodwaters. How he stood smiling over Jonathan's body in my dream, and taunted me with a lion in his fortress before shoving tainted wine down my throat. *Come now, you're not afraid?*

Instantly, the air snaps shut around the thought, and Achish's voice melts, sucked down into the powerful heat filling the glade. It's as though Yahweh Himself stepped into the forest and slammed a door shut. *Enough!*

Trembling seizes my limbs, and I surge to my feet, openmouthed as I search the sky through the branches. At the edges of our company, my guards and commanders snap to attention, seeing the change for themselves. Even though it's midnight, the east is glowing with sunrise, turning the tree trunks red. The brightness pours through the forest, rushing toward me, enveloping my feet in a warmth as thick as oil.

But above me, it's loud and crashing. Like the pounding of ten thousand feet. Twice that. The armies of the Lord are without number. My chest fills with the sound, every sense sharpening to the lightning flashing between the trees.

Joab's voice barely lifts over the thunderous marching, asking me if it's time. But I don't need to answer. I just look at him, and he launches into action, signaling Abishai and the others to alert their forces. Already assembled, we're on the move before my heartbeat can catch up.

I spin Goliath's sword, militant remembrance charging back. When I was an undercover mercenary, Achish had given it back to me, hoping I would continue what the *Nephilim* began. But it was really Yahweh who put the blade back in my hands. To end it.

I grin as the Philistine tents appear in the valley ahead of us. Carried along by the heavy breath in my lungs, I yearn to quicken my pace, but instead, I kneel. With the sword-point in the ground, I press my head against the hilt—the way I would bow to a king.

*This battle is yours, Adonai! Glorify yourself! Let Achish feel the presence of a real Lion.*

The power surging around me lights the night, eclipsing the stars, and I watch as the steady march of God's invisible armies engulfs the outer perimeter of the camp, causing the guards to drop where they stand. Released to move, I signal to my commanders and overtake the king's tent myself, sliding between the hide walls alone.

The cloying smell of incense hits me, awakening a dozen evil memories, and a flame leaps from my chest, lighting the room. Achish jerks awake.

"Who's here?" he mutters, all the arrogance he carries in daylight dropping from his shoulders. Every façade destroyed.

I laugh. It's all I can do with the *Ruach* so heavy around me. I don't even have to explain. The God of Jonathan has come down to avenge His own, and Achish knows it. Without waiting for him to recognize me, I aim Goliath's sword and stare down the blade, smiling as the air turns to fire around me.

"You know Who's here. Now, get off His land."

# SEVENTEEN

*Mephi*

———— •• ◆ •• ————

It's been months since I dreamed of war, but the moment I close my eyes, I feel it pulling me in.

I recognize the frenetic flash, the hissing flight of arrows, and the rush of men covering ground before slamming into one another. My mind tenses, alert in the wildness.

But this time, I'm not crouching on the ground, bound by rock. I'm standing frozen, unable to move, unsure if I can. My fingers grip my bow, but I can't look at it. It's just in my hand. Undrawn, while I take in my surroundings.

I'm in a forest among trees that move, rocking and bowing as one. I hear the rush in the canopy, the ominous creak in the center of the bark as they bend, parting for thunderous steps that rumble the ground. Recognition claws through my veins.

The giants are here.

The *Nephilim* have fought among the Philistines since my father's youth, terrorizing our people with their formidable size and unmatched strength. Until David. The shepherd-king mocked their power once, releasing Israel from the threat of slavery. Will he do it again?

My heart thumps in my ears, covering the sound of fire in the trees. I can see the sparks dancing, spreading smoke that curls around my feet. But the air doesn't cloud. In fact, it clears. Heaviness lifts from my chest, opening the same quiet calm that had slipped into the thicket and found me up against the tree with an Amorite sword at my throat. That same audacious peace, showing up where it had no right to be.

I watch the trees avidly for the source of the rumbling. Is it the giants? Or...

The sparks glow brighter, slowly coming together to form a heavy, lumbering shape. It's running on four massive paws, breathing through teeth. A fiery golden mane streaks out behind it, scattering embers in the path. The lion is more than consumed by flames. Its essence is fire, and its eyes waver and glow like coals, growing more terrible as it gets closer. Its approach mutes the battle sounds, swallowing everything with the heavy whisper of burning.

Mouth open, limbs locked, I wait for it to reach me. To pounce. How do I fight this? Will I feel fire or claws first? But when it's upon me, it simply circles, fire sliding through and around me, sparks darting toward the sky to join the stars. Like dancing.

When I wake up, I swear I still smell the smoke, but Machir's house is quiet. I feel bereft as the walls and ceiling slowly come back into focus, replacing the fiery images. I'd almost wanted it to be real.

I lie there trying to pull the sensation back to my heart— the strength and certainty of being exactly where I was meant to be, even without understanding. Nothing I've seen in the night has ever taken hold of my heart so insistently.

I don't plan to mention it to anyone, but later, when I can't lift my eyes from the table, Machir presses me. "What is it?"

I shake my head, seeing it all over again in place of the room around me. Machir's going to think I'm insane. But how could I have imagined it? It's connected to that moment on the hill somehow, when we prayed for David weeks ago.

I don't understand it, but Adonai came to hear our petitions. I know it. But does this dream mean He's answered? Why would He tell me?

I blurt out the whole dream before I can start to feel awkward, but Abinadab's shout interrupts me before I finish.

"Machir!" He bursts through the door with the elders behind him. Gad's eyes are wild.

"We just got word from Mahanaim. David returned in victory! The Philistines have been routed—double the army, completely driven back. Instead of repeating the previous strategy in the valley, David inquired of the Lord, and Adonai told him to circle through the forest and wait to hear God marching in the balsam trees. Then, he attacked Achish from the rear."

My eyes jump to Machir's, and he smiles through his surprise. "We know," he says quietly, nodding at me. "The boy dreamed it."

Gad looks from him to me, flustered. "What do you mean, he dreamed it?"

Machir lifts his hand at me. "Tell them."

My heartbeat punches my ribs. Somehow, I drag the dream through the thickness in my throat and watch the men's faces change. Amazement smooths the confusion on their brows, and their mouths drop open when I mention what I felt on the hill when we prayed. No one else had seen the lightning or felt what

I felt. I'm shaking from the inside out, wondering where I'm getting the courage to talk like this. When did I start dreaming of things that really happen?

Gad stares at me openly, likely wondering the same. He lifts a finger, addressing Machir. "Who is he again?"

Machir just smiles. "His life was spared for a reason."

But I barely hear him. The elder's question beats in time with my heart. A year ago, I would've answered differently. I told the elders in Ramoth I was nobody. I had no interest in David back then, no ability to decipher my dreams. I'm still not sure who I am exactly, but somehow, my first answer is no longer true. Not by a long shot.

I fold my arms over my wild heartbeat, my wrist brushing the ring under my clothes. I have no idea why, but somehow, Yahweh has a purpose for me. One that involves David. Right there, without telling anyone, I decide to believe it.

# EIGHTEEN

## *David*

---

*Three months later*

My heart crashes while I stand watching the door Michal just slammed in my face. I'm still breathing hard, the burn in my lungs joining the heat in my cheeks. Any other king would be furious right now, chastised by a wife who was unfaithful to him. But then, according to Michal, any other king wouldn't have danced before Adonai in the streets wearing only a linen *ephod*.

I rub the back of my neck, refusing to feel sheepish. My royal robes were too heavy, restraining the powerful exultation pulsing in my veins. After months of uncertainty, wondering if I'd done right to move the Ark, the symbol of Israel's ancient covenant had finally come home to Zion, and I couldn't contain myself.

A rebellious undercurrent tightens my jaw. Why shouldn't I rejoice with my people before our God? The unfettered joy I unleashed in the streets with my praise was the best I've seen Israel celebrate in decades. How could Michal see it as undignified?

Regret stings my throat. It used to be her father who could bring my spirits crashing down at a moment's notice, refusing the joy that could've been his. Now, his daughter is choosing the same bitter path. It's not the first time I've realized I'll never find my way back to what we had before. It just feels more final now.

I'm still standing there staring at the door when the prophet Nathan enters, letting in a cool evening breeze that lifts the hair from my forehead.

I reach out to him, relieved. I'd wanted to be alone, but somehow that doesn't apply to Nathan. The man who anointed me in Hebron has become a trusted friend, bringing the Word of the Lord since I ruled only Judah.

Grinning, he clasps my arms. "My king, the Lord isn't finished with you tonight."

"I'm glad," I laugh, averting my eyes. "I was going to send for you."

Nathan's honeyed smile reaches deep. "I take it, it's not the estimation of Saul's daughter that troubles you?"

I blush, thankful that the old wound is staying closed. "Not anymore."

I'm not sure what I was expecting when I brought Michal back to Jerusalem, but we certainly haven't regained any intimacy. Her caustic assessment tonight was the first she's spoken to me in weeks. The idealistic shepherd who'd been so eager to marry her seems like a different person, locked away in the corner of my heart where the rest of Saul's family lives.

I sigh, pulling a robe over my shoulders. "I thought that Michal would stand with me when I was anointed, but I'm willing to be content that Jonathan did."

Nathan folds his arms, pensive. "You still haven't located his son?"

I shake my head. "No. I'm beginning to think Yahweh doesn't want me to find him. Not yet."

"Why not?"

"I'm not sure. But there's something else."

Nathan inclines his head, and I drag my hand up one of the polished columns supporting the roof.

"When I was in exile, I dreamed of building a house for God. Now here I am, living in a house of cedar, and the Ark of the Covenant still sits in a tent. I'm grateful to have it here, but shouldn't I do as I promised?"

Nathan's face warms. "The Lord has not lived in a house made of hands in all the time He has dwelt among our people. He has moved with us in all our travels from Egypt until now." The prophet's mouth pulls into a smile, and he reaches out his hands. "Listen to the Word of Adonai."

My stomach drops as the air thickens around me. I kneel, and Nathan's hands encircle my head.

"Thus says the Lord, I took you from the pastures to be a prince over my people. I have been with you in all your wanderings and have cut off your enemies before you. I will make your name great in the earth, and your son will build a house for my Name. But right now, I am going to build *your* house."

The words assault my heart with a flood of emotion. The God of Israel is concerned with my kingdom? After all He's already done?

Tears gather as Nathan continues, "My steadfast love will not depart from you, as I took it from Saul. If you walk in my ways, your throne will be established forever."

I cover my mouth, barely repressing a cry of joy. Yahweh's abounding love never ceases to astound me. And yet, it's a small thing for Him to have taken me as His own and raised me up in this way. What's happening here is so beyond me. It's nothing less than instruction for mankind, a glimpse of what Yahweh wants to do with every heart that is submitted to Him.

My heart twists inside out wishing my wife could understand. That's why I danced! The fact that Yahweh's presence goes with me in every battle is the greatest joy of my existence. The greatest grief was seeing the king I loved reject it and fall under a curse. A curse that I can only protect Israel from by humble obedience.

Stretching out on the ground, I raise my voice in worship. Nathan's form disappears from view, eclipsed by the cloud of Yahweh's hovering glory. I want to laugh, picturing my plans for a temple. Even the most extravagant house could never hold Him. He raised me up as king, He subdued Achish under me, He rescued Israel by my hand once again. All my concerns and insecurities melt away in His presence.

My hands shake as I lift them, my seal ring catching the lamplight and reflecting Yahweh's smile back to me.

"Because of your promise and according to your own heart, you have brought this greatness to pass! Blessed are you, Adonai Yahweh. There is truly none like you."

PART TWO

# NINETEEN

## *Mephi*

———◆◆◆———

*Five years later*

L o Debar smiles in the darkness, lit by a hundred torches.

The dirt street through town is full of color tonight, lined with families dressed in whatever precious festal garments they own. From a bench at the edge of the crowd, I settle back to watch the celebration, relishing the extra warmth in the air.

Springtime is the season of feasts, beginning with the offering of the barley harvest, and I feel obligated by thanks. This is the first season that anyone can remember celebrating Firstfruits without anxiety about the coming months.

Across Israel, sheaves have been gathered and set apart in an amber procession from the Kidron near Jerusalem to the upper part of the Jordan. The barley fields that were sown in winter are ready to be cut now that the months have grown warmer. But we set apart the first sheaves to God, acknowledging the surety of His provision.

The feast's processions have become more elaborate in the past few years as the grip of Lo Debar's poverty has eased.

For weeks, men have taken sickles to the fields, eagerly bringing the sheaves to the priests for inspection. The marked sheaves are reaped until the proper amount is obtained. Then, the grain is threshed in the courtyard with rods, parched over an open flame, and winnowed until white chaff dances on the wind.

Amram waves it before the Lord each year, along with olive oil and frankincense, and burns the rest on the altar, which we repaired after hearing of David's second victory against Philistia. Back when I was just thirteen. Even then, I knew that Israel was breathing differently. I knew that things would be different.

What I still don't know is what that means for me.

Amram's ritual words from today's ceremony intone in my head like a steady drumbeat. *Our fathers were about to perish, so they went down to Egypt and dwelt there until they had become a great nation. Now Yahweh has brought us to our own land, a land flowing with milk and honey...*

Our people were perishing, and Yahweh saved us. It's the theme of all Israel's stories, traditions, and feasts, and I've finally been able to step inside them after existing on the fringes for so long. For five years, I've been able to work past survival, growing into strength I didn't know I had. Rather than cutting my wrists, I take pride in the scrapes carved into my forearms from binding sheaves at the edges of the fields. No one asks questions when they see me on my hands and knees doing whatever I can to help.

I should be content.

Instead, I feel lost. Unsettled. Every day increases my yearning for change that won't come. My past still hangs from a cord around my neck, and my present breathes promises I can't interpret.

The bow and crutches Ebenezer made for me sit propped on either side of my bench. I've mastered them both, training every willing muscle to compensate for what I lack, but I've reached a limit I can't ignore. In spite of what I've achieved, I can't go much further with either walking or fighting. And no one expects me to.

So, what does that mean for my future? Is my life to be lived out simply enjoying the safety others have fought for? Struggling to contribute to the work of those around me? It used to be enough that I could participate. But something in me expected more. I'm still young. I'm not an old man who's earned the right to sit on the sidelines.

A burst of laughter shifts the noise of the celebration, and I refocus on the crowd, trying to bury my disquiet. But then, I see Kezi.

She's dancing with the women, her mother's red shawl bound around her waist, and her hair still flecked with chaff from the winnowing. A strange flame leaps in my chest when she moves. I pull my gaze away, trying not to be caught staring. But it's not the first time I've wondered if she's part of what's missing.

The men dance in their own groups, arms clasped around each other's shoulders, legs kicking free into the circle. Laughter explodes from breathless chests every time someone's difference in height causes another to stumble. A few of the younger men beckon loudly to Ebenezer, who shakes his head, edging away.

Five more years of aging haven't slowed him down at work, but he still doesn't dance. And they know better than to ask me.

"If the king can do it, so can you," Abinadab jibes, raising more laughter in Ebenezer's direction.

I roll my eyes. We've all heard of David's dancing abilities. Only a few years old, the stories are already legend.

The news that the *hakkodesh* had killed a man for touching Israel's sacred Ark had held everyone in the grip of fear for months.

268

The golden symbol of Adonai's presence has been described to me many times, but I've never seen it. It contains the original copies of our Laws, given to Moses on Mount Sinai, as well as his brother's staff, through which Yahweh performed miracles to save our people from Egyptian slavery. But for years, this sacred symbol hasn't dwelt close to the king.

Finally relieved of his fear, David had brought the Ark back to Jerusalem amid a cloud of glory, dancing before the Lord in the streets wearing only a simple linen garment. His exuberance earned him plenty of criticism from those who felt he'd shed royal dignity with his robes, but many more people admire him for it.

Given the success that follows him everywhere, Yahweh can't be too offended.

In five short years, David has taken Israel beyond her pre-king existence, expanding our borders into Moab and Edom, enforcing labor and controlling trade routes exactly as our attackers used to do to us.

Three years ago, he took Metheg-ammah back from the Philistines, removing their final grasp on the region. Trade flows easily now, with more merchants willing to make the journey south.

David's defeat of Hadadezer and his Syrian cohorts has given Israel the wealth of the land of Zobah, allies from Hamath, and control that stretches past the great Euphrates River. A mighty garrison sits in Damascus, and the Syrians' tribute fills the storehouses in Zion, waiting for the day David's greatest dream is realized—a house for the Lord.

Gold and bronze are commodities now, and weapons are easily forged without the old Philistine restrictions. David dedicates all the extra wealth to the Lord, including what he's recently obtained striking down eighteen thousand Edomites in the Valley of Salt.

I used to relish the stories along with everyone else. With my first prayer for David's success five years ago, I'd felt drawn in somehow. Included. After seeing Yahweh's presence in my dreams like a flaming lion, ready to do battle for His anointed, I'd been stirred for weeks, assuming it meant something. For me. But year after year, David changes everything. And little changes for me.

I fidget on the bench, my attention still on Kezi. She's been at my side since I got here, and her steadfast friendship always gave me a reason to keep going, conquer another obstacle. Laugh. Her presence has been as steady in my life as the tools of Ebenezer or the bow Machir's taught me to use.

But things are changing for her too, and I'm starting to wonder what's keeping her in Lo Debar. Absolutely nothing, once any one of these amber-eyed dancers figures out he can take her anywhere else in Israel and have a prosperous life.

My stomach twists, and I resist the thought, refusing its power to ruin the day. Tired of sitting still, I reach for my crutches, position them on the ground, and hoist myself up. It's still nearly impossible for me to gain ground on these, but being able to stand upright for minutes at a time is worth the effort it's taken to adjust.

The minute I straighten up, I feel fresh attention on me.

Three young men have been watching the celebration from a distance, keeping apart from the others. I don't recognize them, but when I get to my feet, they leave the edge of the forest and approach me. Once they get close enough, I notice the Canaanite blades tucked into their belts, and alarm quickens my pulse. I have no reason to be threatened by them, but my stomach drops when they move into position, one on each side of me and one behind.

Arms folded, the tallest man nudges my crutch with his foot. "Going somewhere?"

"Maybe," I mutter, angered by the instant offense clawing my throat.

It's been easy to forget how obvious my disability is, since everyone in town accepts it. But all it took to uncover the shame was for a stranger to come here and look at me the way this one is now.

"How'd that happen?" the man behind me asks.

Turning slightly to see over my shoulder, I nearly lose my balance. "None of your business."

The men chortle, amused by the way I caught myself. One of them presses a finger into my chest and pushes gently, but I tense my muscles, refusing to fall. Why did these troublemakers come here? Who are they?

"We saw you today, working behind the reapers," one of them ventures. "Too proud to beg?"

My ears turn hot while he picks up my bow. "What's this for? To chase crows off the fields?"

"It's what all bows are for. To defend our people." Ebenezer answers for me, and I lower my eyes so that I don't see the men's reaction. I can still hear it though.

One of them studies me up and down before aiming his glance at the women. "If you're their best defense, they'd better hope no one attacks."

Dropping the bow at my feet, they move away, leaving me struggling to breathe through the thinning air of my temper. Ebenezer talks through it, trying to reach me. "There's a good branch right over his head," he quips, pushing the bow closer.

I just scoff under my breath and shake my head. I'm not showing off for someone like that.

"They don't have an ounce of your grit; I can tell you that." Ebenezer's glittery smile dares me to look at him. "What do they have that you don't, eh?"

I smirk, lifting my chin at the line of dancing men. "That."

"Mmm," Ebenezer broods. "Is that why you've been silent for five years?"

I frown, feigning confusion. "I haven't been silent for five years."

His shoulders jolt in a gentle chuckle, and when I look at him, he's watching Kezi. "I'm not the most observant man in Israel, but I'm not a fool. Do you love her?"

Heat shoots into my cheeks. "Apparently not enough to bring it up myself."

Ebenezer clucks his tongue. "Truly, boy. You shoot yourself down with better accuracy than any of your other targets."

I shrug. "It hurts less when I do it."

"Does it?"

I drop my guard long enough to read the knowing look on his face. Ebenezer's gruffer than Machir, but the years of working beside me have cracked him open, and I've learned more about him than most people know. He's certain his sons are lost forever, and I can't imagine my presence filling even half of that wound. But for me, it's enough to be accepted.

He clears his throat, rumbling soft advice from beneath his beard. "Remember what Machir told you when you first came here? Before you started becoming the best archer around."

Resisting the warmth of the compliment, I search my memory. *What if you could walk? What would you want?*

I'm silent for a moment, thinking of what I said back then and pondering what I have now. I'm strong. Relatively safe. I can earn money, however little. And my aim is sure. As I always wanted. But this—

I make the mistake of looking toward Kezi again. Spinning and laughing. Breathless with joy. My vision blurs as I realize I've crossed a line. Now that I've acknowledged it, I can't go back. But that doesn't mean it'll happen. I can make arrows and shoot them from the ground. I can work as long as I'm on my hands and knees. But my life still isn't substantial enough for a family.

"I am not able to take a wife," I falter aloud, hoping Ebenezer will leave it at that. For all his arrogance, those three strangers were right. Anyone outside of Lo Debar would look at me exactly the way they had.

I study the crowd, searching for an opportunity to change the subject. As soon as I find the three men weaving their way down the street, I lift my chin. "Who are they?"

"Trouble." Ebenezer's guard tightens. "They're from Rimmon's clan."

I look at him and he nods, his eyes wide with meaning. "Yes. That Rimmon. They're cousins of the same man whose sons killed Bosheth in Mahanaim. Their uncle Japheth arrived around Passover."

My throat turns to ice. "What are they doing here?"

Ebenezer shrugs. "Not welcome anywhere else, I suppose. The clan expected a reward, but David killed Rechab and Baanah on the spot. No doubt they're worried they'll be watched too closely if they travel back south."

I study the ground, feeling scrutinized. I've grown accustomed to hiding in plain sight, but being so close to men who knew my uncle's murderers is a different matter.

Ebenezer folds his arms, keeping his voice light. "They shouldn't cause trouble. The elders will watch them. Just stay clear. And—" he nods toward the women, "for the love of Benjamin, say something before someone else does."

"It'd better not be you," I mutter as he stalks away.

Why did I have to say anything about Kezi? How obvious are my feelings if Ebenezer can just walk over and call them out?

"Did you persuade Ebenezer to dance?" Kezi's voice sings in my ear, filling my cheeks with heat that I hope the dusk will hide.

"I was going to show him how it's done." I force myself to joke, barely smiling. I wish to God I could take more than one step on my own.

Kezi catches her breath around a smile brighter than the torches, but her eyes are swimming. She looks at the ground, and concern pushes through my chest.

"What's wrong?"

Kezi sighs, tilting her head back at the women. "It's just…
my mother should be here dancing with us. It's times like this I
miss her the most." She runs her hand over the red sash at her
waist, and I stand there, absorbing the silence between her words.

"I don't remember mine," I offer awkwardly. "Ama's been…
everything."

Kezi finally looks up, glancing back toward the crowd.
"You're fortunate to have her." She shakes her head. "I knew my
Abba might die, but I didn't expect to lose Eema too. I'll never
forget the way her face looked when the news came from the
battle. All she could talk about until she died was Gilboa."

The breath turns sharp in my chest. "Your father died on
Gilboa? With Saul?"

A tear slides down her face, but she doesn't break my
gaze. "Yes."

My stomach turns over. I'd known she was an orphan, but
I'd never imagined her having to flee because of that battle. It
makes me sick to imagine it. "Why didn't you tell me?"

Her shoulders lift in a deep breath that doesn't release.
She hides a crooked smile, revealing a hesitancy I've never seen

on her. "Because I didn't want it to be the only thing we talked about. The only reason we were close."

I look down before she can find my eyes. But I feel hers burning my forehead.

"Do you remember your father?" I whisper, grateful for something to say while I struggle to sit back down.

"Not really. My mother was Machir's sister. He has more stories of her."

She falls silent again, leaving the memory hanging between us. Two fathers, dead on the same hill. But there's a difference. My grandfather sealed their fate. He's the reason we're both orphans.

Kezi stiffens abruptly. "People acted like my father took my future out onto Gilboa and buried it with him. Women used to say that no one would pay a bride price for me. But Machir taught me…" Her voice slants, and she settles herself. "There's a reason I lived. I've grown up trusting that reason, even if it's something only Yahweh knows."

Coming out of the memory, she looks into my eyes. "Do you believe it?"

"What?" I ask, jarred out of listening.

"That my life was spared for a purpose?"

I sigh. "Of course."

"Then why is it so hard for you to believe the same about yourself?"

Unsettled, I grip the edge of my crutch, my thoughts thrashing like an animal in a trap. Even with all of Machir's kindness, there's still so much I haven't accepted. I can't explain it, but I can't escape it. My life is incomplete.

"My purpose was different!" The words dig through my throat, pulling pain after them. "I was Jonathan's only heir. He knew I would be here after he was gone, but not like this. No one expected this to happen, and nobody wanted me when they found out. I was supposed to be…king."

There. I said it. And it sounds just as ridiculous as I thought it would. I remember the men around the fire at Ramoth, convinced I wasn't a threat as long as I was really crippled. The memory instantly blinds me.

"Do you want that?" Kezi questions.

"No!"

*No, right?* I've never asked myself before. I've never been asked.

"I don't know *how* to want it. I wasn't taught to want it because I couldn't have it after this." I tap my crutches with my knuckles. "I was taught to beg, and steal, and get out of people's way. That's what I was taught, and it's nothing my father would have been proud of. Nothing that means anything to Israel..."

My voice collapses when I remember where we are. Fortunately, the crowds are dispersing and we're not being watched anymore.

"I'm sorry," I exhale, embarrassed. "I never wanted the throne. But my father gave his life for our people. He expected me to follow in his footsteps and defend Israel. It was my birthright. If I can't do that, what other purpose is there?"

Kezi's answer comes quickly, like it was waiting right behind her lips. "Your father's plan for you isn't always Yahweh's. I heard that David wasn't even invited to the feast in his own father's house when the prophet Samuel first came to anoint him."

I scoff, unreasonable anger leaping out between us. That's what she has to say right now?

"David." I toss the name at her, deciding that I absolutely dislike him. It's just taken me years to realize it. Having a dream about him doesn't mean a thing. He's a maddening success story, and he got there by clinging to my father's hem. And now I have to hear his name from the woman I love!

My voice hardens, talking over her. "Of course we need to drag him into this. He's a part of every conversation. What else has he done that we need to discuss? How many wives does he have now? Eight? Twelve? The whole nation is in love with him."

"I'm not."

Kezi says it softly, but a thick tremor pushes through the gentleness of her tone. Something unseen reaches between us and opens a door in my chest, silencing every hint of anger. I'm hesitant to look at her, but when I do, it's clear. In all my avoidance, I've overlooked the desire in her eyes, and it's terrifying. But as usual, I can't go anywhere to hide from it.

It's the slightest movement, just a shift in her posture so that she's sitting on the bench at my side, but it changes everything. She breathes once, then touches her lips to mine. A sharp ache explodes in my chest, but it's different from pain. It's worse.

I can't do this. I wasn't supposed to have this. I have to tell her what I told Ebenezer before it's too late. I have to push her away, say something harsh to douse the flame. I've done it before.

Instead, I lean over, pull her face into mine, and kiss her back. Deeply. She cups my jaw without moving away, then slides her arms around my neck. I push my fingers into her hair, beneath her veil, and my throat burns as my heart lurches into it.

She gasps a little, and I stop short.

"I'm sorry," I whisper, but I can't move a muscle away from her.

Kezi's gaze lowers, her lashes dusting her cheeks. "I love you, Mephi. You and only you." She touches my face again and slips away before we can attract any more attention. Breathing heavily, I let my eyes follow her, no longer caring who sees.

She loves me. I don't know how I dare to believe it, but it's filling every corner of my mind, crowding everything else out. I didn't know she could touch the hunger that's lived inside me for years. But she's found it, coaxed it awake. Dared me to believe that part of it could be eased.

And I don't know how, but I'm going to let her do it.

# TWENTY

## Mephi

— ◆ —

*I'm crazy. This is crazy.*

Everywhere I go, I can feel Kezi's eyes on me. The pressure of her kiss chases after me, demanding I answer the longing it's unearthed.

It's barely been a day, and I can't think of anything else. I've restrung my bow twice and replaced the fletching on two arrows, and my aim is still off. Giving up, I fling the weapons against a tree and stare into the sunset.

How was one moment of passion able to erase years of reason? Machir has been kinder than anyone I've ever met, but even he won't want his niece bound to a cripple. There are dozens of better men who should have her, men who can take her out of this place and give her a better life. How did I not think? Why didn't I stop her? Why didn't I stop myself?

That night, I fidget all through the evening meal, trying not to look Kezi's way. No one's mentioned our kiss, but it doesn't mean people didn't see it. In spite of everything, Kezi seems radiantly at ease, keeping a discreet silence while the men speak. I stare at her, wondering why I'm so captivated by her joyful exuberance, wishing it was something I could create in myself.

After the meal, Ama approaches me as soon as Kezi leaves the room. "Have you spoken to Machir?"

"About…?"

Ama smirks, planting her hands on her hips. "Don't tease me. I can only assume you haven't said anything since Machir didn't mention it, so now I'm asking. How long are you going to make that girl wait?"

I sigh. "The women are talking, aren't they?"

Ama laughs. "You think I need their talk to confirm my own eyes? She's like a living torch around you, glowing from head to toe. It's always been that way. And you. I've spent years trying to get you to smile the way you smile at her."

I roll my eyes. "I smile."

"Yes. At Kezi. And your bow."

I bury a blush, rubbing the back of my neck.

Ama kneels in front of me. "I won't tell you what to do, Mephi. The time for that is long past. But I know what shooting that bow does for you, what it unlocks in your eyes. That's what I see when you're with Kezi. She goes out of her way to be around you, and no one else has spoken to Machir about her. What happened last night wasn't a surprise to him."

She touches my shoulder, looking out through the doorway. Machir is alone, his face tilted toward the sky. "He loves you like a son. Talk to him."

Before I can answer, Kezi comes in from the kitchen, carrying a water jug.

"Kezi…" I stop her, and Ama melts discreetly into the next room. Kezi comes to me, smiling, and I rush to speak before I lose my nerve.

"If your uncle is willing, will you marry me?" I try to phrase it carefully. Everything depends on Machir's decision, but I still want hers. The radiance in her laugh burns through all my fears.

"I will. But only if you ask him tonight." Laughing softly, she skips through the door, touching Machir's arm briefly on her way to the well.

I push a slow breath through my lungs, trying to settle my heartbeat. Caleb hurries over to help me, and in the effort of getting up onto the crutches, I'm able to bury some of my hesitation. But it's not exactly comforting.

The crutches have helped me regain a measure of freedom. But tonight, I resent everything about them. I wish I could fling them in the fire and walk out there to face Machir. At least then, I might believe I deserve to. I may never face a Philistine, but I wonder if all men would rather do that than confront what I'm about to ask.

Machir waits for me, as he always does. He knows it takes me ten shuffling steps to make up two of his. He doesn't offer to help me though, even when I nearly stumble over the uneven stone porch. It's my burden to master.

"All right?" he asks once I've reached him.

"I'm fine." I prop the right crutch under my arm for a second to swipe sweat from my forehead. I'm stuck here now, facing him. If I move, I'll fall.

Machir clasps his arms behind him, his gaze following Kezi uphill. "It seems like yesterday I was carrying her to that well. I didn't let her go many places alone after her mother died. Some of the women…well, you know how people talk, and they're not always kind."

I stiffen, hating the idea of anyone making Kezi feel unworthy. "No one speaks badly of her now. They shouldn't have then."

Machir lifts one shoulder. "It takes time for some people to see the worth in one another."

"Not you."

I let the words hang there like an invitation. He's always seen more in me than I could have on my own. He's the reason I'm standing upright, that I'm strong enough to hold myself here. Working with my hands and sending arrows into trees has tamed the hatred that made me want to turn a knife on myself. I haven't felt the urge in years.

Studying the grass at my feet, I try to think of a way to back into what I want to say. "Everyone in town knows she's worthy. Half the men here were watching her dance."

"I know." Even covered by darkness, Machir's smile is easy to hear. He turns, half his face glowing under the nearest torch. "You've been watching her the longest."

I exhale, my shoulders slackening. "She's like your daughter. I couldn't ask you to give her to someone like me."

"What do you mean, 'someone like you'?"

Uncomfortable, I draw a frayed breath. "You know what I am."

Machir lifts his chin, unfolding his arms from behind him. "I know you love her. But I want to hear you say it."

I try to uncover something insincere in his tone, but there's only the same honesty I've seen since the day I arrived. As hard as it was to believe after Ziba, Machir will not deceive me. I owe him the same honesty in return.

I look him in the eyes and say it without breathing. "I love her." I swallow. "But how could I ask you to surrender her to a husband who can't walk? She would never have her own home or the honor she deserves."

"She has a home. You both do. For as long as you need it." Machir grips my shoulder, his kindness wrecking my defenses. Again. "My answer is yes, Mephi. Jonathan's legacy is more than sufficient for the daughter I have come to cherish. I would be honored to call his son mine."

My throat tightens, my mind flooding with all the thousands of ways I owe this man. It's because of him that the bitter poison of despair has subsided enough for something else to grow. And for the first time, it looks like a future. At the risk of losing my balance, I return Machir's grip, clasping his arm at the elbow.

He glances up the path where Kezi's disappeared into one of the widow's houses. "We'll tell her tomorrow, and I'll begin the arrangements with the elders. They won't be surprised. They've already asked me if I intended Kezi for you."

I study the scattering of stars in the sky, still unwilling to believe this is going to happen for me. It's nights like this when I wonder if I'm merely touching the fringes of why Adonai spared me. Becoming Kezi's husband seems like the greatest achievement, even if it's all I ever do.

Back inside, I hardly sleep, hearing every watch of the night, but when morning comes, Kezi's still missing.

"Isaac is sick," Ama explains. "Kezi's helping Elspeth on the other side of Abinadab's hill."

"Can you ask Caleb to bring a mule around for me?" I ask, my smile matching hers.

I'm not in the mood to fumble with the crutches. Once I'm situated on the mule's back, I urge the animal into a swift trot toward the edge of town. The widows' houses are on the north side of Lo Debar where the ground slopes up past the oldest well dating back to Jacob's day. There's a thin strip of forest to my left that thickens as I leave the market behind.

My stomach catches with excitement, anticipating Kezi's reaction. She's going to be my wife.

But the moment the town disappears behind the hill, the air changes. The silence deepens, growing around me, and a strange feeling trips up my heartbeat, like a stick thrust into a wheel. The moment I sense it, I know I made a mistake.

I should have brought my bow.

# TWENTY-ONE

## *Mephi*

———————◆◆◆◆———————

The stone hits my temple out of nowhere, startling the mule under me. The animal whips around as a thicker clod draws blood beneath my ear. Three figures fling themselves from the trees, and a third rock slams into my ribs. Grappling for control of the rearing mule, I slide too far in the saddle, nearly falling.

My chest turns cold when Rimmon's nephews jog into the clearing, surrounding me. I'd forgotten to look out for them, but I haven't seen them since the feast.

One of them seizes the mule's reins, and another flips a rock up and down in his hand, hostility sharp in his face. "They call you Mephi, but it's Mephibosheth, isn't it? You've been hiding behind half a name for years now, denying your connection to the house of Saul."

I grip the saddle horn, assessing my options. I can't get around them, and the knife at my side will be used against me if

I pull it. "My connection is with the house of Jonathan," I say, too loudly. "I've committed no crime."

Another hurled rock cuts me off, striking my head. Three sets of hands tear me off the mule's back, and I hit the ground hard, instinctively swinging my arm. My fist connects with someone's nose before my wrist is wrenched aside, pinned against the ground.

"Your life is the crime," a voice snarls over me. "You've been hiding here, wearing the bloodguilt of our people."

Recognition spears my mind. Rimmon's family comes from the Beeroth clan, a distant relation of the Gibeonites. No doubt, that's how they heard I was still alive. And I can tell by the way they spit the words, the way they crowd around me like hyenas. They want blood.

Desperate to break their hold around my neck, I bring my knee up into someone's jaw, but I can tell they're going to damage me a lot worse than I'll hurt them. One man crushes my legs with his body, and the two others pin my arms so I can't break free while their brother slams his fist into my face.

After the third blow, my vision doubles, and I flop over onto my stomach, spitting blood into the grass before another kick flattens me again. Choking on dirt instead of air, I can't resist the knife cutting into my robe to expose my chest. A hand grabs at the ring, and then I hear a woman scream.

"Stop!" Kezi's running across the field, calling to someone over my head. "Ebenezer, make them stop!"

The carpenter's form wavers in my vision, holding his staff across his chest like a spear.

"Leave him!" Ebenezer growls. "What right do you have to touch him?"

"He's a disgrace!" The closest man spits in my face, his anger wild. "Why are you alive?" he screams down at me. "What did you do to make them keep you alive?"

The questions I've asked myself for years burrow deep and paralyze me. Rimmon's nephews sneer at the silence.

"You didn't tell them, did you?" They step back, letting me see the shock eating through Ebenezer's expression. "You thought these people wouldn't notice they had the son of Jonathan in their midst?" The man spits again. "Pray no one here will want you for a husband. She would be just as cursed as you are."

Kezi's face torches my mind, and I push up onto my knees, my voice ragged. "Why don't you just kill me, then?"

"And have David behead us like Rimmon's sons?" he scoffs. "He can have your life if he wants. But that doesn't mean you're safe. We can send word to half a dozen men who would be happy to finish the job."

His staff hits squarely in my stomach, burying everything. My sight goes gray, my lungs stretched taut around ruptured breaths.

"Enough!" Machir storms into view, and my assailants scatter, but it's too late. The real damage they did is carved into every line on Ebenezer's face.

"Your father was *that* archer?" he mumbles tightly. "Saul's son?"

Tensing violently, I fold my fingers into the dirt and try to sit up. But the moment I lift my head, pain drops like a rock in the center of it. Blood from my mouth weaves into the grass against my cheek. Machir bends over me, lifting my shoulders. "I'll help you."

"You knew?" Ebenezer's tone is heavy with accusation. "He's Saul's grandson, and you hid that from us?"

Machir straightens, standing in front of me. "He's the son of Israel's most noble prince, and he can't walk. How could I not give him sanctuary?"

Ebenezer's face is more twisted than I've ever seen it. His fists are white-knuckled around his staff. "Because of his grandfather, I have lost sons. Saul's defeat at Gilboa pushed our people to the fringes of Israel. Look any one of these men in the eye and tell them you want to elevate the life of his grandson over theirs."

Shame has my heart clenched in a clawed grip. Seeing the trust and acceptance of five years drop from Ebenezer's face in an instant makes me want to pass out.

Machir lifts his hands toward the carpenter. "Don't say anything. I will speak to the elders. But don't reveal this to anyone else."

Ebenezer's expression flinches. "They're not ready to hear it. They'd cast him out."

Machir's servants help me back to his house in stony silence, and he carries me inside. Pain twists through my head, clenching and receding in waves, and I drop my eyes, wishing Machir wasn't close enough to feel me trembling. He doesn't say anything, but I've never seen his jaw muscles so tightly bound.

He checks my ribs and cleanses my cuts, but my mouth is so split, he has to pull the skin together with a needle. When he tugs the last stitch through my lip, a tear escapes down my face, sliding onto his hand.

"We should've told them who I was."

The look on Ebenezer's face rips into me, opening fresh wounds. The carpenter hovers in the front room, pacing through his anger.

"You exposed us to danger by bringing him here!" he grumbles at Machir. "If Rimmon's clan knows where he is, what other men of violence will be drawn here in search of him?"

Machir's jaw flexes. "Those ruffians will answer for what they did." He moistens a cloth with oil and holds it against the bruise in my temple.

Ebenezer snorts. "You think that kind of loathing can be tamed with words? Rimmon's nephews would rather owe you an honor debt than put up with any of Saul's descendents."

Machir seethes, handing me a fresh robe. "He's going to be my son-in-law. They had no right to touch him."

My throat closes. "I'm not marrying Kezi. What happened today is nothing compared to what the Gibeonites will do if they find me. And to them, it would be justified. They're not afraid of David or of you."

"Or the Lord our God."

"What?"

With every ounce of humor gone from his face, Machir looks like a different man. "Vengeance is His. The life of another is not ours to take at will. The men who neglect that part of the Law in an attempt to satisfy personal justice will never find what they're seeking."

Ebenezer scoffs. "Did the fear of the Lord stop Saul?"

I shudder. "I've witnessed the Gibeonites' hatred." Felt it firsthand. "They'll take revenge wherever they can, and I refuse to have that happen to Kezi. I can't protect her; I have nothing to give her."

"Hold on." Machir lifts his hand, his confident smile returning. "You have overcome more in eighteen years than some men face in a lifetime. You have the compassion of your father and the fierce heart of Benjamin. You're as tough as they come, Mephibosheth."

His compliments loosen the grip of fear, but I'm still too shaken to appreciate them. I swallow twice, my torn lip pulling. "I won't be the reason people jeer at her." Just saying it terrifies me.

"So, you're going to stay here and watch her heart break?"

My shoulders drop. I hadn't thought of that. Even once she forgave me, I would have to watch her marry someone else. Assuming I'm allowed to stay.

Machir chews the inside of his mouth. Turning his back to Ebenezer, he presses a fist into my chest. "You listen to me, son of Jonathan. When you came here, we felt privileged, not fearful. My house has received favor from the king, and we are protected by the God your father served with his whole life. Why shouldn't I extend that favor to Jonathan's son?" Passion shakes his tone.

Ama appears in the doorway, gasping when she sees us. "Kezi said something had happened." Fierceness bites through her tears. "Who did this to you?"

"Someone who knows who he is," Ebenezer growls, facing the door.

Ama looks from one man to another, horrified.

Machir glances at her, then continues, "Mephi, the worst part about Jonathan's death was knowing that his line would die with him. He didn't deserve that. When we heard you were alive, I rejoiced that you would have the chance your father wanted you to have. I will not dishonor someone Yahweh hasn't."

I refuse to look up. "You don't think Yahweh has dishonored me?"

"No. I don't. He brought you here, gave you to us." He touches my shoulder. "Don't leave, my son. Stay with Kezi. All will be well."

Without waiting for an answer, he leaves me to myself for a while. I sit there, my hands folded over my legs, feeling the oils work against the swelling in my face while the men argue outside. The slow burn of the elders' voices mingles with the sharp crackle of Ebenezer's.

"If he stays, he'll bring trouble on us."

"What happened to him could happen to the rest of us if the Gibeonites know he's here. Who else told Rimmon's nephews where to find him?"

"He's the grandson of the king my father served." Machir refuses to raise his voice, but it's still stronger than anyone's. "I will gladly defend him."

Ebenezer grumbles, "You shouldn't. He's not your blood."

"He's of Israel. He shares blood with all of us."

I pull my knees up and set my head on them, refusing to think about where I might go if they force me to leave. The ache crawls between my ribs and climbs my torso while the sun slips across the floor toward evening.

When the door opens again, the street beyond the main room is empty. Machir's face is tightly drawn, fierce as an army with banners. He nods across to me.

"The men who attacked you will leave in the morning. And Japheth will pay your wages for every day you remain injured."

"To you or Ebenezer?" I ask, impressed.

"To you." Machir's expression glows. "You're not indebted to me any longer, Mephi. The elders have granted my request to cancel your bond."

My mouth drops open. "I'll always be in debt to you. That won't change." I plan to say it calmly, but the words break.

Machir's smile softens in the lamplight. "I paid Ziba to get him off my back. I never intended to own you. But from today, you will be bound to me in a different way." He looks up. "Help him, Caleb."

He waits while the servants set me upright on the crutches. The added pressure pulls pain into my bruised side, but my labored steps into the front room are forgotten as soon as I see Kezi standing just outside the door between Gad and Amram. They've woven a hasty garland of greenery and flowers between two trees, forming a makeshift betrothal *chuppah.*

Leaving me braced against the doorway, Machir lifts a small pitcher from a low table and pours crimson wine into a golden cup, which he hands to me.

My pulse is so powerful, I'm concerned for my balance. Propping my crutches safely under each arm, I tighten every muscle in my stomach and focus on grasping the cup's short stem. I rarely see Machir's gold, except on feast days.

Machir beams while the priest intones, "Blessed are you, Adonai our God, king of the world, who creates the fruit of the vine."

Amram locks eyes with me, pulling every bit of heat forward in my face until my cheeks sting. "Blessed are you, Adonai our God, king of the world, who sanctifies us by betrothal."

Machir nods at Kezi, whom I've been too frightened to look at. Betrothal is the binding tie between two people before Yahweh, which cannot be broken. I feel the weight of it drop over my chest as though my father's ring is made of iron.

I slip the cord from around my neck while my mind races, searching for the words. The last I heard them, Japhia was saying them to Milcah, his betrothed. But they feel completely different on my lips.

I look at Kezi, holding Abba's signet out to her. "With this ring, you are consecrated to me by the Law of Moses in Israel."

"So be it." Amram snaps his smile out of sight before I can fully feel it. Machir grips my shoulder while the priest and the elders walk away. They're not pleased about my lineage. But Machir got them to agree to my betrothal just the same.

Kezi breathes deeply, sliding her hand around my wrist. "Come with me."

Caleb helps me onto a mule and Kezi climbs up behind me, as she's done so many times. The night is warm, and the moon is a beaming crescent in the distance. I'm not sure where Kezi wants to go, so I head for the well, but she beckons farther. "Keep going."

At the far end of her uncle's land, the ground drops away into a slight ridge, opening into barren countryside. I tug the mule to a stop, feeling Kezi's words before she says them.

"It doesn't matter what anyone says. Adonai spared your life. He takes the downtrodden and he lifts them from the ashes."

I tighten my grip on the reins. "He also takes princes from their thrones and brings them into disgrace."

The moment the words leave my mouth, I feel ashamed. I still bear the hatred people have for Saul, but what was taken from me has been replaced by mercy that I didn't deserve or expect. A better man would bear his lot in silence, without malice. Instead, I've spent my time resenting my limitations and hating the new king, who's done nothing to me.

"You must despise me," I mutter. Everyone in this town does now.

Kezi shakes her head, the brightness shifting from her tone. "I do not. Why would you think such a thing?"

My whole face burns, everything I want to say locked under my tongue. I owe everything to her family. Without Machir, Ama and I would have still been begging on the streets. Ziba rescued me from Becorath, but Machir's kindness had shown me that not everything was broken. He's the reason I have Kezi. And if they're the only two people in Lo Debar who care, it's enough.

"Your faith is so much bigger than mine." My throat aches. "You should find someone who is like you." Like David.

But even as I'm saying it, I know she won't listen. Sometimes I think she deliberately doesn't listen. She sidles closer, resting her cheek against my back.

"I tell you the truth, Mephibosheth. From the moment you came to this house, I wanted to be your friend. When my uncle told me who you were, I believed Yahweh spared us for each other. I feel at home by your side."

My smile slants into a wince. "You deserve a better home."

Kezi puts both hands around my waist, and I press my fist against hers. "Have you thought about where we'll have to live? What kind of future will our children have if they're not even welcome here?"

Kezi tenses in the saddle, halting my incoherence. "The only future I want is with you. We will trust Yahweh for provision. The One who can turn a shepherd boy into a king can make you my husband."

She moves toward me, her face tucked against my neck, and I smile wryly, turning my head. "You won't wait until my mouth heals, will you?"

Kezi giggles. In her gentle kiss, I feel the fullness of a rich gift I never thought to possess. It'll still be a year before we can marry. But like Jacob of old, the months will pass like days if I know she'll be waiting at the end of it. For me.

# TWENTY-TWO

## *David*

———◆———

*Two years later*

From the balcony outside my council chamber, I watch the men of Benjamin depart toward the Kidron Valley. The violence of our history still stains the air, even now that I have their grudging support.

With the first full month of peace since my arrival in Jerusalem, I was finally able to call the men of Saul's tribe together to solidify our ties. It was our first direct meeting since the days when Abner's men would face mine in the forests of Ephraim, pitting one army's strength against the other.

I still remember how the scattered bodies stained the finger of river running through the glade, Asahel among them. And later Abner. My gut twists to think of Jonathan's son meeting a similar fate, but so far, my efforts to find out what happened to him have come up short. Another reason I called for Saul's kinsmen.

"You know that my priorities these last several years have been military in nature. But now that we will have peace for a time, there's something I'd like to settle."

I had leaned forward, making sure I had their attention. "I am aware of Rizpah's sons and the house of Adriel, but is there anyone left from the house of Saul that I might show him kindness for Jonathan's sake?"

I added the last part to dispel any confusion. But my inquiry was still met with awkward silence. The only name they would give me is a man who used to serve Saul's guard and now lives in Gibeah.

I haven't interacted with him much, but his sons have proven valuable, with half joining the army and the others serving in the household guard where their father has become an advisor. Apparently, he'd attended the recent series of feasts I'd held for the Benjaminites.

But what I heard today surprised me more than it should have. How long has this servant been keeping information from me? It makes me wonder what other subterfuge exists. I've been pacing away my questions, waiting for Benaiah to summon him.

"My lord king?"

I follow the voice to the end of the room. "Are you Ziba?"

The man steps forward, bowing. "I am your servant," he says with a flourish. "As the king knows, I once served under the captain of Saul's guard."

"That's right." I turn to face him fully. Benaiah has spoken highly of Saul's former servant. Now I wonder why I never thought to question him. I pause to breathe.

"Is it true that you are the brother of Naamah bat Ebal, the woman who used to serve Jonathan?"

Ziba's expression remains calm, but I don't miss the shiver dancing across his brow. "My sister remains in hiding, my king."

"From me?" Hadn't Jonathan told her about our covenant?

Ziba smiles wanly. "I was concerned for her safety, my lord. She was devastated after losing the Hassar, and it seemed better for her not to return to Gibeah."

I nod, allowing pity to cover my suspicion. I never met Jonathan's wife, Sheva, who'd died before he did, but I'd always been certain that Naamah loved my friend.

"It was a difficult time for everyone," I acknowledge, my pulse drumming insistently. I gently tap the edge of the table, stroking invisible harp strings. "I was told you might know if there is anyone left of Saul's house."

Ziba blinks. "No one who would threaten..."

"No," I cut him off, and Ziba stiffens. Even after decades of leading men, it still startles me how my voice can silence a room. I soften my tone. "I would show him the kindness I've received from Adonai."

I hear the heartbeat of the room, the unspoken breathing between us.

Ziba's answer is hoarse, whisper-thin. "There is one left, my king. The son of Jonathan still lives, but he's crippled in both his feet."

The servant rushes the last part, and my lungs constrict, pleasure twisted aside by pain. *He's alive! Praise you, Yahweh. But—*

I turn aside to pace the room and sort through what I'm hearing. It's been years since I dreamed of Jonathan's son trapped under rock. And all this time, he's been hiding out in some remote corner of Israel, unable to walk? I can think of hundreds of ways he could have died by now. God had to have preserved him. My senses burn as I search for his name in the memory of Jonathan coming to the cave.

*Mephibosheth. We call him Mephi.*

Tears scald my eyes. I had never seen my friend smile like that. Now I can finally make good on my promise to him.

Ziba's face blurs, and I blink him back into focus, my fists clenched. "Where is he?"

# TWENTY-THREE

## *Mephi*

———◆——

I wake up with Kezi folded against me. Her closeness is like healing oil, warm and soothing, and I never get tired of absorbing it. I keep my eyes closed, relieved that it's still an hour or so before dawn. Quiet moments have become even more precious now that we have a son.

I have a son.

The thought still sends a spearpoint of pleasure through my heart.

Carefully shifting my weight, I drape my hand over Kezi's shoulder to touch the baby. Since Mica was born, I've spent hours like this, untangling the mystery of how he's bound Kezi and me even closer together.

I hadn't thought I could open my heart any wider to anyone. Kezi had filled my life, watering every inch of barren land I thought she had access to. And then, Mica's birth had opened another gate at the far end, revealing a whole other country we had to explore.

There's a whole world in his eyes, and I can't get over how fresh and new it is. How untainted. And while I can't stand the thought of him ever facing the trouble I've known, I also see hope, a chance that he'll have courage to face his own battles because of the things we've fought, Kezi and I.

At first, I had worried that my wife and son might be shunned because of me. Now that the elders know who I am, they keep their distance, refusing to speak to me directly. But after seeing Kezi at their doorsteps year after year lending her hand to every need, the women of Lo Debar were glad to help with Mica's birth.

Elspeth and the widows had spent weeks weaving blankets and garments, and the midwives from Mahanaim arrived to find several women waiting to help wherever they were needed. It was satisfying to see the pleasure gleaming in their faces, softening the hard lines of poverty and loss.

"The birth of a child causes life to begin again. For everyone," Ama had explained.

I don't know what pleased me more, the unashamed awe in her face when she'd first held my son, or the satisfied joy that's lived in Machir's eyes ever since. He happily keeps Mica close when Kezi isn't carrying him in the sling on her back. For months, every milestone of Mica's growth has worked through my spirit like a balm, healing the jagged edges.

Without my wife and son, Lo Debar would be a different place.

The elders hold their peace, quietly avoiding me, but their reticence doesn't hurt like Ebenezer's coldness. The wall that's grown up between us keeps me working within the confines of Machir's property, and I miss the carpenter's gruff company. He'd approached me on the day my son was circumcised, venturing the first words he'd spoken to me in a year.

"I knew there was more to you than Machir was saying. Now I wonder how I missed it. Few people here met Saul face-to-face, or they'd see it too."

He hasn't spoken to me since.

I lean over Kezi, tightening my grip on Mica without meaning to. Now that he's four months old, I wonder if time will continue to quicken. Every minute, something is different. More beautiful than before. I'm afraid to blink or look away, terrified to touch the worst fear lingering in the back of my mind.

Even as long as it's been, I still see the same concern in the elders' eyes, the worry that someone else might track me here, following the word of Rimmon's nephews. Anger isn't even the right word to describe what I feel when I picture their wrath breaking out against my son.

I have to keep him safe. Perhaps it's time to think of leaving Lo Debar. But where should we go?

The rooster at the market's far end shrieks a little louder than usual, and Machir's donkeys bray, anticipating the approaching storm. The thunderous rumble through the ground has become familiar. The countryside has taken a beating under the springtime rains. Ebenezer has had his hands full clearing debris and adding extra pitch to the crumbling roofs in town. I've done what I can from a distance, no longer welcome at his side.

Machir's servants had helped me to build an addition onto the house when Kezi and I married, but the hovels of Lo Debar really should be built up more. We don't even have proper roads, and our guardhouse is ancient and crumbling.

The elders keep saying that David will look to the northern cities once the fighting settles. "Prosperity needs time to take root and spread outward," Gad insists. "But it will."

The rumble outside is growing louder, encroaching. Mica stirs, and I draw my arm up over Kezi. I already hear low, murmuring voices in the main house, feet moving across the floor too fast. Too early.

Machir opens the door and comes all the way inside without knocking. Something he hasn't done since our wedding.

"Mephi…"

The moment he says my name, I hear it—the metallic shouting wound up into the rumble. I sit up sharply. It isn't thunder. It's a raiding party.

Instantly, I remember the reports from Mahanaim of trouble at their borders. My stomach drops when I notice the axe slung across Machir's back with leather straps.

"Amalek?" I say hoarsely. But what does it matter? We're surrounded by enemies, Ammon to the east, Syria to the north. They've been silent for too long, watching David.

"I don't know." Machir's already lifting Mica into his arms, wrapping him tightly against his side with an extra sheepskin. "Gad's servant came to tell me they've been spotted by the back gate. The watchmen have alerted the fighting men."

My mind counts them, comparing them with the way I know Amalek travels. In wolf packs. In Lo Debar, every armed man is connected to at least six or seven dependents.

I pull on my clothes, reigning in anxiety. My bow leans against the wall, and my quiver is beside it, always full. I can fight as long as I stay on a mule. Kezi pushes off the floor, blinking away slumber. "What's going on? Where's Mica?"

"I've got him," Machir says, handing her a shawl. "We're being attacked, Kezi. We have to get you to the river. Caleb has mules outside. Several of the women are taking the children to Mahanaim. Ama is with them." A wordless look passes between him and Kezi before her mouth firms.

We have no time. The sounds are growing louder, more distinct. The screams following the watchmen's warning horn shoves my blood into a boil. There are too many helpless here. Too many.

I pull my knife and bind it to Kezi's belt. "You know how to throw it." It isn't a question. "Don't let any man get close."

Her expression freezes, locked onto mine.

"Let's go." Machir holds the kitchen door open. Beyond the stone porch outside, three servants are waiting, armed with knives and slings. Kezi climbs astride one of the mules they've brought, and Machir hands Mica to her, gripping her wrist.

"Keep moving, Keziah. Do you understand me? Don't stop for anything until you're safe inside those walls."

Kezi nods, the father-respect gleaming in her tears. Watching her from my own mule, I feel a war cry building beneath my breastbone. The last time we ran from the Philistines, we were just children, but we've both spent years fighting for survival. I'd face anything to keep Mica from that stifling succession.

"I'll be right behind you." Machir slaps Kezi's mule, and his grip on my wrist pulls my attention as they disappear down the hill. "My son, I want you to stay with them. If the raiders chase them down before they reach safety, they'll be taken. We might never recover them."

My own capture rushes into my mind. Kezi is a better rider than I was then, but a pack of raiders could easily overtake her. Torchlight bobs closer, and Ebenezer stumbles into view.

"Syrians," he rasps, doubling over. "They're taking livestock in the back fields. Slaughtering anyone who gets close." He looks across to me, his eyes wild. "Don't be crazy, boy. I don't care what your head is telling you. *This* is what matters." He pokes one of my legs, shaking his head.

Machir's eyes are like coals in the dim light. "Get Kezi to Mahanaim. You can gather more fighting men and come back for us."

He slaps my mule, exactly as he did Kezi's, and the animal's gallop joins the sounds of a roof being splintered.

At the base of Lo Debar's hills, the women huddle like harassed sheep, spreading out in a conspicuous group around the low point in the river. My heart burns in my throat when I see Ama carrying an infant in her arms. These women have been harried most of their lives, but they're not warriors, and several of them have children or elderly to hurry along.

Gad raises his staff like a shepherd, his voice lifting over the frantic sobs. "All of you, ride to Mahanaim. Go now!"

"Go, Ama!" I shout to her when she whirls around to look for me.

"Come with us," she mouths, but I'm seeing beyond her, my muscles clenching.

A thickening line of raiders streams in from the northern forest, but there's more. Other soldiers are approaching from the south, at least thirty men on horseback, and the women are fleeing right into them. I barely restrain myself, every sense shaken. I can't let scavengers make short work of the place that's sheltered me.

"Kezi, wait!" Jerking my mule around hers, I rein in closer to the fjord, and Kezi climbs down into the reeds, her teeth chattering.

"There's more coming." I point south. "They'll cut us off. We won't make it to Mahanaim."

"I know." Her throat bobs up and down, her arms stiffly clenched around our son. I glance back up the hill, then ahead at the encroaching warriors. I can't make out their standards in the stormy dimness, but they're riding hard across the plain, and I doubt they'll stop for a handful of women.

"Yahweh, preserve us," Kezi murmurs, and bitterness slides into my heart like a splinter.

We've been faithful, honoring our vows to the God of our people, but it hasn't altered the sensation I still have that He's not watching this side of the Jordan. He's in Zion with His anointed one. My teeth bite together. Wherever He is, I have only one way forward.

I shrug my weapon off my shoulder and reach for an arrow. They'll have to cut this bow from my hands.

"M—" My name dies on Kezi's choked breath, and I barely have time to follow her wild gaze to the edge of the thicket. An armed man crouches there, his sword inches from my wife. Mica kicks awake, oblivious to the fact that death is right behind him. For half a second, I think I'm about to watch it happen.

Panicked rage crackles through me like a shock of lightning as two other men sprint into view. And my pulse wakes up, slamming into my ribs. Against the scar that should have ended my life, but didn't.

My focus sharpens, and I sweep the bow up over my head, releasing the arrow that's already notched in place. The shaft cuts the air over my wife's head, stabbing her assailant under his raised arm. His scream barely reaches my ears over the churn of my blood as I fit another arrow and shoot the second intruder through the heart. And then the third as he swings for Kezi.

Frantic, my eyes grab hold of several more crawling out of the reeds. "Stay where you are!" I shout over the thunder of approaching horses.

Kezi shrieks when they reach us. The massive warrior who leaps from his mount resembles a Philistine. Not exactly a *Nephilim*, but still two heads taller than my height. His men peel out around him, enclosing the fleeing families in a circle while he flings a battle axe into the chest of another raider.

He locks eyes with me once, and I wake up. Arming my bow, I free every arrow I have until the only men left standing are the mystery soldiers who came to defend us. It's over too quickly, leaving white-hot adrenaline pulsing through my body.

On her knees against the riverbank, Kezi sobs over Mica while I force words through the fury burning my lungs. "Is he hurt?"

"No—no, he's fine," she whimpers, holding him tighter as he squirms, starting to fuss in confusion.

Unable to think, I swing my leg over the mule and drop to the ground. Kezi carries Mica over and collapses beside me, unleashing her relief in a flood of tears. Crushing them in my arms, I quake, realizing I could've lost them both. I press my forehead against Kezi's, whispering words I haven't said in years. "Thank you, Yahweh. Thank you."

The giant warrior reins in beside us. "Are you all right?" he asks me.

I tighten my grip on Kezi. The standard of Judah on his clothing looks out of place against the dark tattoos climbing his arms. "Who are you?"

"I'm Ittai of Gath, one of King David's commanders." He squints at the hillside. "Is that the first time you've been attacked by Syrian raiders?"

"So far," I answer, unable to take my eyes off the soldiers guarding Lo Debar's women. What are David's men doing up here? Regaining some wits, I acknowledge Ittai. "Thank you."

It seems more than appropriate after such a narrow escape, but then it hits me. I killed them. With no battle experience, I shot a dozen raiders without even thinking. The same thought flickers on Ittai's face as he studies me. An unbidden smile burns through my fear, and I picture myself back in Gibeah with the bow I'd had as a child.

Then, without warning, my old dream wakes up behind my eyes, and my father's words ride my wild pulse.

*When the Lord is with you, your arrows will fly on the wings of the wind.*

It's so clear, I know it's more than imagination. And it freezes the blood in my veins.

All this time, my father's counsel had been waiting inside me for just the right moment. In the seconds it took me to kill the raiders, the words I've been discounting for years had been pulled into the foreground, infused with strength, and sent flying into the face of my greatest insecurity.

I stare at my son, barely feeling anything else while the shock works its way through me.

Yahweh has had plenty of chances to get rid of me. Instead, He'd trained me for a battle I didn't even know was coming, and then blessed my aim when it did. Just like my father said He would. And Abba hadn't said what he said simply to pacify a little boy. He'd believed our God would be faithful. To me.

Openmouthed, I stare at the raiders' bodies, gripped by the powerful reality that's been hiding in plain sight all this time.

Whatever may have happened, whatever else I am, I am *not* cursed.

# TWENTY-FOUR

## *Mephi*

———◆◆———

Back in Lo Debar, we count thirty dead.

I crouch beside Machir, handing him spices and linen, my heart pulling heavier with each face he covers. Most of them are men, a few women. One child. By noon, Machir and I have bound twelve severe wounds, measuring out frankincense and myrrh like gold. The oils can be replenished, but at great cost.

One man won't recover his leg. The gash goes all the way to the bone, stretching from his thigh to his ankle. Kezi's been working feverishly, stopping only twice to cover her face and wail behind our house. Ama reached her before I could.

The breathless burn of battle has torn through my senses, leaving me as scattered as the streets around me. The groans and screams of the injured keep the flame ignited, spurring me to do something to end the predations of these scavengers.

I'm aching with thankfulness to have my family alive. Ebenezer also survived. But the moment I turn away from the carnage to try and breathe some fresh air, I'm assaulted with the ruins.

Roofs have caved in, a few structures charred from fires that were hastily put out by the rain. The thatch dwellings and market lean-tos are gone, and many of the smaller homes have been smashed in. Piles of crumbling brick and scattered stone have replaced one of Ebenezer's walls.

Crawling over to it, I kneel among the cracked mud-bricks, picking through the dust to see what I can salvage. Sharpness flickers in my chest when I recognize pieces of his sons' shattered bows. If David's men hadn't arrived when they did, this town wouldn't have a single man left in it by now.

Pebbles crunch under Ebenezer's labored steps. "You don't have to…"

I turn away, hiding the rush of angry tears. He's shunned me for nearly two years, but I never wanted to see this happen. I collect the bricks that aren't broken, propping them in a corner. "We can mix some mortar and rebuild the side wall. The roof will take longer."

"Thank you," Ebenezer mumbles, his sincerity covering over the hurt. Almost.

Pain pinches within my face. What's the point of scraping a life together out of the dust only to have it destroyed in a matter of hours? Everyone's safety has been ripped open again like a badly-mended garment.

Ebenezer kneels heavily beside me. "Your family is safe?"

"Yes." The arrows I shot spin through my mind. What if I'd missed?

Ebenezer's hands shake, combing through the rubble. "I can't figure out how David's men knew to come here. Unless they got wind of the attack before we did."

I shrug, my words tasting sharp. "We may be on the fringes of Israel, but we're still within his territory. We've heard enough about his exploits elsewhere. It's about time he started caring about us."

I glance over my shoulder. Out in the street, David's soldiers wander aimlessly up and down behind the Philistine commander. They'd routed the Syrians with little effort, and there's hardly a sign of battle on them. They're dressed like noblemen under their armor, and the way they look askance at Lo Debar's broken pieces inflames my chest. Why did they come here?

"Mephi, I..." Ebenezer ventures, and my defenses tighten, anticipating his attempt at an apology. It took facing death to make him regret treating me like an outcast?

I face him, my voice hard. "I did not choose my bloodline. But my father would have been a great king. Even if it's the only honor I know in my lifetime, I am proud to be Jonathan's son."

Ebenezer nods, grappling for a response. Before he can think of one, Caleb approaches us, leading a mule. "Mephi, someone's at the house looking for you."

I frown at the strange tilt in his voice. "Is it Ittai?"

Caleb shrugs, helping me onto the mule. "One of the soldiers' servants. He wants to speak with you."

Machir's door has been smashed in, but Caleb helps me enter through the side, setting me upright on the crutches before beckoning to the young bearded man in the main room. The soldier steps forward, about to announce his errand. But his eyes work faster than his mouth, taking in every inch of my torn robe before finding my face.

He's wearing Benjaminite colors, with a short leather-bound sword at his waist, but something about his manner tugs at the back of my mind.

He squints through a baffled smile. "Yatom?"

I stiffen, every muscle shrinking away from what Ziba used to call me. The sight of Azarel fills my mind with the image of blood dripping down my arm.

"I—didn't expect to find you on your feet." A smirk pulls his face up, and anger darts my chest.

"What do you want?" I demand, covering my astonishment.

His head tilts to the side. "Come now. Is that any way to greet a…?"

"A what?" I scoff over whatever he was going to say. "What am I to you?"

Azarel closes his mouth, his jaw hardening. "I have come as the closest thing to a brother you'll ever have."

Is that what he thinks? "Why? To explain David's sudden interest in Israel's garbage heap?"

"Watch how you speak about the king," Azarel snaps. "He's the reason you're not dead."

He moves closer, and his nearness arms my defenses. What could he have to gain by reviving any kind of connection with me, real or implied?

"We came following the trail of some reports we'd received of rogue Syrian attackers," he begins.

Convenient. "David's servants need to chase rumors faster," I mutter.

"We didn't intend to stop here." Azarel hardens his tone. A deprecating smirk curves around his exhale. "But my father recently attended a feast where David honored Benjaminite servants who have shown him loyalty."

I wince, the news souring as it folds into my stomach. I can only imagine how much Ziba's convinced the king to give him—from my grandfather's leftover legacy in Gibeah. I see him in his son's face, assessing me.

Azarel's mouth tips. "At the feast, David asked if anyone else from the house of Saul was still alive. My father told him where you are."

The words bite into me until the air starts to sing in my head. The room tilts, and Azarel's form twists out of sight while memories crowd in. Ziba tosses me before the elders, Gimel sells me to the Amorites, Palti turns away, leaving me to the vultures. The air thins around each betrayal, suffocating me. But now, the treachery has walked into my house, bringing the king's soldiers.

I blink, and my sight clears. Close enough to retaliate, I shove one crutch up under Azarel's chin, throwing my whole body against him. Unprepared to support my full weight, Azarel stumbles, thudding to the floor. Familiarity with falling gives me a split-second advantage, and I fling myself over on top of him, grasping at his neck.

"How could he do that? How could your father do that?!" My cry of anger fuels the blaze sweeping through me.

"Get off me!" Azarel struggles for a grip on my wrists, but I keep a tight hold.

"Why does he hate me? Why does he want me dead?" I lean in hard, pinning him up against the wall with my knees. How dare he come here and tell me this now? Triumphantly. Giving me no time to escape.

"Mephi, stop!" Kezi screams from behind.

"Mephi!" Stepping through the door, Machir grabs my collar and heaves me backwards. "Stop this! What's happened?"

Azarel scrambles to his feet, eyeing me while he shakes his clothes straight.

"It wasn't my doing!" he bellows. "I don't know why David's doing this now. But if you haven't noticed, he gets whatever he wants. Yahweh is with him." He pants, edging toward the door. "He's coming, regardless. The rest of his men will be here in another few days with orders to find you. Better face him like a man, and be done with it. There are worse things than living under house arrest in Jerusalem." He scoffs at Machir's broken door before stepping through it. "Like living here."

Once he's gone, I fight Machir's grip. "Let me go!"

"Mephi—"

"I said, let me go!"

He relaxes his hold, and I end up on my knees, my fists pounding the floor. I wish I could break through it, let the ground swallow me. Better than being stuck here, unable to escape.

It kills me that Ziba planned this. For years, he's held my identity like a stolen heirloom, plotting how to exploit it. He'd dumped me here, knowing that he would always know where to find me if he needed to. He's been waiting for David to reveal his true colors so he could know exactly what reaction he could expect. And plan how to come out ahead.

Still, I'd always hoped he would tell a different lie. He could've told David I was dead, ending the search once and for all. But instead, he'd exposed me without any thought to what it might cost my family. I clench my jaw, remembering Azarel's startled look when Kezi had walked in. He hadn't expected me to be married.

"Mephi…" Machir's fingers brush my shoulder.

Kezi kneels in front of me, and I release the breath I've been holding. For years, I've stayed ahead of despair, and now desperation is dragging me back toward the edge of Ziba's old cistern.

I clench my teeth. "Ziba told David about me."

Kezi's hand covers mine. "Are you certain?"

I laugh flatly. "He attended a feast at the king's table. The whole court knows that David is looking for me. Those men out there probably know." I raise my voice, my anger turning wild again. "Do they think I'll just sit here and wait for them to take me to Jerusalem as some sort of spectacle? Like those Moabite kings they made lie on the ground waiting for execution?"

"David has summoned plenty of men without harming them, Mephi." Machir crouches at my side. "He's not a monster."

"But Saul was." Every hunt, every death accuses me. "They all know what my grandfather did, and that's all they're going to see when they look at me."

That, and a cripple who can't possibly profit the king. I can't tell if Machir understands. He's seen too much good from David.

I shake my head. "How can I do this? How am I supposed to give myself up to my grandfather's greatest enemy?"

Machir's voice tightens. "Saul may have been David's enemy, but David never raised his hand against him. He honored Saul's anointing even when his men advised him to take revenge. And he was your father's dearest friend."

I pull my arm away. "Just because people want to remember it that way doesn't make it true."

Silence fills my ears until Machir looks at Kezi. "Bring him what we have."

She steps around me into the next room, and Machir sits back on his heels.

"I can't force you to trust David. You don't know him. But this is the next best thing to hearing it from his own lips."

Kezi returns with a leather-backed folder of parchments. Settling on the floor, she unfolds a wrinkled page from the back and hands it to me. The names of Saul and Jonathan meet my eyes first, and my mind devours the rest of the words before I can breathe.

*"Your glory, O Israel, is slain on your heights. How the mighty have fallen!*

*"Let the mountains of Gilboa receive no rain, no harvest,*

*"For there the shield of Saul was defiled.*

*"From the blood of the mighty, the bow of Jonathan never turned back.*

*"Saul and Jonathan were greatly beloved, undivided in life and death,*

*"Swifter than eagles, stronger than lions.*

*"I grieve for you, Jonathan my brother.*

*"Your love for me was extraordinary, surpassing the love of women.*

*"How the mighty have fallen, and the weapons of war perished..."*

I follow the words to the end of the parchment, then reread the heading: *A lament, written by David son of Jesse.*

"Where did you get this?" I ask Machir, my fingers clenched around the paper.

"After your father died, David had it written into the songbook of Jashar and taught it to all the people of Judah. Copies were sent throughout the tribes. I was waiting for the right time to show it to you."

I stare at the parchment, unsure what to think. This is the clearest proof I've had of the bond Machir spoke of between my father and David. *Neshama sheli.* But instead of feeling touched, I'm still skeptical.

David was likely overcome with relief that he wouldn't bear the guilt of his enemy's death. He may have grieved what Saul once was, even mourned the loss of a friend in my father, but surely his duty is complete now that he provided them with a suitable tribute. Why should this lament dictate his actions now?

He has Moabite blood, but that didn't stop him from setting their thousands to forced labor.

Machir folds the parchment. "Mephi, I wouldn't lie to you. If I thought David meant you harm, I would speak to him on your behalf. But I truly believe that you are not in danger. David proved he could be trusted with Saul's life many times. He can be trusted with yours." His face is settled, sincere. "I say, if he sends for you, go to him. Trust him."

"I'm going with you." Kezi's hand darts to my arm.

A thousand protests spring up behind my lips only to die there when I see her face. She won't be reasoned with. Which means our son will have to come too. I'm not leaving him behind. I lock eyes with Machir.

"Make Ama stay. I'll send word if…" *If what? If I'm dead? If David imprisons me?*

Machir grips the side of my face, shutting the thoughts out.

"David may be a fierce warrior, but he is not one to slaughter those Yahweh has spared. He knows the difference. And Jonathan's life was more precious to him than his own." He aims every word into my eyes, daring me to believe. "I've told you before. You're going to live."

# TWENTY-FIVE

## *Mephi*

———————◆———————

Ittai's soldiers camp on the outskirts of Lo Debar, and within seven days, the rest of David's men arrive.

A contingent of twenty warriors on Moabite stallions carry the Judean flag right through Lo Debar's broken gate. Everyone comes to their doorsteps to watch the retinue pass, openmouthed when the soldiers ask for the house of Machir. Women point out the gleaming armor, and the little children giggle with appreciation, but they don't know why they're here. No one does, except maybe the elders.

When they stop at our doorstep, I'm sitting outside restringing my bow while Mica plays with fragments from the wool Kezi's carding. A commander dismounts while his men study their surroundings with baffled smiles. Their extravagant display would have been a sharp contrast even before the raid. But now, Lo Debar probably looks like a different world to them.

My limbs lock, tension biting through. I wonder if the man standing over me is David's famous nephew, the one who volunteered to kill Saul many times.

His heavy green robe hangs across shoulders plated with thick armor. His breastplate is carved with the face of a lion, and his leg greaves are iron, not bronze. A long sword hugs his side, and he keeps one hand on his horse's jeweled halter.

"Are you the crippled son of Jonathan?" he says in my direction.

"As you see." I hold his gaze, hoping he'll feel my disgust. My crutches are obvious, propped against the doorframe.

The soldier studies me again as Machir steps out beside me. "This is Mephibosheth, the son of Jonathan ben Saul of Benjamin."

His introduction is respectfully firm, but too late. Clearly, Ziba didn't mention my name, and the soldier has already decided what to think.

"We've been sent to bring you before the king in Jerusalem."

His voice betrays no emotion connected to that decision. Behind him, two armed men dismount from a cart, carrying several folded parcels over to me.

I push aside the wrappings, my face growing warmer. The thick cloth inside is well-made, tightly woven, and carefully dyed a deep scarlet. The color is flecked with thin golden thread, making the cloth glisten. Like blood.

I lift my chin. "I'll wear my own clothes."

The soldier's brows lift. "You really intend to insult the king before you've even met him?" Disdain colors his tone.

I twist my fingers in the cloth, resisting the tremors trying to unwind my voice. "My wife and son are coming as well."

The soldier's eyes move to Kezi. "We leave at once. You won't need to bring much. The king will provide whatever you need."

I swallow, hoping the soldiers can't see my dismay. I was worried that they'd march into town and arrest me. But somehow, I feel just as upended by their curt decorum. I don't need to be bound and dragged to be a prisoner. They know I have no choice.

"Are you Joab or Abishai?" I ask the commander.

"Neither. I'm Eleazar. That's Joab ben Zeruiah." He nods to the left, and I immediately find the flinty-eyed man with the fixed expression of a hawk. He's an average height, but built like a giant, with thick limbs and meaty hands enclosing a spear the width of a small tree. My throat closes, but I can't look away.

343

"Your family can ride in one of the carts," Eleazar says. "It might be easier than the chariots."

I'd already noticed the gleaming vehicles hitched up behind the horses. I remember hearing that David kept a hundred of them for himself when he destroyed Hadadezer's army at Zobah. The gold has been polished a hundred times, and the edges are studded with gems.

"You can ride one of the mules. The warhorses are unruly with strangers," Eleazar continues.

He's trying to be practical, but I hear a veiled insult in everything he's saying. He doesn't see the years it's taken for me to attain what I have. I'm not even sure he sees the son of Jonathan. Just a remnant of Saul's house who can't walk.

I feel bereft, everything I've clung to slipping from my fingers. I take Kezi's hand, wishing the soldiers weren't watching.

"You should stay," I whisper, hoping she doesn't misunderstand. I don't know what David will do with us, and it feels harsh to pull her away from everything she's known with only a few moments to say goodbye.

Kezi shakes her head, her firm smile cracking the tension in my chest. "I go where you go." Her voice shakes, but her eyes are dry.

Ama kisses Mica, draping a simple cloth pack over Kezi's shoulder. I hold my breath while the women embrace.

Eleazar moves away, and Ebenezer separates from the crowd, coming to stand over me. He looks abruptly older, like I haven't noticed the passing of time on him. I absorb his silence, swallowing down regret until my throat hurts. Even if they couldn't last, the years of normalcy I'd found with him had meant so much. In time, I may have come to win his trust back. What more can I find in Jerusalem?

Ebenezer studies the ground, his beard lifting as he scrunches up his mouth under it. "From the day I saw you pick up that bow, I knew you wouldn't last long here. People come here to rebuild. And that's what you've done. But you don't belong here." His calloused hand clasps my arm. "If the king sees what I've seen, then you'll have nothing to fear."

I'm almost angry when he steps away. What is David going to see in me? Why should I leave this place for an unknown that I'm completely unprepared for? I'd finally accepted that I would never live the way my father had. Why bring it all back into view now?

Machir lifts me up, folding his huge arms around me. Over his shoulder, Ama weeps through a brave smile.

"Don't be afraid," Machir says softly.

"I'm not," I smile crookedly, lying through my teeth.

Ama kneels down and melts against my chest. "Your father would be proud. No matter what you find in Jerusalem, that's the truth." She touches my face, and I grip her fingers. I don't care who's watching. This has to be said.

"You've given me everything." Even when she had nothing. "Thank you."

Tears spill over, dripping past her smile. "You're my only son, and I love you."

I kiss her palm, the words like nails in my throat. "I love you too." I turn to Machir. "Keep her safe."

"I will."

I wait under his welcoming gaze, sick to think of exchanging it for the contempt and scrutiny of a king's court. "I could never repay you for what you've done."

Machir's face warms. "It was an honor. But it's not the greatest kindness you'll receive."

I force a smile. I'm unsure where he gets his faith in me or his trust in David, but I'll gladly borrow it.

"Let's go." Joab's heavy command snaps every soldier to attention, and Eleazar motions for a few of them to help me. They lift me onto a mule and tie my crutches on behind me.

I reach out to Machir. "My bow." I'm not leaving home again without it.

Machir hands it up to me, and I put the quiver of arrows across my back. Kezi and Mica settle into the horse-drawn cart next to me. Then I look back. The people of Lo Debar have drawn as close as they dare to the soldiers. Every face is gentle, several hands lifted.

"God go with you," Amram says, and the elders repeat the same, their words stirring grief inside me. When did the land of no pasture become home?

Joab shouts, galloping off, and the retinue falls into place behind him, streaming out through the gate the way they came. Every nerve tight, I urge the mule after them, leaving Lo Debar behind.

# TWENTY-SIX

## *Mephi*

We cross the Jordan and ride south into the rocky hills, heading for Judah's territory. No one speaks to me, even when we stop to camp. My defenses mount up like the landscape, looming higher the farther we travel, and the constant alertness keeps me exhausted.

Joab's men traverse the landscape with practiced familiarity. I've grown up on the move; I know how fleeing families scamper across the countryside like scattered sheep, their movements sporadic and frantic. But David's men are precise and relaxed, knowing exactly when to stop and where to camp.

It's still strange for me to sleep out under the stars without fear. Even from their distance, I feel the heavy presence of the southern mountains, watching us like stony giants. I've never slept easily in the open, but more than a dozen sentries stand guard when we camp, and after two nights of keeping my burning eyes fixed on the invisible horizon, I'm finally forced to rest.

Mica sleeps fitfully, unused to constant movement and exposure to the sun. When he cries, I watch the soldiers anxiously.

But no one bothers my wife and son, except to provide them with food and water when we stop. As the open plains crumble into the rocky hills bordering Jerusalem, Joab directs us to a handful of caves for the night.

The shadows are welcome after the heat of the road, but it's been years since I slept enclosed in rock. I watch the soldiers settling in, remembering that they have experience with caves too. Are they thinking of the one in the Negeb where they had my grandfather trapped? People say David had been close enough to cut Saul's robe, but refused to kill him. I wonder how true that is.

The soldiers strike flint and start a few fires as dusk pulls heat from the air. Eleazar's servants bring food to the corner of the cave where we've settled apart from the others. At least here, we won't have to sleep surrounded. Mica slumbers after eating, exhausted from the constant change of pace. Kezi unfolds the extra blankets the soldiers provided. They've treated us well, anticipating our needs without ceremony, keeping me freshly surprised.

But then I remember that I'm a precious commodity. I'm the son that would have been Jonathan's heir. David's men have been instructed to deliver us safely, nothing more. It's so hard to picture this powerful company wandering through caves as fugitives years ago, hiding from Saul. How much of that old fire still burns in them now?

Kezi drapes a sheepskin around her shoulders, folding another to soften the ground. Looking at her makes me think of Machir, Ebenezer, Ama. They're my people, but somehow Lo Debar isn't my home anymore. It's let me go, leaving me in the empty openness between here and David's city.

Kezi studies me. "Are you all right?"

I look down, lowering my voice so the echoes won't find it. "I feel like we're in custody." Shame hardens the words. Doesn't she realize that we won't have any freedom after this? David will keep us like spoils of war, the way he keeps my cousins. My son will grow up in the very shadow I'd wanted him to escape.

I sigh, rubbing my face. "I shouldn't have dragged you into this. I should've come alone."

Kezi squeezes my hand. "You didn't drag me. I came willingly. We belong together."

I pick at the edge of my cloak where the ring is hanging in plain sight. Kezi had insisted I keep wearing it after our wedding. "I didn't want my son to resent his blood the way I did. I wanted him to know freedom. Pride." Now, he won't even remember Lo Debar. He'll grow up in a cage.

Kezi's eyes slant down to where Mica slumbers in the crook of her arm. "He's the son of two survivors, one of them a prince and an expert archer. A man who faces what other men would run from. Mica has nothing to be ashamed of."

I tolerate a smile for her sake, stroking her cheek until her eyes drift shut. Mica sleeps too, lulled by the sounds of the camp quieting. I touch his hand, waiting for his fingers to curl around mine. Kezi's picked up where Ama left off, insisting I'm brave. But they don't seem to notice how I'm forced to face things because I can't escape. That's not bravery. That's just being crippled.

I suppose I could have hidden from David. But what kind of life would that be? My stomach turns over when I remember Palti. How long will that man be able to hide?

Carefully removing my hand from Mica's grip, I place my bow across my lap and move an arrow gently into position, watching the moonlight glinting off the helmets of the guards outside. I should have known I wouldn't be able to avoid David forever. But why all the dreams about him? What does Adonai want from me?

*What am I doing, Yahweh? Are you still watching me?*

Ama says Yahweh's absence drove Saul mad. Yet, people call David a man after God's heart. What does that even mean? Does he hear what Yahweh is thinking, like Moses did? Do they speak to each other? Or is that just the feeling people get from hearing David's songs of worship?

"Are they sheep that you have to guard them?" Joab's voice rumbles toward me from the mouth of the cave. He nods at the men outside. "Nothing gets past them."

*Even you?*

Hearing my thoughts, Joab scoffs and leans his spear against the wall. "Better?"

I bristle, hearing him talk to me like I'm twelve. From the stories I've heard, he doesn't need the spear.

"You're less talkative than your old man; that's a mercy." His wry tone hints at the history he's had with my father, but he folds his arms, cutting it off. "You're nothing like him actually."

I swallow, wondering if he meant to insult me or relieve me of some kind of responsibility. Either way, I feel it like a slur. I grip the bow, steadying myself. Joab's evaluation means little, but there's one thing he can tell me.

"Is it true what they say about my father and David?"

A puff of air comes from between Joab's teeth. He scratches his beard, his jaw braced awkwardly.

"The king's covenant with Saul's son was something I knew would haunt him until one of them died. I'd thought that Jerusalem and the uniting of the tribes would have made him forget. I hoped for it." His eyes glitter. "But Jonathan remains buried under David's rib like an arrow that was never removed. Their friendship is common knowledge in Jerusalem. I'm not sure what stories they've told in that broken sheepfold you were hiding in."

I stiffen at his crude reference to Lo Debar. "They need better protection. You saw what the Syrians did. They're still too vulnerable with so few fighting men."

"Ittai mentioned running into you at the Jabbock fjord. Am I to believe you fought with that?" Joab nods at my bow.

"I killed twelve."

Joab's laugh heaves from his lungs, almost resentfully. "Truly, we thought we were finished with the house of Saul after we returned the king's wife. To think somewhere in a garbage heap up north, the son of Jonathan was fighting with crutches, too stubborn to die."

He's disappointed. I can read that much underneath his grudging respect. Cold remembrance eats its way through my limbs.

"You killed Abner." I'd been gripped with terror when that news came, certain David's vengeful nephew would come after me.

Joab's eyes catch fire, but I don't look away. He won't kill me here. Moving closer, he lowers himself to a crouch in front of me, like a cat hunting. "Abner ben Ner killed my brother. Nothing answers for that. Nothing." His voice is flat and toneless, too quiet for echoes. "One day, David will understand."

"What do your men think about him summoning me?"

Joab scoffs, looking away. "He's our king. He gives orders and we obey."

I frown. Surely, he has more of an opinion. I watch it rumble across his face like a storm cloud before breaking open.

"But we were there for the rest of it, if that's what you're asking. I had to stand by while Saul used David for target practice in the war camp and baited him with the woman he loved." Joab bares his teeth. "That madman stripped David down until he had to crawl to the Philistines, risking everything to survive. We all suffered with him, waiting for the days we're living in now. So yes. The thought of Saul's broken grandson facing David with nothing warms me a little."

I flinch when his eyes find my father's ring at my throat. "You think you had any right to keep that?"

Any other time, I would have protested. It was never David's. Abba gave it to Naamah, making her promise to take care of me. It's all I have from when he was alive. But now, all my defenses are trapped in Joab's steely gaze, tangled up in his accusations.

"The king can have it…if he spares my family," I whisper, my confidence dried up.

"You're hardly in a position to negotiate, son of Saul."

Joab straightens up sharply and walks to the opposite side of the cave, leaving me to grapple with fear that's taken worse shape. I can't tell for certain what David's plans for me are, but I know what Joab's would be.

Jerusalem multiplies my fears.

The massive stone walls dwarf anything I've seen anywhere else. The watchmen up in the guard tower call Joab by name at the gate. The entourage moves through the cedar doors, traveling a wide road straight through the center of the city. Guardhouses and armories tower over the street, and David's palace sprawls ahead, with the harem stretching behind. Gold and bronze glint in the sun, but that's not the only thing keeping my head down.

The people lining the streets number in the hundreds, and I wonder how much they know. Most of them call out the names of several soldiers, and Joab slows his mount, bending to whisper something to an official. The nobleman looks sharply at me, his scrutiny feeding my dread. My body shakes from holding tension at bay. My heart is shrinking, turning colder.

There's nothing to protect me here. The danger I've faced before was always undefined, a general sense that my heritage was like a weapon braced at the back of my neck, ready to cut into me at any moment. But I'd hidden in my beggar's rags, believing if I could become someone else, I'd be safe. The reality of actual death has never come so close since the Amorites took me. Now it's wrapping its fingers around my throat again, tightening as I approach the palace at the end of the street.

For a moment, I think about what it would be like to fall under David's sword, cut down in his throne room. However unlikely that scenario is, I can't push it from my mind. It's more plausible that David will simply lock me away, but how far will his protection extend? After I'm exposed before all Jerusalem, how long will it be before the Gibeonites approach the king with their own demands?

For the first time, I realize that the king himself may have not thought this through.

"You know he won't kill you, right?" Kezi's voice elbows through my thoughts from behind.

I look away, scowling, but there are prying eyes everywhere. My mind pulls back to the dreams I've had about David, but they're every bit as immaterial as my memories of my father. I'm not sure how to use what I do know.

There's life and death in the cords that bind me to David— his rivalry with Saul and his friendship with my father. But which one fills more of his heart? I wonder if my father's covenant with David is the reason I can't shake him. If Abba had lived, I would have already been at David's side, with no rift to consider. There would've been no flight from Gibeah, no broken legs. Instead, Abba died beside Saul, placing my life entirely in David's hands.

The heavy palace doors swing wide, snapping me out of my thoughts, and the weight of the crowd spins dizziness into my vision. I'm no longer hidden; I can't go back to Lo Debar if I tried.

The moment I make it to the row of palace steps, my face bursts into flame. I'm clearly the first crippled man to set foot in David's house. Several dumbfounded looks pass between the guards before anyone makes a move. With so little practice, it's impossible for the servants to make me look like anything but a prisoner. Once I'm off the mule, they manhandle me through the doors and lower me to the floor while they go back for my family.

Across the threshold, it's like being enclosed in a spacious carved-out mountain. The heavy quiet spins every step into an echo, sharpening each whisper. Between the elevated ceilings, the skillfully-cut stone, and gleaming wood, I'm certain Saul's palace didn't rival this one. I feel small under the rich tapestried walls, and every time I look up, I catch the servants mid-whisper, raising their eyebrows.

More richly-dressed officials come through the long doors at the far end, joining the guards' discussion about how I should enter the throne room. I suppose I should have worn the clothes David gave me. But even if I had, I wouldn't belong here.

Then, a side door opens, spitting Ziba out. In the few seconds he's absorbed with the guards, I close my eyes, trying to adjust as the rest of the day goes to pieces around me. When I open them, Ziba's false smile assaults me.

"He's grown," he says to Eleazar, as if surprised. "He looks better than when I saw him last."

Agitation pricks my skin at the way he's studying me the way he used to, seeing only my legs.

"Ziba is responsible for your presence here," Eleazar comments, and I lift my brows in their direction. Am I supposed to thank him?

Ziba's face tightens, and he taps the sleeve of the largest servant. "Better that he says as little as possible. Simply place him before David and let the king judge from there."

I can see what's underneath all his contrived pity. He wouldn't have risked this if he thought the king would be displeased. But he fully expects to see me humbled.

The guards haul me up and force me through the end doors. I can't see between them, so I'm not sure if my family follows. Prayers spring to my mind. *Yahweh, preserve them. Have mercy.*

I haven't determined anything I might say to the king. But it also feels foolish to assume I'll be asked to speak. The carpeted pathway and bright robes blur past me until the guards decide I've gone far enough. They drop me onto my knees, setting my crutches on the floor next to me.

The guards approach David's throne, a heavy ebony chair overlaid with gold, and the servants drop back. A hundred eyes snap onto me, a hundred different opinions seething over my head.

Unsure where to look, I catch the eyes of a woman near the front. For some reason, I feel like I should know who she is. She cranes her neck slightly, but she doesn't smile. Other women cluster around her, each with her hand on a different boy's shoulder. One of them, who looks about thirteen, mimics my stare, his eyes like daggers.

I drop my head to the floor. I shouldn't be looking. David's sons will inherit whatever their father decides to do with me. Wrapping my arms around myself, I listen to the whispers swelling through the room. I hear the name of Saul more than any other.

"You're certain it's him?" The king's rich voice reaches deep into me, but it's younger than I expected. The tenor clarity in it definitely belongs to a singer.

"It's him." Joab strides past me, his voice raised enough for the room to hear. He walks all the way up to the throne, and I hear the gentle rustle of robes and the short echo of a stair as David steps down.

"Mephibosheth!" The king's voice fills the room, rushing over my head to the opposite wall and echoing my name back to me. No one else has used it since the soldiers arrived in Lo Debar.

"I am your servant," I say into the floor, feeling Kezi settling onto her knees beside me.

David steps down again. "Look at me, son."

Slowly, I lift my head and shoulders until my back is straight. The man from my dream stares down at me. Same searching eyes. Thick curly hair bound back with gold. Under the lion medallion, his chest moves, and he half-turns away, a thousand thoughts pulling toward me. When a crooked smile plucks at the side of his face, he sheds three years.

I can see it in his eyes. He thought I was dead.

"He has brought a gift for my lord," Joab announces, his expression spearing me.

My throat thick, I slip the cord over my head and place Abba's ring on the floor before David. The king bends down to pick it up, and he breathes deeply, folding it into his fist.

"Help him," he orders two servants without releasing his gaze.

The guards lift me up carefully this time, replacing my crutches under my arms, but I felt more comfortable on the floor. Standing, I have to rely on the instability of the wood and my crooked ankles to hold me up. I have to feel the dismayed attention of everyone fixed on me again.

David is too close already, but he's coming closer. I stiffen, anxiety clouding my chest. I won't bow my head. I'll face him for my father's sake. But it's getting harder the longer I can't read what's on his mind.

His impossible eyes keep changing color, deepening into brown and then dancing with gold. I'm not sure what to do with my expression, since I can't possibly mirror his. David seems both awestruck and overjoyed, neither of which makes sense. But then, this is the dancing king. The warrior poet. Everything about him scatters the imagination.

David grips my shoulders. His hands match the warmth in his face, but I can feel his fingers trembling.

"Don't be afraid, son. Your father—" He shakes his head, the bewildered smile returning. "Your father was my closest friend. I've been waiting to show you kindness for his sake. You were hard to find."

He chuckles brokenly, but my face tenses. I feel more unsteady with him holding onto me. Like I'll just end up at his feet again.

David's expression relaxes, but the sparkle stays in his eyes. "I am going to restore to you all the land that once belonged to your grandfather, Saul. I've rebuilt most of his estate in Gibeah, so I want you to stay there. With your family." His attention shifts behind me briefly. "But you will eat at my table for the rest of your life."

I hear Kezi gasp, and whispers pull through the crowd. Heat doubles in my face, and the sudden sting of shame is unbearable. Why such an extravagant display of honor? Any other king would have burned his rival's palace to the ground.

*Saul's house deserves to crumble until there's nothing left.*

It's no doubt the opinion of most of the people in this room. Instead, David wants me to live in the same home I was torn from as a child. Why should he do that when even the people in Lo Debar resent me? I'm the lowest in Israel. No king wants to honor someone like me. David's only exposing himself to ridicule.

"Why?" My voice breaks, and I look down, unable to bow the way I should.

Unsteady, I stumble as one of my crutches clatters to the floor. But David's arms come up around me. "I've got you."

I have no choice but to grip David's sleeves. Up close, I don't feel the largeness of the room so much. My face stinging, I turn my head, speaking into David's arm.

"Why should you show regard for a dead dog like me?"

David exhales sharply. His fist lifts my chin, my father's seal ring wound up in his fingers. "You're no dog, Mephi. You're worth more than all the treasure in this room."

His words shock me, but they're like pure water, not muddied by flattery or irony. I stare deeper, letting him in, every assumption I've ever made dying a slow death the longer I look.

For years, I've scoffed at the idea that Jonathan meant anything to David, but now I know I was wrong. This truly is the man my father loved as a covenant brother. As a friend. The reality is astounding.

One arm firmly set around my waist supporting me, David clasps my hand with his opposite one and turns me to face the room.

"Israel—behold my son!"

The room erupts with applause that takes my breath. I search the faces for animosity, but can't find any. The surprise is still moving through me, gradually working its way to pleasure.

Under my hand, held against the king's chest, I can feel the wild dance of David's heart.

# TWENTY-SEVEN

## *Mephi*

———— ◆◆ ◆ ◆◆ ————

The longer I watch the king, the more I realize that none of the stories were exaggerated.

David is every rumor fleshed out. I can see the battles he's fought stretched across the breadth of his shoulders, wound up in the strength of his arms. And yet, there's a tenderness about him that makes me picture a child running up to embrace him. Is it because of the way he lived for so long, in caves among the outcasts of Israel?

Years of playing the harp and gripping swords have turned his hands rough. I'd felt the callouses when he'd gripped my arms. His face holds a strange depth of sorrow that could surface at any moment. But his teeth flash in a persistent smile that never seems to fade.

David lifts his hand, his purple sleeve hanging down. "Ziba, come here."

"My king?"

Ziba separates from the crowd, bowing while I try to keep the scowl out of my face. He's waiting for a reward, no doubt.

David's voice fills the room. "All that belonged to Saul, I have given to your former master's grandson. You and your servants will manage the land for him. Your sons are already living in Gibeah, so they will serve as his guards and attendants. They will work the ground to bring in the harvest so that Saul's fields do not lie fallow. But your master's grandson, Mephibosheth, will eat at my table."

I turn my head, but there's nowhere to look. Ziba's sons are scattered throughout the crowd, and each one is wearing the same expression—like they've had cold water thrown in their faces. I feel exactly the same, but for a different reason.

"You may report to Benaiah for anything you need," the king continues.

David's massive household manager stands straighter when his name is mentioned.

"As you command, my king," Ziba responds, not daring to look at me. His acknowledgement is carefully respectful, but I know this wasn't what he planned when he offered me to David.

Perhaps I should be encouraged that he misread the king so profoundly.

David steps between us, blocking Ziba's sour expression. "Is this your family?"

"Yes," I turn toward them, immensely grateful that they're here. "My wife Keziah, my son Mica."

Kezi comes closer, with our son in her arms. She bows down, but David takes her hand, lifting her up.

"Shalom, my daughter." David touches Mica's head. "What do you think of your son becoming a prince of Israel?"

Kezi blushes, lowering her gaze. "He will be happy to serve your kingdom, as you serve Yahweh."

"Well said." David turns the sunlight of his smile on me. "You are blessed to have the confidence of a close family unit who loves you. An excellent woman, a firstborn son—these are some of the greatest signs of Yahweh's favor."

I nod, wondering at the longing in his tone. In spite of his many wives, is it possible that the king isn't truly loved by any of them?

"Japhia, Shaphat, show them the way to the banquet chamber," David orders, and I flinch hearing the names of Ziba's sons. The king is immediately surrounded by his family and servants, who lead him through a door on the right.

"This way, my lord." Shaphat sneers into my shoulder. "Or should I say *Geber?*"

Master? Absolutely not. Despite the irony, I refuse to smile, imprisoning Shaphat with the calmest gaze I can muster. "I'll settle for my name."

After years of having it replaced with insults and curses, Mephi will be shocking enough without hearing Ziba's sons call me *master* with that much disdain.

"We will be working closely with you, it would seem." Japhia leans in to my ear, his hands tightening around my arm. "Close enough to know if you tell the king any lies about our father. Remember, there's plenty we could say about you."

Once the threat works its way through me, I realize how weightless it is. The stories Ziba could tell now would merely be a humiliation, revealing the way I've lived for years. But that can't really hurt me. What I have to watch out for is Ziba finding a way to paint me as a traitor.

I smile wanly. "Trust me, the king is not interested in anything I have to say. Your father will not lose any position with David on my account."

"Good," Japhia purrs through a false smile. "Our father knows more about life in the court than you ever will. One word from him can take everything David gave to you and make it his."

My heart thumps harder, but I dare to look deeper. There's a chance that he's bluffing. It must burn him to watch his father spend years scheming for power only to see David hand me something I never asked for. But no doubt Ziba thinks more highly of his position than he should.

I'm relieved to know that he will answer to the king's steward. Benaiah is the most intimidating man I've ever seen. His heavy arms are crossed over a chest of iron, and his fierce black eyes never leave David.

"We're not children anymore, Japhia," I remind him coldly. "We're servants of the king, and unlike Ziba, there is nothing I have to hide from David. I was content with what I had before, and I'm not afraid to go back to it. Your father has the most to lose."

I expect a comeback, but Japhia stays silent, annoyance pinching his expression. He knows very well his father kept me in a cistern, and I could tell David all about that. I can play this game too.

I expect to feel relieved once we're settled in the long banquet hall, but fresh amazement keeps me alert. David's family sits at a raised table of strong cedar planks covered with a crisp linen cloth. The servants keep piling the table with food long after our cups are filled.

David's prayers stretch across the table, enveloping the room, and Kezi squeezes my hand, her eyes glistening. My heart lifts to see her happy, seemingly unconcerned with the contrast. Amid the resplendent colors of the polished room, we look like shepherds brought in from the fields. It's hard to imagine that David was one as a boy. I wonder if he always looked like a king, even following his father's flocks.

David settles back against his chair. "Ziba said you've been staying with Machir son of Ammiel. He never told me you were with him all this time."

I straighten, unprepared to speak. "I asked him not to say anything, my lord. With my lineage, my lord, it seemed better that..."

"I understand. Machir has always been a trustworthy man. And I promise you won't die if you forget to say *my lord* one time." He laughs, comfortably, tearing bread in half. "The first time I called your father *Jonathan,* I thought Abner would appear and throw me out a window." His face sobers almost instantly. "I'm sorry about him. And your uncles. I made sure they received honorable burials in Hebron."

"Thank you." I keep forgetting that he knew everyone my father knew, everyone I wanted so badly to meet. I wonder vaguely what might have happened if Abner would have received Ziba's letter about me.

"You should meet my children." David lifts his hand at a dark-haired fifteen-year-old seated near him, and I hear the distinct note of pride in his voice. "My firstborn, Amnon, the son of Ahinoam of Jezreel."

I look over, but my eye catches another boy mouthing David's words as he says them. David follows my gaze. "That's Absalom, son of Maacah of Geshur." He gestures to a beautiful young girl with matching eyes. "And his sister, Tamar."

*Date palm.* It fits. She's excessively beautiful for someone who can't be older than thirteen. Her brother stares at me, intent on one thing. "How long have you been like that?"

One of the women clears her throat, looking sharply at David, but he says nothing, still watching me. I realize he may not have heard the whole story either.

"I was five. I fell on the hills outside Gibeah when we fled the Philistines." I'm struggling not to shake, my heart jumping around in my throat like a caged animal. I've never really told the story out loud. I've just lived with it.

David's tone slants, turning sad. "I didn't know what had happened to you. I looked for the woman who raised you, the one your father loved."

I blush, hearing him acknowledge that so plainly. It's strange how kind he makes everything sound. The feeling that David knew my family better than I did grows around me. "Naamah stayed in Lo Debar with Machir."

I'm almost relieved she's not here. It's bad enough that Ziba and his sons are so close at hand. I need time to understand what David wants before I expose him to more people who really know me.

David straightens. "She is to be commended. She's been a faithful servant since the days of your father. If you want to send for her at any time, just say the word. I'd like to make sure she's well cared for."

"Thank you, my lord," I whisper, wishing my throat wasn't so dry. I lift my cup and taste the smoothest wine I've ever had, nothing like the sharp, raw bite from Lo Debar. Everything in this place speaks of wealth and power, and it seems impossible to believe that I was born into it only a few miles from here. In the very house David just gave me.

I wonder how long it will take the king to realize that I know nothing of wealth. I never expected to run a household with servants. But if I don't learn, Ziba's sons will waste no time undermining me. The life David's offered me will require a level of vigilance I haven't attained yet. But perhaps it won't be so different from how I've lived already, keeping one eye open, testing people's motives before entrusting myself to them.

A woman speaks brightly from the other edge of the table. "My husband was overjoyed to hear that you were alive, Mephi."

David's face warms in her direction, relaxing. I wonder if she's his favorite wife. "This is my Abigail, the mother of Chileab," he points out another boy whose grin matches his mother's. Instantly, I know they're safe. Absalom and his mother are not of Israel. Maybe that's why I feel pinpricks on my neck when I look at them.

David continues, "This is Adonijah, the son of Haggith, Shephatiah, the son of Abital, and Ithream, the son of Eglah. There's Shammua, Shobab, and Nathan."

The names of David's other wives and children bounce off of me. The last three are probably concubines' sons, since their mothers aren't at the table. Nathan's name sounds familiar, probably after the prophet who attends the king. But each son, each wife represents more than family. They're power—David's influence over Israelite regions and other kingdoms. In a short time, he's expanded our borders beyond anything Saul had accomplished.

I taste metal, remembering. My grandfather's reign had been cut short by disobedience, an unwillingness to fulfill Yahweh's mandate to defeat the remaining Canaanite tribes. How long have they harassed us because of that?

I lean forward, reminded of Lo Debar's broken walls. "My lord, the land I came from remains largely unprotected. It's populated mostly by refugees from Gibeah, and many of them have already lost everything. Before you summoned me, we were attacked by Syrian raiders. They killed thirty men and wounded several more before Ittai arrived."

The chaotic grief of that day tightens my stomach, and I feel vulnerable again, thinking of how soon another raid might happen. Perhaps I should get Machir and Ama out of there.

Concern puckers David's brow. "We should set men to rebuilding their wall. Benaiah oversees the laborers. Tomorrow, he can send a contingent of the Cherethites up that way. We need to answer these threats."

He strokes his beard. "I'm concerned that the Syrians are hiring themselves out for raiding again. We put down thousands under Hadadezer. But Joab fears the king of Zobah has licked his wounds long enough and is ready to seek revenge. Abishai thought the Ammonites might join him, but Nahash was a friend of mine. He died recently, but I'm confident his son Hanun will follow in his steps."

"Are you, my lord?" Abishai questions. "My servants have taken several trips to Ammon recently, and from what they've heard, Hanun is nothing like his father."

I'm startled by his boldness, but David takes it with practiced ease, shrugging. "I forget that fathers don't always duplicate themselves."

"You would know that better than anyone," his nephew affirms softly.

I'm impressed by the undertones of friendship in their banter. The king is blessed with the ability to attract the loyalty of fighters who will spend their lives on his welfare, believing that building his kingdom is the best thing they could do for Israel.

I listen to the beat of my own thoughts against David's strategies, realizing there's nothing these men wouldn't do for their king.

After the meal, David's family rises together, the women melting into the background while servants come for the children. David kisses each child on the head, touching Abigail's cheek and squeezing Ahinoam's hand.

Watching them, I realize there's someone missing. The woman who hadn't smiled, the one I felt like I should know. Once we're alone with Benaiah and a few others, David clasps my shoulder.

"My servants will see to your family, but I want you to come with me. There's someone else you should meet."

Benaiah's arms are like tree trunks. He supports me with little effort up a set of stone stairs and down a long corridor, but I don't think I'll ever get used to being hauled around. Let alone here. Benaiah mutters something about getting me a chair that servants can carry from place to place. I've never considered that, but I can't deny it would be easier.

David grows more subdued the farther we go into the harem. His smile stays, but it's muted, hesitant. The end of the hall is darker, with fewer torches burning along the walls. David taps his fingers on a wooden door, and a handmaiden opens it, bowing out of the way so that Benaiah can help me through.

The room is warm and comfortably furnished. Green tapestries cover the walls, and soft silk coverlets hang over the low furniture. A small fire snaps in the corner to ward off the chill from the open window where a middle-aged woman is watching the moonlit Kidron Valley.

"Michal?" David murmurs, and she turns her head to her shoulder, not moving her body.

Now, I know who she is. And I can guess why she keeps apart from the others.

As soon as I'm settled on my crutches, David announces, "This is Mephi, Jonathan's son."

My chest lifts, and her brow slants in my direction. There's nothing I recognize about my father's sister, but the more I look at the shape of her face, the more I can believe she's a relative. It's something hidden, though. Beneath the surface.

"I'll leave you alone," David says, disappearing behind the door.

Michal breathes without opening her mouth, letting a low, thoughtful note vibrate through her lips. "So, he found you. I don't remember Jonathan saying you were crippled. Then again, we didn't speak once I moved to Laish."

"I wasn't. I fell outside Gibeah when we had to flee." I wonder if saying it will ever feel as commonplace as it's starting to sound.

Michal lifts her chin in response. Then a smile comes out of nowhere, lighting the dullness in her eyes. It looks foreign on her face, though. Out of place. "It's so strange to see you like that. My brother, younger. And on crutches."

I swallow. "I wanted to find you," I venture, for whatever it's worth. "I wanted to find anyone. But we had to stay in hiding." I decide right there that I won't mention Palti. I never want to think about that man and what he did. I vaguely wonder how long he'll manage to stay hidden from David if I couldn't.

Michal's mouth pinches shut, and she grips her elbows, creasing the blue shawl wrapped around her. "I used to wish I was like you. Lost. Beneath David's notice. I wished for your sake you were dead."

Her bitterness burns, but somehow, I can tell she's hurt herself more than she could ever hurt me. She looks down, her voice dropping. "Sorry. He's gone. I have no one left to fight with."

"David or Abba?"

"Both, I suppose." Michal chuckles mirthlessly, shaking her head. She inhales twice, each breath more unwound. "Jonathan was the one person who I felt certain would never abandon me. As you probably thought. But for me, David died a long time ago."

A heaviness is creeping into my head, like the fog of too much wine. I've sensed it with Ama before—too many untold memories tossing between us. I'm not sure I want to know what happened between David and his first wife. But I know what I want to address.

"My father didn't abandon anyone. He did what he had to do. He died fighting for Israel." The words feel wooden, but I know they're true.

Michal sniffs, dabbing her eyes. "Perhaps it's for the best. You think he would've been happy to see all this? You crippled, me..." She waves her hand, not finishing. "No. I don't suppose he'd care. He'd be too overjoyed to see David crowned. It was his mission those last several years." She looks up at me. "You're fortunate you had him to yourself for a while. All he ever thought about was David."

"Not true." He never abandoned Saul to follow his friend, even though it would've been easier. And might have spared him Gilboa.

Michal shrugs, her voice shivering through tears. For an instant, I consider trying to get closer, but I'm too unsteady on the crutches. And she's clearly not comfortable with my inability to walk.

"I suppose you're satisfied," she mutters. "You've convinced yourself you've done right by your father."

I stiffen. She's been trying to test me since I came in this room. To see if I'm willing to live in the place she does. For the first time, I'm seeing what a pit it is. I breathe deeply, realizing I might never be alone with her again. I don't know that I want to be.

"My father would have grieved many things if he'd lived to see them. But I know this. David was meant to rule, and if Abba were here, he would agree with me."

Michal looks shocked for a moment, but her face adjusts quickly. "Yes. I think he would too." Folding her arms, she studies me deeply. I feel colder the longer she looks. How do I feel safer with David than with her?

"None of Merab's children look anything like Saul," she murmurs. "There's more of him in you." Satisfied, she goes to the wall and touches a small bell hanging there. "You can go. I don't need to see you again."

# TWENTY-EIGHT

## Mephi

———————— ◆◆◆ ————————

Michal's bitterness crawls after me into the hallway, and I'm annoyed that I can't easily shrug it off. Benaiah brings me downstairs, setting me on my crutches to wait for David, and I welcome the darkness. My thoughts fill the empty armory while I try to work out what I'm doing here.

I wish Ama were here now. Every dusty story she's told me about her former mistress is returning, sharp with fresh meaning.

"Michal was David's first wife. Saul took her from him when he had to flee Gibeah. Her marriage to Palti was unlawful."

Perhaps that's why she's locked away with no children of her own. She and her father had humiliated David, though it was likely she had little choice in the matter. It's evident that Michal resents David for more than just forcing her to return to him. She's probably the only person in Jerusalem who hasn't made peace with his kingship. Have I?

Everything I said in defense of the king and my father runs through my mind, and I wonder if I meant it. Do I believe that David was anointed by Yahweh, or have I simply adopted what everyone else has told me? Was he really so purehearted, or was he just an ambitious young solider who'd exploited Saul's weakness and stolen the kingdom?

Seeing my father's sister holding on so fiercely to a darker story makes me feel the way I felt in front of the elders of Ramoth, hearing my father's name being tossed around over my head. Like my own blood didn't know me. I'm caught between a dead world and a living one, both waiting to see what I'll choose.

I have no idea how much time passes. Outside, I hear the faint changing of the night watch, but I can't move. I'm still braced against the wall where Benaiah left me, my reflection staring back from every bit of polished metal in the room.

I resent what Michal's comments have unraveled inside me. The way she'd been able to fumble with cords I didn't realize were there. It unnerves me to see her trying to claim me for Saul, as if I need to pay homage to his side. But how much sense does that make now? Saul failed. He dragged my father down with him. Why follow a doomed path?

I pull back from it, trying to focus on what I know. I'm not Saul. I'm Mephibosheth. The crippled son of a fallen prince, the grandson of an apostate king. I was the boy who had to survive by begging, picking through garbage. For years, I've had to live knowing that I might never have a home of my own.

And now, I'm in Jerusalem with King David. The man whose heart had prompted Yahweh to choose him over my grandfather. The man I always thought would kill me if he got a chance. That man wants me here. I'm now completely beholden to a generous king with such a violent past that I'm not sure I can trust him.

Easing myself down onto a bench against the wall, I lose my grip on the crutches. One of them clatters against a black polished spear as a door opens, pouring light into the room. Thinking it's a servant, I don't turn around. Until David's voice fills the space.

"Are you any good with spears?"

Startled, I catch the crutch before it can fall again. "I've never had much use for them, my lord."

David looks almost wistful as he walks over. "I saw the bow you carried with you. Your father would be proud." His eyes glisten in the lamplight, and he reaches up to adjust the spear on the wall, regarding the weapon like an old friend he wishes he'd never met. "There was a time when all I could think about was fighting for King Saul. But shedding blood comes with a cost."

A cold tightness edges my heart. "How many have you killed?"

I don't know how I dare to look at him. I'm not sure why I want to know.

"Too many." He folds his arms. "The first was a Philistine who was attacking your father. I didn't think. I just swung the spear, and nothing was the same after that. Jonathan was the first to put one of these in my hands."

The image that jumps into my head uninvited pinches my throat shut. Somehow, with all the bows I've handled, I'd never really considered what it would've been like to have my father teach me how to use them. I'd grown accustomed to dismissing the impossible without grieving it. Even now, my heart's turning over, shrinking away from territory I've never explored. There's a reason I haven't.

I fold my arms over the ache, and I notice my father's seal ring on David's finger. I'm such a fool to have given it to him. I'd been caught in self-preservation, thinking I was about to die. And now, David's wearing it like just another piece of jewelry— the ring that was all I had for so long.

I fidget, hating the yoke of resentment trying to force its way onto me. I shouldn't be surprised. It's the way of conquest. One line obliterated to pave the way for another's glory. I've always known that David would take control of everything I couldn't. But he achieved all that a long time ago. If that's all he wanted, why am I here?

David's smile holds a pleasure that baffles me. "You can speak to me," he says warmly, and the invitation pokes a rebellious ember inside me. I can feel the poisonous smoke being released, filling my chest.

I've been silenced my whole life, but now I have the ear of a king. And not just any king. The beloved psalmist of Israel. My father's covenant brother and my grandfather's replacement. So, if he wants me to talk, I'll talk. But he's going to hear something real.

"What are you doing?" I ask him. Now that the initial shock is over and he's been thoroughly praised for his generosity, I really want to know why he would do this. After thirteen years of not caring where I was.

Strangely, David doesn't seem to mind my change in manner. In fact, his smile widens, and his voice drops even lower. "I'm speaking to my best friend's son."

He says it with wonder, and everything pulls tight in my chest, drawn down into the empty pit that opens when I'm hurt. He was expecting to summon me here so that he could see my father. But if he wasn't disappointed before, he will be soon enough. Jonathan is gone, and I'm nothing like him. Maybe now that I'm here, David will see that. Then he'll send me back to Lo Debar, where I belong.

I glance down for a moment to gather my nerve. "I mean, why have you done this?" My voice turns hard, and suddenly I'm speaking through a boulder in my throat. I pull as much steel into my expression as I can before aiming my distrust into David's face. "I can't serve you. I can't follow you into battle. There's nothing about me that can profit you except…"

My death. For a second, the old fear is back, sinking icy claws into me. Revenge didn't seem to be David's motive in the throne room. But it's easy to believe because it makes the most sense. There are still plenty of people who hate Saul, who want restitution for what he did to them. No doubt David's already being criticized for turning me into a prince instead of a sacrifice.

David reaches for my shoulder, and I flinch away. What is he touching me for? Then I see the gratified look in his eyes, and outrage fires my blood.

He doesn't want me to die. He wants to keep me here like a trophy of his goodwill. At every feast, people will see the defenseless son of Jonathan at his side and laud their king's mercy. And he'll get to look at me and remember that he won. After all that my grandfather did to him, David won the throne, and now his last enemy is crippled at his feet.

David's voice pushes through the indignant tides swelling around me. "When your father swore friendship with me, I had nothing to offer him either."

His tone hints at a longer story, but I close myself off, resenting his efforts to identify with me. He might not be the villain I was imagining, but his motives still sting. More than likely, he felt guilty when he heard what happened to me. Now he wants to satisfy his old vow with my father so that he can rule with a clear conscience. My grip on my crutches is so tight that my fingers ache.

I'd finally accepted everything and found a life in spite of myself. I'd closed the door on the past, refusing any connection to what had been taken. Why couldn't David have left me alone?

"I'd forgotten. There's something you should have." Interrupted by his own thoughts, David moves halfway down the room, glancing back as if he expects me to follow. I smirk at his ignorance. How much of a shock was it for him to find out that Jonathan's son couldn't walk?

He opens a small cedar box on a table, returns to me, and places two gemstones in my hand. Their bright red fire startles me. Even with their moderate size, one of these would have changed my life back in Ramoth. And now, David hands them off to me as though he has fifty more where these came from.

I'm annoyed by how much I admire him without wanting to. Even if I can't put it into words, it's evident why the people love David. Everything about him speaks of the wealth and self-assuredness a king should possess, but his open manner invites trust. And his eyes won't stop dancing.

He points at the stones. "These are from the belt of Goliath the Gittite."

Of course. The giant Saul had been afraid to fight all those decades ago. My face stings, and my hands get hot around the stones, fresh anger charring my appreciation. It makes so much sense. Why not give the son of a defeated prince a token from your greatest victory? Just so he knows who he's dealing with.

I turn them over in my hand, trying to muster an appropriate response. If he was telling the truth about the land he's given me, I'm already wealthy. Why would I need these now?

David doesn't wait for me to ask.

"I gave these to Jonathan to symbolize the two arrows the Philistines had put in him the year before. I was just a shepherd then, and I had nothing else of value to give your father. But that day, he made me a prince. He gave me his robe and his bow, and he offered me his protection as a brother. He made a covenant with me, a promise of friendship that he kept until..." His voice stops, and he looks at me.

"Gilboa." The word shakes the walls around my heart.

David keeps shocking me, contradicting the image I have in my head of a ruler like Ziba. Cold, vengeful, jealous for his own name. Easy to hate. Somehow, this is worse than finding him that way.

If he'd been some sort of selfish tyrant, I could've avoided him. But David has more memories with my father than I do. It's like he's spread a feast before me and made me realize how little I've been living on for years. My stomach clenches, warning me back from the hurt. But it's too late. Everything in me wants more.

Caution dropping away, I pick up each memory David's dusted off, turning them over with the rubies in my hand. I let myself imagine my father giving a shepherd boy everything that he should have given me. David handing him the gemstones of a *Nephilim* giant who had threatened our people. Their arms clasped in covenant somewhere in my grandfather's war camp. But what stands out to me is the image of my father with Philistine arrows in him.

That stops me cold, like a fist to my face. I'd never let myself go there. Never pictured what happened on Gilboa in my father's final moments. All I'd known as a child was that my Abba wasn't coming back. I was afraid of what that meant. I'd learned not to ask questions because I was told no one cared. But now, the edge of what I never knew is turning on me. Tearing me open.

"Did he suffer?" I ask quietly.

David doesn't move, but pain darts across his face like a muscle clenching. "I don't know. He didn't deserve to."

I flinch violently without meaning to. All my life, I've heard the opposite. That my father deserved death. For being Saul's son. Saul rejected Yahweh, so He'd rejected them. And cursed me for belonging to them. It had become so easy to believe that I almost can't bear the alternative.

The idea that my grandfather had rejected a God of love, that Yahweh had honored my father's trust and still let him die, is more painful than anything I've ever felt. Right there, I know

I would've gone through that night in the ravine over and over if I could've had my father.

But he's dead, and I actually feel it. For the first time.

The fresh grief carries the power of a tempest, slamming against the doors of shame that have held it back. It's terrifying. But I can't do anything to stop it. There's nowhere to hide. And I can't run.

My shoulders cave and I clench my fists, letting the sharp edges of the rubies bite my palm. David didn't bring me here so I could weep like a child. My father died thirteen years ago. But I never knew that my dreams about him were closer to the truth than what Ziba always said. I've spent so much time masking my grief with anger when I never even *knew* him. Now I'm standing here with someone who did, and everything in me aches with the void.

The moment I make a sound, David's arms turn me away from the wall and pull me into his chest, kicking through my last defense. Undone, I decide to stop fighting. This isn't Ziba. This is David.

He's holding me tighter than anyone ever has. Even Machir hasn't heard me grieve like this. I sob freely, overtaken by something stronger than fear. David says nothing because there's nothing to say. He's stood at this cliff before, realizing my father wasn't coming back. I'd never known how much that hurt him until now.

When David's grip relaxes, I lean away from him, my head lowered as my old enemy slithers back into view. What have I done? This is the king of Israel, not some long-lost relative.

I rein everything in, shuddering. "Forgive me, my lord."

"I won't criticize a son who grieves for his father." David's voice is quiet and deep, like water at the base of a canyon. Silently, deliberately cutting through rock that has stood for ages.

"Where's yours?" I ask without meaning to.

"He died in Moab more than ten years ago. Along with my mother." For the first time, the hint of a conflict shifts the confidence on David's face. "He was a good man, but I rarely heard him tell me he loved me. For a long time, I didn't think he did. Your father was the first man who ever made me feel worthy."

His sincerity pulls my gaze back up.

David's eyes flood. "He would have done the same for you. When I was in exile, he came and found me. He strengthened my faith like no one else could have. But he was different that day. The burden he always carried had been lifted and replaced with a joy I couldn't understand," David beams. "It was you. I wasn't a father yet, but that night, I saw what it was like. In his eyes."

My pulse burns in my throat. "God knows, it's enough to know that," I whisper.

The mention of God seems to awaken David. He leans over me, his eyes deepening, as though he's seeing another realm beyond the room.

"God knows, Mephibosheth. He saw you the night you fled and were injured. He was the one who bound your father and me together. All those years ago, Yahweh established that solemn oath between us—for your sake. He was my Shepherd when I hid out in caves all over Judea, running for my life. And He was yours too. All those years I couldn't find you, He already knew where you were, and He had reached ahead of all of us to save you."

I blink so I can see clearly. After living bound by Ziba's words for years, I'd never guessed David's would have the power to knock the chains off. Except, maybe it isn't David. He's a great king, but he's still only a man. He's failed and fought just like anyone else. And yet he doesn't sound like everyone else. He sounds like what they call him—a man after God's heart.

He's not just saying this. He's not just reciting the words of Torah for some ceremony. He's somehow lived inside them. Yahweh's faithfulness is real to him. Because he's found safe pasture in it when he had nowhere else to go. That's how he can offer it to me. That's why his words touch Israel's heart. That's why he was chosen.

My pulse turns wild as it dawns on me. David knows our God. And for the first time, I feel certain Yahweh offered the same chance to Saul. Which means He might be offering that same chance to me. My heart splits, thinking of the hint of His presence I'd felt when I faced death. It wasn't my imagination. All that time I ignored Him, hid from Him, even cursed Him… He'd been right there?

I shake my head, stunned by the time it's taken me to see it. Only Yahweh could've spared me while Saul's descendents were being wiped out clan by clan. Only He could have brought me to David, a king who actually understood what my life had been like, what my father had been like. Instead of letting me live out my life in obscurity, closed off from what I could have had, I've been brought here, given the chance to see Yahweh in the eyes of Israel's king.

The king my father had helped build.

I shake my head, bewildered by a joy I can't fathom. I can't even begin to know what to say. "It's too much. I can't contain it all."

"I know." David's answer is soft. There are years of travel in his face, but somehow, his experience has humbled him, not puffed him up. "Don't be afraid to believe. Just do it. Yahweh is bigger than any of us ever imagined." He takes my arms again. "We're His dream, Mephi. You and me. Israel. But what we see here is just the beginning."

# TWENTY-NINE

## *David*

— ◆ —

Tonight, when I close my eyes, Jonathan's face smiles behind them.

But this time, he's younger. Brighter eyes stare into mine, and a deeper-colored beard skirts his jawline without the flecks of gray. It's Mephi's face.

Thankfulness burns in my chest, the most welcome pain I've felt in years.

"You've done it, Yahweh. You had your eye on him all this time, and you finally brought him to me."

I feel the glow of Yahweh's smile warming the walls around me as Jonathan's voice joins the silence.

*Our children could end up playing in the same halls where you used to sing for my father.*

I'd been afraid to believe it then, but the boy my friend loved is finally going to be safe and regain the inheritance that was always his. I open my eyes in the darkness and stare at the moon filling the window across from my bed.

*He's everything you hoped, brother. You would be proud.*

It will be up to me to help Mephi believe that. He doesn't yet. I could see it in his eyes, in the things he called himself. I wonder how many insults he's taken, what he's had to do to survive. All these years, he couldn't even get onto his feet, take one step out of whatever ash heap he was hiding in. But he's fought.

Why else would a crippled man bring a bow with him? Mephi has found his way to his father's weapon and learned how to fight for his people. And he's become a leader. Even in that land of no pasture, he's stood out. He's struggled alongside the people there, and he wants to defend them, to see them prosper.

The desperate courage in his voice had reminded me of the feeling that had pulled at my heart in the caves, watching Uriah spar with Joab or Ezra training the younger boys with wooden swords. I had known I was looking at the future of Israel, and I was ready to face whatever I had to in order to help them. To spend my life on their welfare, one step at a time.

We had done the best we could as fugitives empowered by Yahweh's mercy. And now, we can do more.

I smile, a plan taking shape in my mind. I will ride to Lo Debar along with Benaiah and the laborers. I will leave behind a contingent of warriors to defend the forgotten city that sheltered Jonathan's son.

And I know who else I will take with me.

# THIRTY

*Mephi*

———— •• ◆ •• ————

"The king wants me to ride with him to Lo Debar?"

I'm half-expecting Azarel to be mocking me. But after spending the night in my grandfather's old fortress in Gibeah, nothing should surprise me. My wife and son are still sleeping in what David assured me was my father's old room. I'd spent hours the night before trying to fall asleep myself, only to dream of a shepherd boy playing his harp in every corner of this house. I'm tempted to think this whole journey was a dream.

But this room alone is larger than most of Machir's house, and now Ziba's sons are standing over me, tossing fine linen garments in my direction.

"Trust me, the king was very specific. He's on his way here now, and we have to make you the prince David thinks you are."

Three of his brothers join him, dragging me onto the floor and forcing the clothes onto me. When they're finished, Zarethan props me up on my crutches, and Shaalbim drapes a green robe over my shoulders. "Satisfied, Sar Mephi?"

I smile tightly. "Handle me like that again, and I'll have Benaiah get me new servants."

Azarel folds his arms. "You're enjoying this, aren't you?"

I roll my eyes. "I will when I'm certain it's real."

Azarel lifts his brows when we hear the king's men downstairs. Gibeah is barely a few miles from Jerusalem, and half a battalion is waiting in Saul's courtyard in an arrow-shaped line behind David. Amnon, Chileab, and Absalom sit beside him atop the finest horses I've ever seen.

Benaiah has sent me a chair with long bronze poles for servants to carry on their shoulders. It should be much easier than the crutches, but I refuse to watch Azarel's expression when he has to help me up into it.

When Ziba's sons bring me outside, David dismounts, grinning. "Ready to go, my son?"

"You do me too much honor, my king," I respond, ignoring the way Absalom's rolling his eyes.

"Actually, you're not ready yet," David continues. "Azarel, bring me what I sent to the armory last night."

In a few moments, Azarel returns with a polished plated vest, a pair of leg greaves, and a gleaming sword.

"They're your father's," David announces proudly. "The men of Jabesh stole them back from Ashtoreth, and I had them purified. No one else has used them since then. No one else should."

I don't breathe while Ziba's sons snap the armor into place. When they're finished, I slide my father's sword into the sheath at my side, still unable to comprehend that it was his. To have him with me like this means more than I could ever say.

"Jonathan's bow was broken, but I see that you already have one of your own," David says, his eyes sparkling at the weapon beside me.

"Yes, my lord." I'd expected a measure of disbelief from the king, but he acts as though it's the most natural thing in the world that I can shoot.

David squeezes my shoulder, his eyes skirting the fields. "Saul's property goes all the way past the stream of Ezel. Jonathan and I spent hours out there practicing. You'll have to shoot for me when we return."

It'll be a miracle if I can display any skill with the king of Israel watching. But David already looks impressed. "Your father would be proud," he declares loudly.

Absalom and Amnon snicker quietly while the servants help me onto a horse, but Chileab talks over them, politely echoing his father's praise. He's the only one who doesn't show visible annoyance when David sends them back toward Jerusalem.

"The Sars stay here?" I ask David as soon as they've ridden out of earshot.

"For now, yes." David turns sheepish. "They're not much like me, my sons. I'm still trying to figure out how that happened. They were born amidst upheaval, as you were. Yet somehow, you picked up right where your father left off, even without him. How is that?"

The humble longing in his question embarrasses me. I twist the reins, trying to decide. "I was desperate, I guess."

All those years, I would've done anything to find my father. If anyone had told me I would end up outside Jerusalem's north gate, ready to ride out with David's mighty men, I would've laughed.

I listen in awed silence while David points out the soldiers around him. They're polite, but I can feel their agitation. Carefully-controlled disgust passes back and forth between them like angry clouds in a summer sky.

When I spot Uriah the Hittite, I wonder why I haven't heard more stories about him. He was in the caves with the king as a servant to Joab until he'd fought his way through the ranks. But he seems to put everyone at ease, so I ride up next to him.

"Are they offended by me?" I ask him quietly.

Uriah's expression twists. "No. We had some disturbing news this morning." He angles his horse into the trail. "The king sent his servants to Jericho with gifts of condolence for the son of Nahash of Ammon. He was an ally, but his son Hanun rejected the gifts and cut the servants' beards and clothing. He humiliated them, so the king told them to remain in seclusion for a while."

I frown, wondering what kind of ruler would challenge David now when an alliance was already in place. "Doesn't the king have Ammonite relatives?"

"Yes," Uriah acknowledges. "He has connections with Moab too, through his great-grandmother Ruth."

"Why did David conquer Moab, then? Didn't his parents live there for a while?"

Uriah nods. "During his fugitive days, yes. But our lord didn't realize the new king would betray him. Once he took power, he was instrumental in plotting to kill Jesse and Atarah. They had already died, though. They were very old."

I smile, hearing how Uriah won't address the king by name. The open loyalty David attracts isn't forced or contrived. It's the most genuine thing I've ever seen.

Uriah bows his head as David reins in closer.

"Did you ever learn to fight on horseback?" the king asks me.

"A little, but we didn't have many swords in Lo Debar," I remind him.

"Eleazar can teach you."

I smirk, my face getting hotter. "I'm grateful, my lord, but I'm not foolish enough to think Joab would want to command me in battle."

David laughs comfortably. "I have more than enough capable men out on the field, but every Israelite should be able to defend his family. You've come far enough by yourself."

"I had help." I briefly describe Machir and Ebenezer, how they helped me put my skills to work, giving me the courage to push past my limitations. I keep my stories short and simple, but appreciation fills David's face as he listens.

"Machir has always been honorable. And Ziba was your guardian before Machir found you, yes?"

I can't control the darkness filling my expression. "He kept me for eight years. That doesn't make him my guardian."

I don't say more, but David's silence seems to understand. "What did Machir say when I sent for you?" he finally asks.

"They all told me to trust you. They said you wouldn't put to death someone Yahweh had spared."

Shadows push into David's face. "If it were up to me, there would be no more Israelite deaths. Now that Jerusalem is mine, I want to build a place to install the Ark of the Covenant permanently. And yet, it's still in a booth, waiting for that day. As always, we have enemies to deal with first."

I squint past him at the hills. "Do you think we'll ever be completely rid of them?"

"Perhaps we'll drive them from this land. But enemies will always find the people of God. That is why He's always telling us to be strong and courageous," David grins, quoting Yahweh's words to our ancestor Joshua.

I smile with him. "Machir told me that you would worship in Saul's war camps before leading your soldiers into battle."

"Yes," David acknowledges. "I miss that."

I lift my brows. "You don't now?"

"Not in the same way. But you're right. Why not? Men!" David shouts, and every soldier snaps to attention. "We should give thanks to the Lord our God as we ride out. It has been too long since we've rejoiced before Him together!"

The army's appreciative laughter builds into hearty cheers and shouts of encouragement as David lifts his voice in a bold melody that carries through the ranks.

"Sing unto the Lord for what He's done! Make a joyful noise, all the earth!"

I laugh as several men eagerly add their voices behind David's, lifting powerful praise that plucks chills along my arms. I can't muster enough boldness to join in, but it's no wonder Yahweh loves this man. He's like sunlight, waking up the army.

In a few days, my grudging admiration has increased tenfold and become purer, the cynicism dropping out of sight. David has flaws, I'm sure of it. But right now, I don't want to see them.

Once the singing dies down, David laughs in my direction. "My new son is giving me the same look they all do."

I hide my smile in the army's hearty laughter.

"Crazy lion of Judah," I mutter before realizing David heard me. "No disrespect intended, my king."

"None taken." He tries twice to finish. "Your father used to call me that."

David's smile is unbound, letting me see what I saw before—the weight that Jonathan holds in his heart. Once we leave the gates of Jerusalem behind, I ask him, "What happened with you and my father?"

I was afraid to know before, but now I feel foolish for assuming their friendship was only legend.

David doesn't answer right away. He studies the hills ahead of us.

"I still don't know. I had heard stories about him, but when I met him…" He shakes his head, something vulnerable appearing on his face. "I wasn't prepared for what happened. I didn't expect him to pledge his honor to me, especially after he found out that I'd been anointed."

"Did you tell him?" It's hard to imagine David as he was back then. A young commoner with a dangerous secret. The story goes, he was anointed king by the Roeh Samuel when he was still a boy.

David's smile deepens. "He figured it out. So did your grandfather."

"And Saba tried to kill you," I finish quietly.

David's shoulders sag. He's not angry. But it's still something he wishes never happened.

"I didn't want to accept it. Saul was like my father. He pushed me into things my own Abba didn't believe I was capable of. After I married Michal, I thought things would improve, but—" He stops. Abishai looks away, and Joab keeps his gaze straight ahead.

David lowers his voice, continuing, "It hurt your father deeply to see the rift that was growing between Saul and me. Jonathan loved his father, and I couldn't imagine him ever going against Saul, even for me. But he still helped me escape with my life. He was the reason I made it out alive."

"Why did he do that?" After all this time, I really don't have a satisfying answer.

David smiles, thinking deeply before answering.

"When a man gives himself to Yahweh's purposes, he can see more clearly than those around him. It's a gift of closeness with Adonai. Jonathan could see deeper than most of the men in Saul's army. He knew that I had been set apart, so he lent me his strength to honor Yahweh. To help Israel. And to save you."

If anyone else had told me that, I might've written it off. But there's a permanence in David's eyes, in the strength of his words. Everything he's lived through has carved Yahweh's truth deep into him. He means what he says.

"Do you believe me?" David questions.

"I don't know that I could ever believe anything as passionately as you do," I admit, embarrassed.

David smirks. "I think you can. You're Jonathan's son."

I shrug. "No one expected me to be like him. No one said I was."

David's voice softens, pulled back into memory. "You've learned a better way, then. Your father grew up in Saul's shadow, and Saul was…a force of nature. He wasn't an easy man to live under. No one envied the Hassar the burden he carried. Jonathan wanted it to be different for you. He always knew you would be your own man."

Twisting Abba's seal ring off his finger, David holds it out to me. "You should keep this. It's always been yours."

I take it, impressed that it fits me now. "It felt pointless for the longest time. Nothing qualified me for what it represented."

David's face warms. "If it helped you keep fighting, it wasn't pointless. He knew that when he left it with you."

Without the old dread weighing me down, the journey north goes faster than the one to Jerusalem. When we reach the hastily-repaired gate of Lo Debar, I immediately sense how my eyes have adjusted to the glittering city of David. Glimpsing the ramshackle town through the king's eyes, I keep my gaze forward, realizing that he's getting a clearer story of how I lived than if I'd told him.

David's heralds have gone ahead of us, so the elders and Machir are already gathered, waiting. Overwhelmed, Gad and the others go to their knees, but David is already off his mount, approaching to clasp their hands.

I can see now why they call him the shepherd-king. It's not merely a reference to his upbringing. He looks as comfortable here as in Zion, lifting up each elderly man the way any Israelite son would.

"Machir, I have brought you an ambassador who will act in my stead to see this town rebuilt and armed against further attack."

Machir laughs aloud when he sees me, and I easily slide off the horse into his arms. He keeps one hand around my waist, supporting me as he always did. "I didn't expect to see you back here so soon. No one should be homesick for this place after seeing Jerusalem."

"I have you to thank for his safety, Machir." David squeezes his shoulder. "You have my gratitude."

"Mephi!" Ama's shriek reaches me seconds before she does, flinging her arms around my neck. Staggering, I drop heavily to my knees embracing her, and someone hands Machir my crutches too late.

"He's given me Saul's land in Gibeah," I tell Ama, my throat thick as I watch the magnitude hit her. "Kezi and Mica are there now. He's made me like one of his sons."

Ama's wet eyes open wider in David's direction. Her lips quiver. "Thank you, my lord. I knew you wouldn't have forgotten Jonathan."

Bending over, David takes her hands in his. "He would have been grateful. I knew if I could find you, I would find Jonathan's son safe."

Ama lowers her eyes, swallowing a sob. "I failed him, my lord. Mephi's injury was…"

"Not the death of him, thanks to you." Turning tender, David tips her chin. "I'm leaving Machir with money for you. If you choose to marry, I want to know about it so that I may give my blessing and make sure he's as worthy as the man who loved you first."

Ama's eyes are riveted on David's face, but every bone in her body is trembling. "Thank you, my lord," she manages before Machir lifts her up.

"I'll take care of her, my king." His eyes go to the army beyond us. "With your reinforcements, this town should no longer be a dangerous place to stay."

"Mephi told me about the Syrian raiders who attacked you," David says, the fight building back into his tone. "I received some disturbing news from my spies before we came. It seems my Ammonite allies have turned against us. They've armed at least twenty thousand of Hadadezer's old army, along with a thousand more from Maacah and Tob."

Fearful murmurs sweep the crowd that's gathered, and Machir frowns. "Hadadezer? He's come out of hiding?"

"Not yet," Joab weighs in, his face twisting scornfully. "He's hoping for revenge, but he'll put as many Syrians ahead of him as he can."

"My guess is they'll go to Helam and amass under his old commander Shobach," David explains. "They'll try and draw us to the Euphrates so they'll have the option of sending out more reserves after we defeat them."

419

"Are you attacking with just these men?" Machir blinks.

"No." David points west. "Joab has summoned the other commanders to meet us at the Jordan with their units."

"What about Ammon?" Gad asks. "Won't they come out against us once you defeat Shobach's men?"

"I certainly hope so," Joab answers boldly. "Then we can finish them once and for all."

David smirks. "Joab is the only man who would dare answer for me, but he's right. After we deal with Syria, I'll send out more troops to besiege Rabbah before the springtime feasts. But Lo Debar should be rebuilt before then. And I'm leaving a unit of warriors here to defend it and train up more fighting men. You've been forgotten long enough."

"What if the fighting pushes past the Jordan?" Machir asks.

David's smile turns fierce, making my pulse race. "It won't."

Machir smiles at someone behind me. "Ebenezer, Mephi's back," he announces as the carpenter steps forward.

I turn around, but he's not looking at me. His attention is fixed on the men behind David, and years are escaping his face like frost lifting from a field. He mouths a name, and a hoarse cry escapes one of the soldiers. "Abba?"

One of David's armed men leaves his mount and rushes forward, stopping for one breathless moment before catching Ebenezer in his arms.

The old man sobs, every ounce of coldness broken on the rock of his son's chest. I gape, struggling to comprehend what I'm seeing while I explain it to David. "His sons escaped Gilboa. But he never heard if they made it to you. He thought they were dead."

David's smile is laced with pain. "Zebulun arrived in Hebron alone. His brother fell in the wilderness." Watching the men embrace, the king folds his arm around me. "Praise Yahweh, I'm not the only one who gained a son today."

Long into the night, the elders sit around fires, their attention rapt as David's war plans and rebuilding strategies trail off into singing. He starts with some battle songs he wrote after he and Joab struck down the Edomites in the Valley of Salt. After that, the haunting melodies begin.

Even up against the fire, the music scatters chills across my skin. David's praises fold gently underneath the melody he coaxes from the harp he carried with him. The notes mingle with the breeze, lifting up over our heads to join the stars. The wind parts the branches of Ebenezer's olive grove, like Yahweh has stepped into the clearing to listen.

"Because the needy groan and the poor are plundered, I will arise," David sings, speaking for Adonai. How does he dare? "I will place him in the safety for which he longs."

David leans back, letting his own heart respond. "The words of the Lord are purer than silver, refined in the furnace sevenfold. On every side, the wicked prowl, but you, O Lord will keep us. You will guard us from them forever."

I fold my arms around my bow. The fresh confidence settling into my bones is almost enough to make me stand to my feet. I wonder if David knows that he's speaking for all of Israel, for men who can't put such things into words.

I finally sense the safety Yahweh has surrounded me with. I'll spend my life trying to understand it. But at last, I believe it. I know that He's been building a warrior even before I knew I was one. I could camp inside that assurance forever.

In the morning, David prepares to meet the rest of his troops beyond the Jordan, leaving me behind to oversee the rebuilding of Lo Debar. The wall will need to be reinforced and lengthened, the guardhouse expanded, and a watchtower installed. Better homes will line the inner edges of the market, and a secret tunnel will connect the town with Mahanaim.

Before David leaves, he turns to me. "Will you come back, my son? After you're satisfied with the work here?"

I search his face, taken aback. I hadn't realized I had a choice. But now that I do, the answer is easy. "Yes, my king. I will come back. Please send someone to watch over my family. This is all new to them, and Ziba isn't exactly someone I've been able to rely on in the past. I want them to know that they'll be taken care of until I return."

David embraces me. "You have my word. They'll be treated as my own family."

I can't answer such kindness. I can only respond to it. "God go with you, my lord."

"And with you."

In the rumble of the fleeing horses, Ebenezer appears soundlessly at my elbow. All the years we've barely spoken had dropped away last night. Now, there's nothing between us.

He watches me, a playful grin working beneath his beard. "So, you're going back to the shepherd-king. With a smile. What's happened to all your caution?"

I shrug, too amazed to laugh. I feel somewhat stranded without the dread I've carried, but I know I'll come to relish the freedom.

"I was wrong about him," I admit quietly, watching the trail of dust behind the army. I know it already. Even once Lo Debar is rebuilt, it can't be my home anymore.

"I have to thank you." Ebenezer's gruffness is gone, replaced by a shaky joy. "I never thought I would see either of my sons again." His tears spill over. "I'm grateful."

"So am I."

Their reunion, like my elevation, was beyond me. It's still startling to know that my grandfather's home is waiting for me back in Gibeah, along with the king whose name I've dreaded hearing until now. Not only does David not hate me, he wants me. The way a father wants a son. He's not willing to let me disappear from the world my Abba once ruled. He wants me to be as much a part of it as I can.

I'm wondering how long this newfound freedom can be trusted when Ebenezer grasps my arm, his eyes shadowed.

"Just be careful, son. Even in the best kingdoms, there are things going on beneath the surface, storms brewing that only certain men see coming. Until everyone suddenly does. Jerusalem is not like this place, where everyone knows everyone and every decision is discussed openly."

I frown, not wanting to go back to distrusting David's every move. "I don't think David would turn on me now."

"I'm not saying that. Just keep alert. Things can happen in the blink of an eye that have been building for years. You could find yourself in the middle of something you didn't begin and cannot finish."

I don't know whether to be concerned or annoyed. Ebenezer's always been wise. But he's never been one to talk like a prophet. "How do you know?"

He shrugs, devoid of specifics. But the certainty in his face tells me he's serious. "It's just the way of things. You'll see."

# THIRTY-ONE

*David*

———◆◆◆———

*Five months later*

I've worn out the floor, pacing miles from one end of my terrace to the other.

It's the worst kind of journey, one where you don't get anywhere. My mind has traveled farther than my feet, stretching and straining against an impassible barrier that I should have noticed before.

Up till now, I've tried to ignore the way the bricks have piled up, refusing to believe something like boredom could have such an effect on me. But now I'm staring down another nine-foot giant, an inner wall that couldn't have been built overnight. And I can't break through.

Staying in Jerusalem while my men faced Ammon in battle felt like a good decision at the time. The first real reprieve I've had in years. I've been fighting since I was fourteen, and all my generals encouraged me to rest. But it only took a few days for me to regret staying home.

I understand now why Jonathan rarely did before he was married. But then, he only had one wife. Most of mine have become sharp-clawed politicians, and it was a mistake to give them even more access to me. Their main concern is the elevation of their sons. Nothing else. Few of them have the ability to reach the emptiness that's been growing inside me. The cavern has expanded so slowly that I've barely noticed.

I refuse to believe I miss the old days, the ones before my rule. When I rode into Zion years ago, I'd thought the richness of everything I'd been promised would fill my heart indefinitely. But I can't recall the last time I celebrated like that. I've been living on empty for too long, trusting the succession of battles to occupy my heart. Not singing. Not worshipping.

That should scare me. It would have years ago. But I can't reach the part of me that's real enough to feel it.

I stop at the edge of the tiles where the view stretches over Jerusalem's rooftops. I've never felt this vacant during wartime.

Joab has assured me we'll be victorious over Hadadezer's troops. Our previous successes secured us a powerful hold over

Syria, sending their allies running scared. But for the first time, I don't know where I should be. What I should do.

*Wake up, David. Wake up.*

But even my inner drive seems wilted, tired. I know it in the instant I glimpse the flat roof of the house in the near distance.

The sight of the woman bathing there wakes me up, shaking me out of the strange slumber hanging over me. Almost. The part of my brain that might ponder how strange it is that the height of my roof allows me to see things like this stays asleep. The rest of me continues to watch, too captivated to wonder why.

The woman is half-covered by a thin screen, but the shadow of her frame isn't hidden, and she's taking her time, dragging each limb through the water before stepping out into the robe her maid hands her. Her dark hair is like a curtain down her back. The images are brief but powerful, pulling me down a path I didn't realize I wanted to follow.

I'm still watching the unknown woman, but my mind is back in Saul's fortress. The heavy, curtained walls of the king's garden surround me again, giving me a few precious moments alone with his daughter. It almost didn't matter that she might not ever be mine. Having her in my arms made me feel like she already was. That kind of passion is tossing inside me now, except ten times more intoxicating.

Because this time, nothing's in the way.

I have no idea who the woman on the roof is, but my aimless heart is following her through my eyes, refusing to back down. No one has taken control of my imagination so completely since Michal, and all I have to do is acknowledge it.

I'm not a shepherd boy anymore, forced to wait and watch while some king dangles a woman in front of me, making me risk my life to earn her love. It's different now. I can feel whatever I want to feel.

And no one will stop me.

*Nine months later*

Nothing will be the same.

I kept waiting for it to be difficult, for some sign that I was doing wrong. But things just kept falling into place.

I called her. She came. She looked terrified for one second, and then melted in my arms. I'm not sure I would have stopped even if she asked. That should scare me. But it didn't. Doesn't.

Nothing's been the same since Bathsheba.

It's been almost a year since I saw her bathing, but from that moment, everything was different. Every step afterwards drew me to the daughter of Eliam like a moth to a flame.

Except now I'm the flame. I can consume everything in my path and nothing will stop me. And no one did.

But I'm not the type to set those kinds of fires. I'm the shepherd-king. It's my job to stay vigilant. When did I decide to stop? When did I decide it was too hard? I've been pacing the length of my terrace for hours trying to figure it out, but all I can see is Bathsheba's face.

She's so beautiful. It still makes my chest ache to think of the passion that had been stirred awake by her touch. From the moment she came, I didn't see her as anyone's wife. She was just... Bathsheba. It felt right to have her in my arms, to let unbridled pleasure cover over every wound that Saul's daughter carved into me. But it wasn't enough.

I couldn't be apart from her. Couldn't stop even once I found out who she was. Gripping the stone railing, I unfold the message Joab sent.

*Read it again, David. Feel something.*

It was Uriah. The loyal, valiant youth who'd followed me in the caves, willingly pledging himself to me during my exile. It was his wife I slept with. His life I tossed aside in a recent battle. He's dead now. And I don't care.

When I found out Bathsheba was pregnant, I tried to get Uriah to come home, maybe think the baby was his. But he wouldn't leave the army for more than a few days. And then he unknowingly carried his own death warrant back to Joab. I tried to tell myself it was unavoidable. Inevitable. Better than him finding out the truth. Something even Bathsheba doesn't fully know yet.

The irony that I've basically copied Saul's preferred tactic should feel sharper than it does. Uriah was just as innocent as I was back then. Except I survived the dangers Saul put me through. Uriah didn't.

But I don't feel much of anything. Not remorse or grief or triumph. Not even now that Bathsheba's my wife.

I squint into the sunlight. The day should be hot at this hour, but I don't feel that either. I could go inside, eat something, but it doesn't matter. I'm dazed, not tasting food, not relishing sleep. Every night, I just lie there staring at her. And our son. Not even ten days old, still uncircumcised and unnamed. Why can't I think of a name? What's happening to me?

"My lord." My servant barely comes onto the terrace, but his message is like a sharp drink of cold water. "The prophet Nathan is here."

*Thank God.*

Since the beginning of my reign, I'd rejoiced to find a faithful prophet who would stand by me as Samuel was meant to stand by Saul. Whatever Nathan has to say, wherever he goes, he brings clarity. And he always seems to know when I need him before I ask.

I turn around, but he's already upstairs, standing in the doorway.

"Nathan—" I stop with his name halfway out of my mouth. His expression looks like a piece of rock with a fissure, ready to split any moment. He doesn't approach me, doesn't open his arms.

"I have brought the Word of the Lord," he says, his manner making me feel like a stranger in my own house.

I come inside, dismissing the servants. "I thought as much. What is it?"

My heart is moving up into my throat. He's probably going to rebuke me for avoiding battle. I really should be at the head of my armies, facing Ammon. Perhaps there, I can find myself again. Avenge Uriah. Inactivity isn't good for me.

But when Nathan begins to speak, I'm a little disappointed. It sounds like the sort of case that should be tried at the gate. A commoner's problem with sheep, nothing to do with me. But the more I listen, the more I'm drawn in.

"There were two men in your city, one rich and one poor," Nathan says, punctuating each word. "The rich man had many sheep, but the poor man had only one ewe lamb. He loved it like a daughter and fed it from his own hand. But one day, a traveler came to the rich man's house, and instead of killing one of his own sheep to feed his guest, he took the lamb of the poor man and slaughtered it for the man who had come to him."

My fingers clench, and suddenly I'm remembering the orphaned lamb I raised as a boy. Now I know why Nathan brought this to my attention. Such blatant cruelty deserves to be dealt with by the king himself.

Anger is tossing my insides, and I can feel the heat in my answer.

"As the Lord lives, that man deserves to die! He should restore the lamb four times over before he suffers. He showed absolutely no pity! How could he do something like that?"

The second the words leave my mouth, the pain behind Nathan's eyes cuts to the surface, and my stomach drops. The fissure in his rocky expression carves deep, splitting open to reveal the darkest chasm I've ever seen. Nathan lets me stare into it for four breathless seconds before disarming every defense in my body with four words.

"You are that man."

# THIRTY-TWO

## *Mephi*

———◆◆◆◆◆———

I sit by the window, my disappointment staining the walls alongside the setting sun. It was the last thing I'd ever expected of David. My mind still refuses it. It's an ill-fitting garment I'd rather not wear, an unwelcome visitor I'd rather bar the door to.

I'd been surprised when the king hadn't gone out with his armies to face Ammon in the spring, never guessing that a married woman was holding his attention back in Jerusalem. But now it all makes sense, and every muscle in my body is trying to unwind after being clenched for days.

Unable to do it on my feet, I let my mind pace, following Kezi from one end of the room to the other while she straightens curtains, kicks baskets under tables, folds and refolds coverlets. She's been agitated ever since we returned to Zion and found out what everyone else knows by now.

David's new wife, Bathsheba, was already pregnant with his child when she came to the harem. And worse, she was already someone else's wife. Uriah's, of all people.

David had slept with her while her husband was fighting the Ammonites. And now, Uriah is dead. Kezi's anger follows the path of the kingdom's dismay, growing more exhausted as the focus shifts to Bathsheba's son, who's burning with a high fever, refusing to nurse.

Kezi's expression is pulled taut, her face carved with old tear marks. "What did Azarel say they were going to do?"

I lift one shoulder. "What can they do? The word of the prophet was clear."

Nathan had come to the palace and destroyed David, leaving him flat on the floor with grief. He'd told him a story of a poor man who had cherished his one beloved lamb, only to have it taken away and slaughtered by a rich man with many sheep. David had reacted in anger, assuming Nathan was asking for justice for someone. But the prophet had declared that David was the rich man in the parable, taking another man's wife in cold blood. With no regard for Uriah's loyalty. And in direct violation of Yahweh's Law.

My heart had stopped when Ziba's sons brought the news. I'd been certain they were going to say that David would die, and I was ready to strangle them rather than hear it. It's too soon for Israel to lose another leader, to be thrust into upheaval again because of a king's sin.

But David still lives, if you can call it that. According to Benaiah, he's been facedown in his chamber, covered in sackcloth, begging Yahweh for mercy.

A new kind of pain has taken hold of me since then. I haven't been able to think, let alone share the indignance Kezi has filled the house with since the news came. She seethes, her fingers biting her elbows. Resisting what still isn't right and can't be altered.

"How could he do this? Didn't he know that he would make her an adulteress? What kind of life will she have in his harem? Her family will disown her, and she will be despised by every other woman in the palace! I thought…"

"I know." It's all I can say. Because we all did. We thought David was the one person who wouldn't be caught in that kind of snare. He's a vigilant warrior who loves Yahweh. It shouldn't have been so easy to let his guard down. Perhaps it had been happening gradually for some time.

Kezi stops at one wall, her consternation filling the space between us. "I never asked what you were thinking."

*Fine with me.* I feel like a fire has blown through my mind, and I don't know how to spin all the smoke into anything coherent.

I'm still searching for words, trying to find what's buried beneath my agitation. I didn't want to see David die. That's all I could think for the endless seconds it took Azarel to tell me he wouldn't. It's taken days for that fear to release its grip and let me feel what else is closed in its fist.

When I'd heard Nathan's exact words, something like hope had slipped in to scatter my terror. But even the reality of Yahweh's mercy has left me unsettled. Deep inside, something I've built my life on is being shaken, like a quake in a foundation about to split the underpinnings that have held me up.

I glance out the window, remembering. "Nathan is coming here."

Kezi flattens against the wall. "Here? Why?"

"I need to speak with him."

She twists her shawl, disconcerted. "Do you want me to leave?"

"No, you can stay. Just make sure Mica stays with the servants."

Kezi's eyes are huge, but I'm grateful that she doesn't press me. It's not likely that Nathan will be able to do anything about the disarray inside me, but maybe he can help me find a way through it.

For my whole life, David's been upheld as more than a man. He's a symbol of what Yahweh can do with a heart that continually follows Him. David's faithfulness has led Israel into the prosperity we've been seeking for decades.

He's been set apart as the opposite of the judges of the past who would fight under Yahweh's blessing for a couple decades only to be corrupted by idol worship or Philistine women. The ensuing demise that would lock its iron grip around Israel's neck afterwards seemed cruelly inevitable.

It tears me apart to imagine David like one of them— another charismatic leader who let his guard down and left his sheep to the wolves. I'm not afraid anymore. I'm angry.

The moment I realize it, a servant announces the prophet, and I don't have time to wrestle my tension out of sight before Nathan walks in. I'm lacking the options most men have. I can't take refuge in pacing the room or leading the prophet to the balcony.

I try to push off the bench to kneel, but Nathan waves his hand.

"Stay where you are." He stands in front of me, waiting.

"You know who I am?" The moment the words leave my mouth, I feel foolish. He's a prophet of the Most High God. He probably knows more about me than I know about myself, depending on what Yahweh has revealed to him. The thought thins the air, making me dizzy.

A smile enters Nathan's face without moving his mouth. "Speak, son of Jonathan."

His direct manner is what I admire. It's also what I fear. Where do I start? Do I even have a right to ask this?

"I don't understand." That's a beginning. "I didn't think this would happen to David. I thought he would stop it." I clench my fists, feeling the dagger of disappointment twisting. Several men in our nation's history have dragged our people into disaster because of their rebellion against Yahweh. But...*David?*

"He's the king," I press on. "An offense of this magnitude affects everyone beneath him. Everyone sustained by him. How could he do this? How could he risk everything?"

Nathan's eyes turn dark. "Yahweh's chief warning has been lusting after other gods, pleasures outside His path. It's a poison that is hard to resist once it takes hold."

I rub my head, trying to uncover the source of the ache digging through it. "But, he's seen it happen before. My grandfather was removed for a smaller offense than this."

I shake when I say it, my words turning thick, like I'm speaking through frozen lips. That's what's beneath all this. Saul.

He'd been rejected as king after offering an unlawful sacrifice, refusing to wait for Yahweh's instructions. He'd failed to destroy the Amalekites as God commanded. All sins, yes, but somehow not as despicable as what David's done. And yet it was enough for him to lose everything.

"Rebellion is not a small offense. No matter how it unfolds." Nathan speaks gently, hearing everything I'm not saying.

I breathe over the sharpness that's cutting me open. "I thought you were going to tell us that David was condemned. I thought we were going to watch him die."

"And that grieved you?"

"Of course!" I can't even begin to explain what David has done for me. In the year and a half I've known him, he's shown me more kindness than Ziba ever did. But—

I spread my hands. "What is the meaning of this mercy Yahweh has shown him? How can David walk free of this sin and not be consumed?" It makes me tremble to think it through.

Something like pride swims in the prophet's eyes. "When I laid the words of judgment at David's door, I did not hear one excuse from him. His face turned gray, as though he were dying on his feet. He prostrated himself, screaming like he'd lost a relative. Even now, he begs for the life of his child, hoping Yahweh will show mercy. It was not that way with Saul."

I swallow that down as Nathan continues.

"Saul fought for the position he believed he deserved. He defended his actions to Samuel, using your father and others as a covering for his sin, making them bear the consequences over and over. He took matters into his own hands, as though the kingdom were his possession instead of Yahweh's. He was offended by the idea that he could not do as he pleased. And he refused to repent. Even the pleadings of his favorite son didn't move him. His heart did not chase after Yahweh."

I nod, feeling the grief of it for the first time without taking it onto myself. It's the truth. It's what happened. But I don't have to carry it.

Nathan's voice lifts, passion doubling its strength. "David's heart clings to Yahweh for sustenance. When the veil was lifted from his eyes and he understood what he had done, he knew the worst of it was the violation of Adonai's Law. David sees what Saul was not able to—that Yahweh's Word isn't just our guidance. It's our life. It's the life that David is desperate to regain."

And Yahweh will let him. I know it without asking. It's like that moment in David's armory where I'd realized that Yahweh hadn't been waiting to fail my grandfather. He'd given him a clear chance to repent. But Saul hadn't recognized it. Too busy grasping at power, often at my father's expense.

I unclench my fists, settling into the truth that grips my heart with a thousand cords. I want to be different. For Abba's sake. For David's. Yahweh is worthy of complete devotion. I want to give it to Him, but I don't know if I have it in me. Does any man?

Nathan touches my shoulder, and I get the feeling the conversation has to end soon.

"Let me remind you that it was Yahweh who sought His people before they were ready to be found by Him. He has made it clear what He requires of you, Mephibosheth. Your very name speaks of devotion. And what Yahweh requires, He has made provision for. Hold fast to that in the days to come. It will be your anchor in all the storms."

I'm afraid to wonder what that means, what storms might be coming. But there isn't time to ask. A moment later, Japhia's wife comes in and whispers to Kezi. Her sharp gasp cuts the room, and she can barely get the words out before she's begun to weep.

"The baby's dead."

The sun doesn't shine for days as Jerusalem mourns for the king's child.

I keep Mica close, unable to shake the heaviness. Is David really better off having escaped death only to watch his son suffer for his sin? Will Bathsheba ever be able to look at him the same way? Will he be the same?

I can't imagine it. So, I don't.

As grieved as I am for his loss, I'm one of the few who isn't surprised when I hear that David has washed his face and ended his fast, allowing his servants to bring him food to eat and royal robes to replace the sackcloth.

His elderly court official Hushai brought the news, quelling the confusion with gentle perspective. "Why should he fast now that the child is gone? He has to find some way through the days ahead, and he'll need strength for that."

I'm hesitant to join the king's sons in the palace, afraid that David will come down for the evening meal. But I'm still disappointed when he doesn't. I'll probably never understand what happened or why. But it's time for me to see him.

I send servants upstairs with a discreet message that the king answers before we've finished eating. "Come up to the antechamber," Benaiah whispers in my ear, bending over the table. I nod, refusing to answer aloud. David's older sons are already on the edge of their patience.

"I'd like to see any of us get away with something like this," Shephatiah mutters, not lifting his eyes.

"I got a good look at Bathsheba," Amnon sneers. "My mother says Abba's a fool to have caused all this trouble on account of her."

"He's going to lose his mind," Chileab sighs, "knowing it's his fault that the child died. My mother's relieved that Abba listened to her and finally ate something."

I study Abigail's son out of the corner of my eye. Of all David's children, he's the one I admire most. He has his mother's gentle nature and compassionate wisdom. Kezi's told me Abigail has been the only one who's shown Bathsheba any kindness the past seven days, letting her weep with her head in her lap.

Absalom's scorn cuts the silence. "I don't know why he's so devastated. The bastard only lived a few days."

My head comes up so sharply that I ram my arm against the table, rattling everything on it. Absalom's iron attention snaps onto me.

"You have something to say, son of Jonathan?"

Dumbfounded, I finally pry the words from the roof of my mouth. "I would only beg you to show respect for the king in his grief."

A smile flickers on the side of Absalom's face, and his eyes become more dangerous. Pushing his chair back, he comes over and bends down in front of me. "I tell you, when your father has a dozen other wives, including your mother, and he obsesses over a harlot he saw bathing, tell me again how I should behave. But then, you'd have to have a father to understand."

He surges to his feet, knocking my crutches onto the floor on his way out of the room. Everyone else turns away, rolling their eyes.

"What's wrong with you?" Ithream sighs. "Don't talk to him. We've told you before. He hates all of us, but you…"

I settle back, my heartbeat still scattered. "I know he hates me."

Ithream lifts his head from his hand. "Do you care?"

"Not really." I only care what he'll do about it. "Benaiah, send Azarel in here. I need to get upstairs."

Benaiah's brow pulls, heavy with sorrow. No one else has seen David lately besides Bathsheba. Azarel helps me into the hall, wearing the same closed expression he always does before the princes. But as soon as we're alone, he removes his arm from my waist and shoves me into the wall.

I push back at him. "Azarel, stop this!"

"No, you're going to listen to me!" he hisses, his eyes wild. "Don't you see what's happening here? I know you're still blinded by what David did for you. But you shouldn't make Absalom your enemy. He's the last one you should cross—"

"He's made himself my enemy, Azarel. He's hated me since I got here. He insulted the king, and I defended him."

"You shouldn't. You don't know what happened. This is all David's fault, and there's more coming." Azarel pulls a wrinkled parchment from his belt and shoves it into my hand. "Look. Hurry."

"Will you let me go?" When he relaxes his grip, I slide down the wall to the ground, unfolding the message. It's a letter from David to Joab. "Where did you get this?"

Azarel folds his arms. "Who's on trial here, me or the king? Read."

Sighing, I glance along the lines, my expression dropping the more I take in.

*"Set Uriah in the forefront of the fighting,"* the letter instructs, *"and then draw back from him, that he may be struck down and die."*

A burning coal lights both of my eyes, pain erupting behind them. I grip the paper harder, wishing I could tear it to bits. But I can't as long as there's a chance it's true. "You have three seconds to tell me who forged this."

"It wasn't any of us. David wrote it himself. Only the king's letters bear his seal." Azarel points at the bottom of the page. The red lion emblem smears in my vision. "Mephi, David murdered Uriah to take his wife. To cover up the pregnancy. Uriah was his friend. If he's willing to have a man like that killed, who else wouldn't he remove if it served his purposes?"

I feel the ground shift under me. I crumple the paper, throwing it back at him.

"He repented, Azarel. Nathan said Yahweh had put his sin away."

"And yet the baby died. Nathan told David that the sword will never depart from his house because he'd scorned the Word of the Lord. He said a man would take David's concubines and defile them in broad daylight, the way David defiled Bathsheba in secret. He said evil would spring up from David's own house."

Azarel's words are adding wood to the fire that's licking up the ground around me. The air bends until it's hard to see through the flames.

"This is the calm before the storm, Mephi. It's all going to come apart. My father and the rest of us just want to be on the right side when it does. You should think about that because when everything crumbles, you'll be one of the first to crumble with it."

Azarel hides the message, but the words are painted all over the walls around us. They're draped like evil talismans around my neck.

"Now," Azarel slurs, "you wanted to see your king."

I barely feel the grip of the servants who bring me to David, or the floor underneath me when they set me down beside the low table in his antechamber. It's obvious that he has eaten. Empty cups and plates wait at the end to be cleared.

David is fully clothed in a long white sheath of linen and a purple robe edged with gold. He's sitting by the window, his harp beside him, sunlight warming his face. He opens his eyes before I'm ready for him to. *Adonai, help me.*

I don't know what to do with what I'm carrying. But I can't cause him more pain. The king already knows what Nathan told him. I can't control what will come of it.

The smile that breaks open David's expression wrenches my heart. He's sinned. But he also repented. Whatever happened, he's still my king. Still a man who's lost a son.

"Thank you for coming, Mephi."

"It's an honor," I whisper, meaning it.

"Honor." David's face disintegrates, and he presses his face into his hand, breathing heavily through his fingers. He bends almost to the ground, his shoulders caving in like a mountain bowing.

I don't move. Grief stings my heart for Uriah. He didn't deserve to lose his life this way. Neither did the child. And the king knows it.

David straightens, trying to smooth out his expression. "Forgive me. I don't want to embarrass you."

"I will not criticize a father who grieves for his son," I murmur, the words David said to me a year ago coming effortlessly.

Another sob tumbles out of David, and he quickly covers it, reaching for me. I edge across the floor and clasp his outstretched hand.

"How are my sons?" he asks.

"They're all wondering why you're up, eating, when you've been locked away for days."

David's voice is a shadow of itself, whisper-hoarse and ragged. "Yahweh's mercy is everywhere, even in His judgment. I thought, who knows? Maybe He will show mercy on..." His voice drops out of sight for a breath, and tears drip onto his lap like rain. "Uriah saved us. He rode out to divert Saul when we were trapped between the mountains."

I sit back on my heels, realizing he's referencing his years in exile. Some story I've never heard.

David forces a stormy breath over the memory, wiping his face. "Jonathan was there that night. He told me that when I failed, I should run to Yahweh. Repent. Even if there are still consequences, it's always worth asking for mercy."

"Is that why my father went to Gilboa?" My mouth says it before the full truth of it works through my mind.

David looks confused, but I know he'll understand. He always does.

I spin my father's ring, searching for words. "I used to think Abba was foolish to follow Saul into a doomed battle. But maybe he was just hoping for mercy. He couldn't run from his duty. Or from the consequences of Saul's sin. What else should he have done but fight to the end, faithful to the work God had given him?"

David's face glows, even as more tears slip down the fresh lines in it. "Your father saw things no one else did. He saw me break over and over, but he always reminded me that Yahweh would never abandon me. Even in my failures. In all that he faced, Jonathan never despaired. Which tells me Yahweh never left him."

My spirits lift. "He hasn't left us," I summarize.

David shakes his head. "No."

I breathe deeply, allowing myself to feel relief. If Yahweh hasn't left us, then we have hope to carry into the future, whatever happens. Even if violence threatens our borders, or mistrust erodes tribal bonds.

David and Jonathan weren't perfect. But they kept after our God and refused to let Him go. Therefore, they always had hope.

As the truth lights a wick behind my eyes, I look at the king bent over on the floor and realize that he and my father are the two bravest men I've ever known.

# THIRTY-THREE

*David*

———◆◆◆——

*A year later*

**M**y new son slumbers in the moonlight, peacefully ignorant of my writhing. His tiny chest lifts and drops in steady succession beneath the blue coverlet, quieting my fears. Bathsheba is curled up beside me, asleep after hours marveling over him. The beautiful starlit night drew us out here to the balcony, but I'm still too unsettled for rest.

When our first son died, I thought my heart wouldn't resume beating. The fact that I'd killed him made me want to bury my face in the floor and never rise. But Solomon's tiny fingers around mine are holding me together, his every breath prophesying that amazingly, there's still life in me. Life that Yahweh will bless.

I remove the crown from my head and set it down next to the baby, bending so that my hair dusts his forehead. I don't remember the awe being this weighty, this profound. He's perfect.

His tiny form has filled up Bathsheba's aching arms and is slowly stitching our hearts back together. But what have I done for him? Made him a prince who will be hated by brothers who want the position I'm sure will be his.

I know it more with each beat of my heart. It's going to be him. Not Amnon, not Chileab, not Absalom. Somehow, Solomon will rule Israel after me and build the house for God's Name. How can that be?

I back off slightly so I can see him more clearly. His lips pull in sleep and his brow wrinkles, an expression I've felt on my own face working behind his closed eyelids. I touch my lips to his head, holding back tremors that might wake him. I've been afraid to touch him for fear something will happen.

"Solomon..." I whisper, and the side of his mouth lifts, tugging at my heart. I feel the weight of it like an avalanche in my head—everything I should have sown into the others, but didn't. This one will be different. He'll be dedicated to Yahweh like the others should have been.

I bend to the floor, keeping my hand on my son. "Lord, I know my transgressions, and my sin is ever before me." Waiting like a dagger behind my ribs. Only Adonai's mercy has removed the knife and washed the wound. Only His grace enabled

Bathsheba to reach out to me with merciful love instead of resentment.

I spread my body across the floor in the pool of moonlight. "Wash me thoroughly, and cleanse me from my iniquities. You delight in truth in the inward being. Teach me that truth. Teach me your wisdom in the secret heart."

When did I let go of Yahweh's Word and come to despise it, as Nathan said? It was the delight of my life! I'm terrified to believe that I can return to it.

"Purge me with hyssop, and I shall be clean; wash me, and I shall be whiter than snow. Let me hear joy and gladness, that the bones you have broken may rejoice! Create in me a clean heart, O God. Renew a right spirit within me. Cast me not away from your presence, and take not your Spirit from me. You're life to me! You're life to him!"

I reach down and take Solomon up into my hands. My *hands*. He's so tiny.

"Oh Lord, teach me your ways again. Teach Solomon. May he drink deep of your instruction all the days of his life. You will not despise the sacrifices of a broken and contrite heart. Don't turn away from Israel because of my failings. Bless Zion with your good pleasure. Build up Jerusalem as you promised."

"He will." Nathan's voice from the door launches my heart into my throat. I hear Bathsheba's sharp inhale as she wakes up. Handing Solomon to her, I kneel and touch my head to the floor.

"Get up." Nathan crosses the room and takes my head in his hands. "Take heart, my king. Adonai has sent me to tell you that this boy is greatly loved. In Yahweh's eyes, his name will be Jedidiah, beloved of the Lord. He will put into action the dreams that are in your heart."

The simple words carve out what's left of the thorn in my spirit. Bathsheba's voice cracks around a sob, but it's the most joyful sound she's made in a year.

I thought I had no more tears, but a waterfall fills Nathan's hands while my son's beautiful face blinks in my mind. Without a doubt, he's the miracle my heart needed. The one Israel needed.

Solomon. Jedidiah. Loved by Yahweh.

# THIRTY-FOUR

## *Mephi*

———————•◆•◆•◆•———————

We reach the back gate of David's palace as dusk is covering the path. My servants pause at the edge of the street, watching for Sar Amnon's guards, but no one stops us.

All I have to do is lift my cloak enough to show my face, and the guards at the watchtower nod, resuming their conversation. They have no interest in the fact that I haven't exactly been invited to this gathering. And they won't find out.

"Stop here," I tell Azarel, hating the insidious look he's giving me. "Shaalbim is waiting inside to help me."

Ziba's son tugs on my mule's halter, tying it up before lifting his eyes to mine. "I never thought I'd live to see you working in tandem with my brothers," he scowls, letting me brace against him so he can help me up to the door.

In the years they've served me, I haven't seen any major discrepancies, but that doesn't mean they don't exist. And they've made no secret of their contempt for the job.

Once, I'd been encouraged by their attempt to show respect in public, but now I realize that it's not a good sign. They're confident that I won't be their master forever. Which is another reason I need to learn as much as possible.

Ebenezer's warnings carry more weight after what happened with Bathsheba, and I'm determined to keep my eyes on the horizons to spot any storm clouds before they form.

Azarel shoves his shoulder up under my arm, fixing his grip on my waist. "Are you trying at all?"

I sigh, heavily. "Believe it or not, I hate this more than you do. Just get me to the threshold."

I made my own way on my hands and knees long before I had their help.

If I were bolder, I would've told David more about our history and asked him for different servants. He always understands when we speak in private, but in the cacophony of the court, he often forgets the promises he makes.

Besides, there's other things on the home front now. David's latest victory razed the Syrian armies, leaving Ammon without an ally to hide behind. They're not numerous enough to challenge David without help, and it finally looks like we might be finished with them.

If I were living in Lo Debar, I would have assumed everything was settled. Another triumph for Israel, bringing more stability to the tribes and feeding more wealth into Jerusalem. But it's never that simple. No one in court can seem to agree on the ramifications of David's achievements.

I hate the way people cover their words in front of David, looking askance at me as though they don't want to reveal anything. Which is why I've done what I never thought I'd do. Approach Ziba's sons and ask to appear uninvited and unseen among the princes at one of their private meetings.

Shaalbim had assured me I'd be concealed up in one of the battlements. He and Zarethan had agreed to get me in without alerting the servants who usually guard the doors. Of course, they're probably planning to use this at some point. But I can't see why David would be angry if he found out. The Sars often let their friends come. I've seen David's young nephew Jonadab there plenty of times. I just can't let any of the princes see me.

Arriving after dark will help.

"Why do you even need to do this? I thought you believed in everything David does."

Annoyed by Azarel's grip on my wrist over his shoulder, I avoid answering until he's lowered me to the ground.

"This has nothing to do with my loyalty to David. I'm tired of being told what everyone wants me to hear. I want to hear everything. Just get me inside."

Azarel's face twists again, but he knows the hold I have over him. I've watched him and his brothers for too many years, and I know the bribes they've accepted from the princes. If any of them tries to double-cross me, I can reveal anything I choose to David. I really have to find other servants though, before my son gets old enough to be influenced by them.

Azarel raps at the door with his foot. "You think you're so different from us, Mephi. But mark my words, one of these days, you'll be coming to us for something more serious than a prince's meeting."

Before I can probe further, Shaalbim opens the door. His sour expression looks oddly triumphant. "The king just left. Half the men here had to step out of sight, but if he saw anything, he didn't say."

"Why was David here?" I ask, hating the thought of being coupled with the lowlives assembled in Amnon's house. The young prince already has as much wealth as his father, and he takes nothing for granted, inviting every worthless youth in the city to waste the king's food and wine.

"Amnon's sick, and the king went to see him. It's why he never rode out to Rabbah to meet the others," Shaalbim explains.

I roll my eyes. Amnon's finally feeling the pressure of his absence in his father's army. At his age, he should be commanding his own cohorts, establishing himself as Hassar. I'll wager pretending to be ill is his last excuse these days.

Shaalbim beckons. "Don't worry. Absalom will talk more freely without his brother there."

I wince. Amnon is a foolish boy, dissipated with luxury. But Absalom's charisma is dangerous. Unrivaled in the training camps, he's already left his brother in the dust, outshining him everywhere they go. Amnon is usually too drunk to care, but when I look at the two brothers, I see an ignorant shepherd lazily dragging his staff around the sheepfold while a rogue hunter lurks in the background.

For the first time, I realize that Amnon probably won't be king. David's preference for Solomon is clear, but I can't imagine Absalom stepping aside gracefully to let Bathsheba's son rule.

Zarethan comes to the door, looking over his shoulder. "Come on. Absalom's distracted by his sister."

"Tamar's here?" This is hardly a place I would expect to find the Sarrah.

"The king sent her. Amnon asked her to come and cook something to tempt his appetite."

"Doesn't he have servants to make his bread?" I groan.

Zarethan scoffs. "That's what Absalom said. Let's go."

They help me up the steps and down the back corridor. Fortunately, the kitchen servants are too harried to notice us, and we slip easily up to the battlements.

"I'm going down there," Zarethan announces once I'm hidden behind a heavy wall of spears. "I'm actually supposed to be here."

I watch him go, assessing my position. I can pull a thick tapestry down over myself if I need to, but I have a clear view of the activity below. Only the smoke from their massive fire is smearing my vision.

"Why are you staying?" I ask Shaalbim. "If anyone finds you with me, you'll need an excuse."

He snorts. "Trust me, I don't need to hide the way you do." He studies me, arms folded. "What are you planning, son of Jonathan? You already have your precious grandfather's estate. What more could you gain from the king's sons?"

"Nothing." By any account, I would have more to lose. "I'm past explaining myself to you."

Shaalbim is trying to decide if he has an ally in me after all these years, if he should reveal whatever conspiracy he's involved with these days. What I can't decide is if it's worth knowing about. I glance at him. "All I want is stability for my family."

A wry smile splits Shaalbim's face in the dark, and my pulse scatters. He knows that's still in question.

"David won't be king forever and when he isn't anymore…" I let my words drop off, tasting the sharpness of betrayal on my tongue. But I'm not plotting anything. Far from it. "I just want to know who my closest ally would be if it wasn't David."

In the royal household, there's Benaiah. Back in the north, there's Machir and Barzillai, David's old friend from Rogelim. But they're old men, servants David has enriched by his support. They won't have power to stand against the princes.

Shaalbim studies me. "I would have thought your ambition carried further than that. We all expected more from the grandson of Saul."

I scoff, disgusted. "No, you didn't."

Shaalbim shrugs, watching the group below. "Why do you think Abba tried so hard to crush you? He knew Jonathan's son would be made of iron."

Unsure what he's trying to put on me, I shrug him off. "Just get out of sight and keep watch."

Ziba's sons were always deceptive, but I can't decide what game they're playing now. Trying to clear my mind, I focus on Jonadab's voice below me.

"The king brought back twice the spoils this time. Did you see the stone in that crown he took from Ammon? The gold was almost a full talent's worth."

"So, Jerusalem is richer, and we have more laborers than we know what to do with at the brick kilns. The decimation of

Ammon doesn't answer our problem here," another young man declares.

"David barely even took Rabbah," Jonadab sneers. "Joab sent word that if he didn't join them by the end of the battle, the city would be called by his name instead."

Absalom leans back in his chair with his fingers crossed. "Joab hasn't lifted his nose from the grindstone since my father was wandering around in caves."

"Which one of David's sons would Joab prefer as king?" someone asks.

Absalom's face tightens. "When has it mattered what he prefers? Amnon is the firstborn."

"But he won't be king," Jonadab says, and everyone looks at him.

"Why do you say that? I thought you liked him." Absalom makes it sound like a character flaw.

Jonadab shrugs. "I like him. I just don't see David elevating him. He certainly doesn't try the way others do." He pops his eyebrows at Absalom.

Shephatiah leans forward. "Do you think Joab would follow Amnon? Or will he go his own way? He's said more than once that he thinks you would make a better commander, Absalom."

Absalom shrugs. "He's not blind. I'm better at everything on the battlefield. That doesn't make Joab an ally of mine."

"He's too dangerous," Adonijah determines. "He walks a narrow path between honor and treason, and he's the only man who's able to live there comfortably."

"Who would you prefer?" Ithream wonders aloud.

"Over the army? There are several other choices…"

Absalom cringes, shoving his chair forward. "Listen to yourselves! What does any of this matter? All your plans will come to nothing. Just like my efforts at the training camps. We're all invisible since Solomon was born. Mark my words, that's who Abba wants."

"To rule? Over his firstborn? That can't be," Jonadab frowns.

Absalom stares into the fire. "He hasn't made anything public yet. But I can tell that's where his heart is. He's probably promised Bathsheba in secret. But we'll never get it out of her. She doesn't talk to the women."

"We have to get him to mention it aloud," Ithream says. "Then we'll see who else is against it."

"Amnon should have the throne. He'd be easier to deal with," Zarethan speaks up, and several others voice agreement. "We need to convince the king that his firstborn should reign."

My throat tightens. Amnon would be the worst option. Stronger men would run the kingdom behind his back and dispose of him whenever convenient. Hopefully, David will see that and elevate a more capable son. Solomon is still an infant, but he already has enemies, simply by virtue of being his father's favorite.

My own position in the kingdom is precarious, not because of David, but because he's the only one who keeps me in it. I still don't know what would happen if David were to fall from favor. As much as I hate the thought, I've shed the naivete that deemed it impossible. Will those in charge of Solomon be trustworthy enough to take care of him until he's of age?

*Guard him, Adonai.*

A sudden screech shreds the quiet along the corridor, ripping through my nerves even as my mind tries to explain it away. The cry of a night bird shouldn't be that intense. And close.

There's a rustling struggle, followed by a thud, and after a few moments of deathly silence, tight, inhaled sobs cut the air, high-pitched and breathless. Sliding to the floor, I crawl into the dark, keeping along the wall where the shadows are deepest.

The battlements are connected to Amnon's chambers by a long hallway where windows create patches of moonlight on the floor. Feeling along for a door, my hands find a bench, and I grasp it to pull myself forward. The crying sound pulls up into a tight gasp, and Tamar slides into the slice of moonlight.

"Mephi! What—?" Shaken by sobs, she doesn't finish.

Tamar's long hair is mercifully unbound, the only covering she has with her royal robes torn to ribbons. Her cosmetics are smeared across her face, and I can't tell if it's kohl or a bruise under her left eye. She's huddled outside Amnon's door. Amnon, who was supposed to be sick.

The reality of what's happened leaps from the shadows like a raider trying to slice my throat. I press against the wall, gripping the leg of the bench until my fingers feel splinters. But I can't outrun the knowledge any more than I could an Amalekite. For an instant, I consider that someone might have broken in, killed the prince, and…

But the door is obviously locked, because Tamar was clinging to the latch, trying to budge it. Voices float toward us from below, and Tamar shudders, putting one finger to her split lips. In that instant, she looks so much like David that my stomach turns inside out, and an unreasonable fury floods my limbs. My useless limbs.

I'd probably write my own death warrant if I could walk. Because Amnon's door would be splintered, and I'd have my hands around his neck.

"Get out of sight. Don't let them see you. Absalom will help me." Tamar's warning shudders toward me.

Her brother's approaching voice pushes through the flames in my mind, and I feel a glimmer of dark humor staring at Amnon's door. *Good thing it's locked, Hassar.*

I pull back behind the window covering, concealed while Tamar keeps screaming her brother's name. Amnon won't be able to hide for long. Whatever despicable thing he's done to his sister, his crime will be answered for. And if the bastard escapes, Absalom will hunt him down.

It's almost midnight by the time I make it home. The chaos erupting in Amnon's house provided a substantial cover for my escape. Kezi is waiting for me in the upstairs antechamber of my grandfather's house.

"Where were you?" she demands, barely giving the servants time to settle me onto a bench by the window.

His usual manner scattered, Azarel leaves us alone.

"You did it, didn't you? You went to another one of those gatherings at the prince's house." Kezi plants her hands on her hips, her chest heaving up and down. "Why are you doing this now? I don't understand."

I gape at her, dumbfounded. "Kezi—"

"Isn't this enough for you?" Her voice inches upwards into a near sob. "Isn't it enough that we're safe, that your son is being raised like a prince instead of a beggar?"

"I would *never* have let my son beg!" I yell blindly, then quickly lower my voice. I rub my face, wishing I could erase what I just saw. And heard. "Can you just tell me what's wrong?"

"No, you're going to tell me!" She closes the door and comes to stand in front of me. I've never seen her this unwound. "Azarel said you'd gone to Amnon's house for some sort of meeting that the king didn't know about. And then David showed up."

"He was there for three minutes. He should have stayed." The burn in my stomach intensifies.

"Did he see you there?"

"No." Now I can interpret the fear in Kezi's eyes. She's afraid David will catch me in some kind of subterfuge. "I'm not doing anything wrong. I swear it. I just get tired of being treated like I'm supposed to sit here and live off of David's gold and know nothing about the kingdom my son is growing up in!"

Kezi's eyes spark. "And what did you learn, Mephi? What are you going to learn from Amnon and his foolish friends that you couldn't ask the king yourself?"

Tamar. I squeeze my eyes with my fingers, trying to bury the sting. Nathan had said violence would attack David's house, but... Tamar?

Kezi grabs my shoulders. "Talk to me, Mephi! What are you trying to find out? Can't you just trust David for once?"

"For once?" My head snaps up. "It isn't enough that I came here and faced death at his feet? That I risked your life and Mica's before him?"

"That's what this is about. Still." Kezi bites her lip, a tear sliding down over it. "Death. You're still afraid you're cursed because of Saul."

My throat closes. "This has nothing to do with Saul..."

"No, it does! You're afraid that you'll die like your grandfather and your father. You're afraid we'll all die."

I open my mouth to protest, but she's right. That may not be why I went tonight, but it's certainly curling into my stomach now. Along with the image of Tamar with her robe torn and anguish streaking her face. If David can't see through his own son to protect his daughter...

I grit my teeth, trying to speak evenly. "Kezi, you don't understand. What I saw tonight. I..."

But I can't say it. I can't breathe around it. It's too horrible. I'm seeing Kezi's face, but in my mind's eye, I'm seeing other women.

Bathsheba, with her name tarnished, her first husband and son in the grave. And now, youthful, innocent Tamar—sobbing in Absalom's arms as she told him how she was raped.

By the king's son.

I look at my wife, refusing to admit my deepest fear out loud. But it's burned into my mind, and I can't remove it.

*Who will be next?*

# THIRTY-FIVE

## *David*

———————◆◆◆◆———————

My fingers dig into my elbows as I try to ward off the chill chewing my bones.

Since my daughter left, I've been staring at the same wall for endless meaningless hours, thinking of my father. He didn't live to see me have my own children. He never talked to me about it. I haven't pulled his face to the forefront of my mind in years. But he's here tonight, with little effort. And I know why.

I haven't used my old sling in decades, but I keep it close, beside my harp. It's in my hand now, my fingers rubbing the faded curve of the leather. All I have to do is touch it, and I'm back in the valley of Elah, facing Goliath with the *Ruach* pulsing in my veins. My awareness of Yahweh's presence had grown over time, diminishing the fear that I was destined to fail the father who rarely spoke to me.

Jesse's only gift to me had been the slingshot, but he'd given it to me hoping I would bury myself in the pastures so no one would have to see his bastard son.

Yahweh's anointing and Jonathan's friendship gave me the confidence that was lacking on the home front as I fought to do something no one thought I was capable of. I learned that walking in step with Adonai meant I wouldn't stray, and I'd managed to keep my actions in line with His voice in battle. I was finally certain I'd grown past my insecurity and apprehended true success.

Who knew my failure would lie in the one area of life I'd thought would fall easily into place?

The irony eats into me like corrosive poison against metal. My father had little reason to be ashamed of me. It was his own fears that kept him prisoner for so long. But where can I go from the shame of what Amnon did?

Amnon. I let myself remember his birth in Hebron, recalling the disappointment I'd felt when I realized my firstborn would be Ahinoam's son. It hadn't been the first time I'd wished I'd married only Abigail and not been coerced into marriages that left me paying relational interest on political alliances. Ahinoam had hardly spoken a dozen words to me. We had done our duty to one another, but it was difficult to believe that something so platonic would have given me a son.

Yet, as soon as I held him, I'd felt every old expectation melting away like dross in a flame. He was my son, a miraculous mixture of myself and his mother. When I'd seen a hint of my father in his eyes, I'd promised myself I would do better than Jesse did. My sons would always know that I loved them.

But how did I plan to accomplish that? Somewhere along the way, it had become relegated to gifts. With all the spoils I brought back from war, it became easier to impress my boys with lavish presents. Things I never had at their age. After a while, that was all they had an appetite for. Their mothers watched me like vultures, privately calculating the value of everything I gave and comparing levels of favor. As they do now, with worse effect.

But Amnon's lust for wealth had never given me reason to think he would…

Angered, I start to tear the nearest tapestry from the wall, but it's no use. I can hide my face from Amnon, send him away, lock him up, but it won't change the damage that's been done. My beautiful daughter hides in Absalom's house, refusing to be seen, at a time when she should've been counting suitors. I had never even asked if she favored any particular man. If she'd been married already, she would have been safe in her husband's house.

*Like Bathsheba?*

The evil voice rippling through my head is the darkest thing I've ever heard. I rip the rest of the purple covering from the window, and the sharpest moonlight spears my eyes. How could I expect Amnon to do any different with the example I've given him? Why should he have scruples I didn't? I had seen what I wanted and taken it. Because I had the power. Amnon was more powerful than Tamar. So, he'd done the same.

I drop to my knees, feeling the cold hardness of the stone against them. Tamar's sobbed assurances cut into me. *It wasn't your fault, Abba.*

Even in her own grief, she'd tried to ease mine. But she can't because I know the truth. I'm failing as a shepherd, as a father. I deserve to suffer. Not Tamar. Not any of my other children. Who else will be endangered because of my failure? Solomon? Mephi? I shove my hands up over my eyes, my heart bleeding.

If my sin is gone, why does it hunt me down?

I know the answer already. Even though I'm forgiven, violence plagues my house because I let it in. Rather than feasting on the abundance that was already mine, I grabbed the door of unrighteous passion, believing it held only pleasure, and flung it wide open to release all manner of evil.

And I will suffer, as Nathan said. But the worst of it is that I'm not the only one who will.

"Who can bear up under this, Adonai? If you kept a record of sins, who could stand? But in your goodness, there is mercy and forgiveness." I whisper it into the dark, my tears smearing the moonlight. "My soul waits for you, Yahweh, more than watchmen for the morning."

Just a hint of the *Ruach* entering the room trembles my core, and I spread my hands, shaking, more terrified than I've ever been in my life.

"Don't leave. Don't leave. Don't leave."

# THIRTY-SIX

## *Mephi*

———— ◆ ————

*Two years later*

Mica's little arrow sings, finding its way to the wooden target about a yard away. Propped up against a tamarisk tree, half-hidden among the grasses of Saul's south field, it's not the easiest target, even this close.

"Did you see that one, Abba?" Mica warbles while a servant retrieves the arrow. "It went over the target, but it hit the tree! It hit it!"

"I saw. You're getting good." I grin, trying to tickle him while he dances out of my reach. Regret tightens my throat when Zarethan grabs him instead, swinging him around high enough to make him squeal. Mica's happy enough, but Zarethan is watching me over his head.

I squint past them, gripped by a shiver of gratified jealousy. Ziba's sons all notice how much skill my son has developed at such a young age, and they love to mention it for my benefit, enjoying the fact that one day, he'll do things I can't.

Mica isn't much older than I was when I broke my legs, and it's frightening to have a fresh realization of how vulnerable I was. How young. He already talks about fighting for David. And unlike the princes of Israel, he has more understanding of what that means. I've schooled him in our history, helping him comprehend what we fight for and why. Still, I doubt I'll ever be ready to watch it happen.

Mica's still abuzz with energy, clamoring for more attention, but Zarethan sets him down. "That's enough," he says, giving him a little push in my direction. "Go back to your father." It's almost a sneer, aimed directly at the rock where I'm trapped, unable to get to my son without help.

I've watched Ziba's sons carefully in the years they've served me, and I haven't noticed any outward signs of betrayal. But I know Mica has heard things that are trapped inside him. Things that come out randomly when we're alone. I wait for it now, watching him wear himself out doing somersaults in the grass. Scrambling to his feet, he leans against the boulder I'm sitting on.

"I want you to play with me out there."

His honest desire stabs me through, but I talk over the pain, refusing to let Zarethan see me defeated. "I can't get very far on my feet, son. That's why I wait for you to get closer. So, I can do this."

I throw my arms around him and tickle him until I slide onto the ground. Laughing hysterically, he rolls over on top of me and wrestles my hands away until he's bored.

"See? I have secret skills no one else does," I tease him.

On his back in the grass, he turns his head. "Then, why don't you fight?"

There it is. Mica knows I've trained on horseback with a few of David's men, but he hasn't missed the talk about why I don't ride out with the army.

"What do you mean?" I probe, shifting up onto my elbow.

Mica sits up, his eyes serious behind the curtain of his hair. "Azarel said the king doesn't need you to fight. But you can, can't you?"

Wounded pride pounds in my temples, and I wait for the sting to pass before I answer. "Our honor doesn't come from riding into battle. It comes from Yahweh. There will always be something to fight for. But there are other ways to serve the king."

I tug absently at one of Mica's curls. As grateful as I am that he's been raised in safety and plenty, I can already see him growing restless, eager to stretch past it. His skill will certainly be noticed one day, and David will place him wherever he wants to be, treating it like a favor.

I'm not convinced it is anymore. Over the past few years, I've learned what Ebenezer meant about the troubles arising from a king's court, and I can't help wishing for a different future for my family.

Kezi doesn't say much in response to my concerns. Around the court, it's safer to keep your most cherished opinions to yourself. Anything released in public is picked up by someone to be twisted, sharpened, and used against you later.

But whatever I come up with will have to be soon, before Mica becomes old enough to start drawing the attention of the commanders.

At least he sees the value in continuing to fight for what's been given. Most of David's sons seem content to enjoy their positions without preserving them. Their entitled apathy reminds me of what I've heard about my uncle Ish-Bosheth. He rarely joined my father in battle and was not ready for the onslaught that came against him when his position was challenged.

David's sons are the same way. But what else can be expected when their father still hasn't answered the clearest threat in his own house?

Tamar's rape at the hands of Amnon had shocked everyone enough to eclipse the scandal of Bathsheba. The women in the harem still watch her closely, and little Solomon has more guards than I do.

But Amnon has yet to be punished outright, and after two years, few believe he will suffer at all. There hasn't even been a clear discussion about him losing the birthright. Are we to assume David might still give him the throne, setting a precedent that the king's sons are immune from the Law? How am I to entrust my son to a man who won't answer an attack on his own daughter?

It galls me to see what all this has done to my trust. For all David's kindness, I rarely get an opportunity to broach my concerns, and it's insulting to think that he believes my loyalty is settled. Does he think the wealth of Saul's estate has blinded me to the fissures in the foundations of his own?

"Look, Abba!" Mica scrambles to his feet, pointing excitedly uphill. "It's King David!"

Looking over, I catch the glint of the king's crown in the late sun. I pull myself up against the boulder as David rides down the slope followed by his guards and servants. Maybe I shouldn't think about the king so hard. This isn't the first time he's appeared on the heels of my thoughts. Though I haven't seen him more than six times since Tamar.

I wave Zarethan away when he tries to help. "I'm fine." Positioned against the rocks, I press one of my crutches into the ground, forcing my posture to straighten by the time David reaches us. Mica giggles, prancing like an unruly colt as David dismounts.

"Mica," I reprimand him, and my son instantly sobers, dropping into an adorable bow.

"My lord king," he lisps.

David's smile looks like it hasn't come out of hiding in days. Maybe years. He opens his arms, and Mica scrambles into them. The king's eyes shift to mine over my boy's curly head. "Shalom."

I nod, stiff with formality. But David doesn't seem to notice.

"Practicing?" he asks, releasing Mica.

"Yes! I mean, yes, my lord. I'm almost as good as my Abba."

David's brows jump. "Show me."

Mica eagerly notches an arrow, resisting Zarethan's efforts to help him. He pulls the bow up against his face and takes aim. David watches pensively, his thoughts tangled behind his eyes. He seems to wake up once the arrow hits. "Well done."

"I'm going to be a warrior like my Saba," Mica crows, straightening his posture.

David's smile slants at the reference to Jonathan. "You're already a warrior, Mica. A true son of Benjamin." He glances at me while my son chases the arrow ahead of Zarethan. "You've trained him well."

"He still has much to learn. He's so young." My fingers grip the wood of my crutch.

David folds his arms, watching the fields. "I know. And yet Yahweh calls to us even from our youth. It's from the mouths of infants that He ordains the purest praise. And that is the best weapon. So, in that sense, our children are already warriors. It was like that for me in the sheep pastures. From my youth, He has been my God."

"Are you still holding onto Him?"

Out of the corner of my eye, I see David breathe deeply. I didn't mean to challenge him, and yet every muscle in my body strains after the answer. Our hope as a nation hinges on the king's faithfulness, and I must know if Israel's future is secure.

David's voice rides a whisper. "Sometimes it seems as though my grip is weakening. And then I open my eyes and realize He's still holding onto me. That renews my strength."

The weight lifts from my chest, allowing peace to flow in, uninvited. My countenance relaxes, softened by a smile. I can't resist the wealth I feel in David's presence. As much as the current circumstances pain me, I can't deny that Israel's king is still one of a very rare kind.

"I've got it!" Mica yells from a distance, sprinting toward us with the arrow raised in his fist.

David shakes his head. "It's unfathomable that in a few short years, Solomon will be ready to do that."

I squint, pain stinging my eyes. Kezi's always telling Mica not to run with arrows, but that's all I want to do. In every sense, I already see my son getting farther away from me, running ahead into trouble where I can't protect him. It's another reason to hate my inability. And question David's.

"I've been worried about your son," I hedge, covering my concerns by referencing Solomon. I've learned it's the best way to get through to David. "The prince is still so young, and there are many who don't approve of your preference for him. Are you certain he'll be safe?"

David's manner stiffens. "I'm certain he's beloved by Adonai. That has to be enough for me. It was enough for your father."

Always. We always come back to that. As grateful as I am to know someone who appreciated my father, I'm different. David has to stop assuming I'll do everything the way Jonathan did. I don't have that luxury.

I tighten my expression. "I assume if something were to happen to Solomon, you would react differently than…"

David's head pivots slowly to face me. Our gazes lock together while Mica puffs between us. "Did you see how fast I am?"

Ignoring him, David nods at me a few times, his smile shrinking. "Do you question me about my daughter?"

*Yes! For the love of everything holy!*

The insistence knocks against my ribs, my heart like a battering ram in my chest. But aloud I say, "My only question concerns him." David follows my eyes down to Mica, and his forehead softens.

"Your son will have anything he needs. Just ask."

"I am asking." I refuse to blink. "Where does justice stand in your kingdom? What if someone chooses to look unfavorably on the covenant you had with Jonathan and unleashes wrath on my family? Who defends us from that?"

David's mouth drops open, as if the answer should be obvious. But I'm not finished.

"Because God is my witness, if you don't, I will."

My own fierceness exhausts me. I'm tired of spending months planning how to confront David, only to have him come here and look at me like a wounded father. How can I love him so much and be so unsure of him? Mica looks between us, confused. I feel Zarethan's stare on my back.

David steps closer. "Do you trust me, Mephi? Do you trust me to protect your life?"

I can tell he wants an honest answer, but I don't like the one I have. Pain turns hard in my face. "I trust you to defend the covenant you had with Jonathan. But I'm not Jonathan."

"You're his son." David's voice is so small, it's disappearing.

"And he's mine." I reach over and draw Mica to my side. Jonathan trusted David enough to leave me with him. I'm not sure I can do the same with my son. Not now. The king trusts too many people that I don't.

David inhales, clearing his throat. When he speaks, it's with a tight voice he rarely uses. "What would you have me do?"

"I would have you *know*." My heartbeat is leaping up into my throat now. When did I get the gall to talk to him like this? Deep pain hooks my chest, reminding me. Violence attacked David's own children because he walked away from the door of the sheepfold. And I'd rather fight to the death than let that happen to my son.

Instead of growing angry, David stares at the ground for a moment, slowly lifting his gaze as the wind picks up to toss in the trees. He stays silent for so long that I don't think he'll speak again. Incredibly, Mica remains quiet too.

But when I start watching the trees also, David says, "I brought you here because of my covenant with Jonathan. But I keep you here because I *want* you." His eyes move over again, directing Zarethan to give us some privacy. Once he's walked away, David faces me.

"I have many sons. But not one of them is like you." His words run together like a current, gathering strength. "You know what it is to be cast on Yahweh from birth, with nothing but His protection to shield you. You've survived on little, so you've been able to receive my gifts without being corrupted by them. When I speak to you, I know it's you talking—not some sycophant who's holding a knife at your back. You don't know what that means to me."

I shut my eyes briefly, my whole face aching with trapped emotion. Why does he save disclosures like that for moments like this? If he appreciates my openness, why doesn't he listen?

The appeal in David's tone is maddeningly sincere. "Don't be afraid, son. Yahweh has smiled on this city, on Israel. There is so much more He will do, and we must persist in spite of the battles."

*Then let me see you fight the ones in your household with as much valiance as you confront the Ammonites!*

I'm considering whether I should say it out loud when another voice shouts across the field. David's servants who were keeping watch at the fork in the path are running toward us, pointing back the way they came. "There's a rider approaching, my lord! He's distressed. Something's happened!"

I grab Mica's wrist when he tries to dart around David. "Stay here."

The rider is coming from the direction of Ephraim's territory, too ashen and breathless to explain. He flings himself from the mule, collapsing into the dust before I realize his face is stained with more than just sweat. He's weeping, his chest wild with trapped breathing.

David steps around the mule. "Ahimaaz, what's wrong? Are you hurt?"

Zadok's son is shaking like a tree limb in a storm. He can barely get the words out. "It's Sar Absalom. He…"

"Has something happened to Absalom?" The edge of fear slips into David's voice.

Ahimaaz shakes his head, tears spilling over. "I ran from his feast at Baal-Hazor. He—he's killed all the sons of the king. Not one is left."

I take the news like a fist in my gut. "Mica, come here," I whisper hoarsely, needing to have my son closer while the storm clouds roll over me. I'd expected retaliation against Amnon, but all the king's sons? What did Absalom hope to gain from that?

David is bending at the waist, as though he's been stabbed through the heart. He sways, then grasps the collar of his garment, ripping it down the middle. Tears flash in my eyes as he collapses in the dust, wailing aloud, "God! My God, no! *No!*"

Mica hides his face in my arm as the servants begin tearing their own clothes.

"Abba, will Sar Absalom kill us too?" Mica says into my shoulder, and I tighten my grip, readying a swift answer. But there's more dust in the road, another messenger approaching. I recognize Jonadab's irritating voice even from several feet away.

"Ahimaaz! Ahimaaz, wait—" He pulls his mount up sharply, looking anxiously from the king to me.

I can't resist a scowl in Jonadab's direction. *You escaped? How convenient.*

"My lord, I—I was trying to get here faster," Jonadab wheezes.

David rears off the ground like a wounded bear and grabs the young man's collar, jerking him off the mule. "Tell me truthfully who you saw dead! How did you escape to tell me?"

"My lord, please!" Jonadab wails, cowering in David's grasp. "It wasn't everyone! Please don't think it was everyone! Only

Amnon…it was only Amnon who died. Absalom commanded his servants to kill him because of what happened to Tamar. But he's the only one who's dead, my lord! I swear it!"

David sets him on his feet, and the boy chokes on his own fear, embarrassed.

"And where is Absalom now?" David pants, trying to believe it.

"He's gone, my lord," Jonadab whimpers. "He rode north toward Geshur. He fled right after Amnon fell. But your other sons are alive." Looking around wildly, he points toward the mountains. "Look! Here they come now."

I glance over Mica's head at the procession of mules rumbling along the Horonaim Road. Zarethan touches Mica's arm as the princes get closer, but I hold my son tighter. It would have been better that he didn't see this, but I don't want Mica out of my sight.

The king's sons dismount in disarray, already in tears, and David's tortured gaze counts them: Adonijah, Shephatiah, Ithream, Shammua, Nathan. All except little Solomon who's back in the palace, out of harm's way. For now.

David embraces each of his sons, every one of them ending up on the ground beside him. Their bitter weeping cuts the sky like discordant music, and I dig my fingers through my own son's hair, unsure what to pray. Unable to watch the strongest man I know leveled by one of his own. Again.

Grief surges into my stomach, but I hold it back, desperate to be strong for Mica. Desperate to believe I can shield him from this. But I know there's only one way. And this is hardly the time to bring it up with David.

*I want to leave, Adonai. I want to leave before more death comes. This isn't home anymore.*

# THIRTY-SEVEN

## *Mephi*

———————•• ◆ ••———————

I ride up to Machir's old gate, realizing it's been years since I've breathed so easily.

The place of no pasture has grown since I lived there. Thanks to David's attention, the old broken sheepfold is now a sprawling marketplace with an imposing guardhouse and a thick wall that follows the curve of the hills. Lo Debar no longer means exile. But will it be the refuge I'm hoping?

Machir greets us exactly as I knew he would, shouting for the whole town to hear.

"My son! My daughter! Mica—you've grown so much!"

By the time he has us in his arms, half of Lo Debar has gathered to greet us, marveling at the time that's gone by since we were here last.

I had sent word ahead to Machir, but he hadn't told Ama we were coming. Her eyes flood, and she sobs against my chest, pulling me to the ground with her.

"My son, I've missed you," she gasps once she can speak.

"I've missed you." I touch her cheek.

Watching Kezi weep over her uncle while Mica hangs on Machir's back, I have to wonder why we ever left. Of course, it had made sense at the time. The king my father loved adopted us, gave us back the wealth my grandfather didn't have the power to save for me. But how could we stay there with the upheaval of David's household pushing so close to home?

This is the inheritance I want. Simple safety. To watch my son grow up free from the clutches of kings and princes and their warring factions. Is that too much to ask? My family's laughter is music to my ears, and I focus on it, refusing to acknowledge the pull of regret.

"What did David send you to build this time?" Ama asks with a wry smile.

"David didn't send us," I murmur, sensing the immediate change in Ama's expression. "We just needed to get out of Jerusalem."

"Why?" Her eyes search mine, and I realize I haven't decided how to talk about this.

I set my jaw, my thumb twirling my father's ring. "I'm not sure."

I've wanted to leave Jerusalem since Amnon attacked Tamar, but now I feel transplanted, yanked up by the roots. It'll take time to regain my freedom, remember what it's like to be a common man. I heard David say once that he'd feared becoming king, preferring to stay a shepherd forever. Already, I'm relishing the openness of the plains beyond the gate, the smell of the river, the safety in everyone's faces.

That's all this is. A respite to remember who I am. My son will come to appreciate the change of pace. I'm not a prince, and it's time I stopped trying to be one. It's too dangerous.

The men of Lo Debar prepare a feast in the center of town, and Mica stays up late chasing other little boys in circles until he collapses from exhaustion. Later that evening, I lean on my crutches at the gate, watching the sun stretch its arms across the eastern hills until Machir joins me.

"They're sleeping," he says, keeping his voice low. The sunset warms his gray hair, sharpening the lines behind his eyes.

Everyone's aging, but not seeing him for years has made it seem abrupt in his case. Deep wrinkles bend when he smiles, following the curve of his peaceful grin, but he's earned them.

"It's good to have you here, son," he says warmly.

I smile back, refusing to think about why there's a pang with the word. I'm Machir's son. Why do I need to be David's?

Machir pulls the thought right from my head. "The king has been good to you. Why have you come back now? Didn't it grieve David to see you go?"

I adjust my grip on the crutches, my throat aching. If the time it took to get permission to leave is any indication, I've hurt the king deeply. But I have to stop seeing it that way.

"It's not about him. I couldn't wait any longer. There's too much death, too much crime and mistrust. Another few years, and Mica would be caught up in whatever happens next." The words tumble out of me, irritation sharpening.

"You're so sure something else will happen?"

I shrug. I wasn't before. But something insidious lurks on the periphery of my thoughts. Will Lo Debar be safe if something worse takes place?

Machir's soft laugh displaces my anxiety like a stone dropped in a stagnant pool. He places his hand on the back of my neck, steadying me. "Lo Debar is your home, Mephi. You know you're welcome here as long as you like. But you weren't meant to stay forever. I knew that when you first came. Just promise me you'll keep your ears open, and obey when Yahweh calls you back to Jerusalem."

I glance at him, but he's still watching the sunset. Why does he have to be so enigmatic?

"For a man who isn't a seer, you sound an awful lot like one," I mutter, picking at the golden edge of my crimson robe.

For years, I've worn the heavy colors of a prince, discounting the wealth the king's laid at my door. Still, all my grandfather's money didn't mean as much as knowing David wanted me close by.

I twist my father's ring around my finger. "Why should Yahweh call me back?"

I thought I would feel foolish saying it, but the words make my nerves dance. I know the answer even before Machir says it. Without wanting it to be true.

"Because whether or not he realizes it, David needs you."

Machir is right.

For a few weeks, I remain alert. Agitated. Watching the sky each morning, straining to hear something. But there's nothing. Eventually, I decide to relax. David will call for me if I'm needed. Which I'm not.

Each successive season in Lo Debar rolls into the next, with no pressure to return. I deliberately stop counting the months, aware that one year is stretching into two, then three. But I'm not counting.

As Mica grows into his strength, I continue training him with his bow, more relaxed now that Ziba's sons aren't watching. I lay aside my royal robes, and join Ebenezer and his son at the workbench, helping the craftsmen from Mahanaim to add fresh bows to the city's armory.

At first, David sends messages every other Passover, sometimes promising to come up north. But he doesn't. The word is, he's grieving the loss of Absalom, who remains in Geshur with his grandfather. A few others have escaped to the land of

Aram as well, including Palti and his cohorts. After I learn that, the messages stop coming.

I try not to care. The pace of life here is easy to adjust to. Kezi is content, and Mica relishes the loss of servants watching his every move.

But Machir was right.

I'm both gratified and flustered when I realize it.

After nearly five years of respite, I dream of the lion again. The one who'd circled me on the evening of David's victory against the Philistines. When Yahweh marched in the balsam trees.

When the lion appears this time, I nearly wake up from shock. Except this time, he isn't burning. He's dragging his tail, licking wounded paws as he follows a man across the Kidron Valley. The man's face is covered, and he's weeping as he stumbles barefoot toward the Mount of Olives, leading a large retinue of men, women, and children. The moment I wake up, I know it deep in my bones.

It's time to return to Jerusalem. Why? I couldn't say. But it's time.

PART THREE

# THIRTY-EIGHT

## *Mephi*

———— •• ◆ •• ————

*Five years later*

I stare out the stone-framed window of my father's old house, trying to read something in the slant of Zion's hills.

*I'm back, Yahweh. What now?*

Preparations to return had moved quickly, faster than our journey north. Anticipation sped us on our way, and after a fortnight of travel, we're back in my grandfather's old walls, facing the City of David. I'd been certain of our course up until we arrived. But now, I feel scattered. Exhausted without cause.

We've barely been home for a day, and Mica has already disappeared with Ziba's younger sons, going to shoot in the back field. I sent word ahead to the king a week ago, but it was hard to read pleasure in his curt reply.

I've kept in touch with him during our time in Lo Debar, but it was hard to explain how easily the weeks with Ama and

Machir multiplied after so long apart. Lo Debar was my home for so long, and I had needed to prove to myself that I could have a life outside Jerusalem. It's been impossible to tell what David thought of that from a distance.

I have to get to the palace and see for myself. I'm still not sure what to do about the dream, if anything. Perhaps it was merely a call to return, not a warning.

My mind gallops in a hundred directions while Azarel and his brothers apprise me of everything I've missed. After having the run of the Gibeah estate for several seasons, they can't be happy to see me back. It'll take some time for me to discover exactly how deep their influence has gone in the years I've been away. But Jerusalem has a pull to it, and I'm already feeling the draw toward the palace. To David.

Kezi watches me out of the corner of her eye as she follows the maids from room to room, unpacking. "Don't worry. He'll be overjoyed to see you."

I unwrap my bow from its casings. "I didn't realize it would be this long."

"You're not sorry though, are you?" Kezi grins, unfolding the long blue garment Ama wove for her. I smile back. The time at home had refreshed her too.

"No, I'm not sorry."

Kezi dances over and kisses my cheek. "You should tell David about Machir and Ama. He'll be so proud to know that they want to get married in Jerusalem."

I shrug. "Maybe. Machir said he wanted to be the one to tell him. He won't wait too long. I wouldn't be surprised if they come within another month."

Machir and Ama's betrothal was a development I should've seen coming. She couldn't be much closer to being my mother. And Machir has been family for years. It would be easy to tell David, use the news to distract him from any slight he might be feeling.

I call toward the door. "Zarethan, send a message to the king. I want to come tonight if he'll see me."

"If," Zarethan mutters on his way past.

I frown. I'd expected Ziba's sons to act strangely, but the wordless conversations they've been passing back and forth all day are starting to annoy me.

"What's wrong with you?" I demand when Azarel walks by. His broad grin worries me.

"Your timing is impeccable, that's all."

"Why?"

Amusement crackles in Azarel's eyes. "Someone else is back."

"Who?"

"You didn't see him in town? He always draws a crowd."

The broad-shouldered, thick-haired image that enters my mind stirs my defenses. "Absalom's back?"

Azarel sets my bow against the wall, his smile widening. "Along with his wife, their three sons, and their daughter *Tamar.*"

"The king let him return from Geshur?" Why haven't I heard about this?

Shaalbim enters the room, interrupting. "No, that's the best part. Joab did. He sent for a wise woman from Tekoa and had her tell David this whole elaborate story about her sons. Basically, she got the king to admit that Absalom should be forgiven and come home, without knowing the story was about him. So, he spoke his own judgment, like he did when Nathan told him the story about the lambs. You know, when Bathsheba…"

"I remember," I cut him off. "Did David figure out that Joab was behind it?"

"Yes. He still complied, though. That general will be running the kingdom one day."

Yahweh forbid. The room condenses around me and chills crawl my arms. I feel trapped, sitting there while Ziba's sons watch everything run through my mind.

"You were always close with Sar Absalom," Shaalbim derides. "Would you like to see him?"

"No." I tighten my guard, but it's too late to hide my dismay. "Send for Joab."

I hadn't imagined Absalom would ever return. The last I heard, David had decreed that Absalom should stay with his mother's father, Talmai, the king of Geshur. If Joab made David change his mind, that's disturbing enough without having to consider Absalom taking hold of Jerusalem again.

The effect he always had on the people was uncanny. Even as a youth, people expected more of him than they did of Amnon. The younger sons always stepped aside as though they couldn't compete with Absalom and wouldn't try. I refuse to believe it's only because of his looks.

Azarel continues, "Did you know he weighs his hair now? Two hundred *shekel's* weight every year when he cuts it—"

"Do I look like I'm interested in Absalom's *hair?*" I snap, annoyed that he's still standing there. "Just send Joab up when he arrives."

"He's here now." Shaalbim follows the general inside. "He was passing by on his way from the king."

Joab strides over to me without ceremony, his rumpled riding clothes and sweaty brow adding to his aggravated demeanor.

"So, you're back. Glory be." His flat tone stirs the embers of my temper.

I stiffen. "So is the Sar, I hear."

"If you're referring to Absalom, he's been back for almost two years now. He's been living in separate quarters with his wife and children." His eyes snap. "Why should that surprise you? Even in Lo Debar, you should've heard that."

"I heard that David wasn't going to bring him back from Geshur. But you did."

"So?"

"Why?" I demand.

Joab flings his arms. "Since when did I have to explain myself to you? Absalom is smart and capable, and he did something that no one else in this kingdom could've gotten away with—dispose of that disgusting prince who raped his own sister. And I am tired. I'm tired of seeing David age before his time. He's had enough of that in his day."

He paces in front of me, his neck muscles bulging. "You weren't here to see him wither away every day that boy was gone. It was ridiculous to keep Absalom in exile over something that should have been done anyway."

Fair enough. Tamar's brokenness is etched in my mind like an incurable cut in flesh. I can't imagine it was any easier for Absalom to live with that. And I don't blame him for his anger. What bothers me is how efficiently and casually Joab turned the king's head.

I find his eyes. "How much did you pay that woman from Tekoa to deceive him?"

"Don't speak to me of deception!" he explodes, towering over me. "Your own father wouldn't have lived as long as he did if he divulged everything to Saul. I merely gave David the same encouragement Nathan did—wisdom in the form of a parable."

"You didn't trust the king to judge whether he should bring Absalom back?" That's what unnerves me. What else could he convince David to do?

The general bends, planting both hands on either side of the wall behind me. "David is nothing like me. He loves deeply. He grieves deeply. He has a hard time distinguishing enemies from friends. Which is why you're here."

My mouth drops open, but he continues. "It's also the reason I'm the head of the army. David knows I can be trusted to carry out decisions he can't. Why do you think Uriah is dead?" He pushes off the wall.

I set my teeth against the sharpness in my stomach. "Uriah didn't deserve to die."

Joab's protest stops unspoken. His jaw twitches. "No. I'll give you that. But you still have no right to question me or the king. We both carry burdens that would crush you. You were never meant to rule. You don't understand what it takes."

I set my teeth. "Maybe that's a good thing."

His brows jump. "It is. So, why don't you stick to the lot you were given and stop interfering where you don't belong?"

"My lord!" Joab's servant hovers near the door. "Absalom—"

"Yes, I know!" Joab snaps, rolling his eyes. "Tell him I'm busy being chastised by Jonathan's son. That should please him."

I nod, hoping he feels every bit of my disdain. "Why is he sending messages to you? Are you his ambassador now?"

"I serve no one but the king!" Joab shouts. "It should interest you to know that Absalom hasn't seen his father in almost two years. He's been sending me messages for months asking me to set up an audience, but have I done it? No! Because—"

"My lord!" His servant pushes into the room, his hands shaking.

Joab spins around. "*What?!*"

"The message from Absalom is about your fields. He…he's burned them."

It's probably the only time in my life I'll ever see Joab look so shocked. He crosses to the window, trying to see south toward his property, then turns to me, aiming a finger in my face. "Don't say a word! Yours may be next."

He storms out of the room, right past Kezi, slamming my door downstairs.

Her eyes wide, Kezi hands a pile of blankets to her maid. "What was that about?"

Buzzing with agitation, I won't look at her. "I'm pretty sure that man is made of stone. One of these days, someone will try to stab him, and the sword will just break in half."

Kezi smirks lightly. "Maybe that's why David keeps him around." She waits, studying me. "Why is this bothering you? So, he showed a little compassion for the king and brought his son back. David probably wanted to, but couldn't because it would seem like he was condoning what Absalom did."

I sigh, looking out at the smoke smearing the southern border of Joab's fields. "There's more to this, Kezi. I can't find it, but it's there."

It's an instinct, the same one I used to feel around Ziba. Azarel's right. We did choose our return perfectly. Not only has Absalom been back for two years, but he's choosing today to actually see his father?

"I came back for David, not Absalom. First, the king let Amnon have his way, and now..."

"But why should that affect us?" Kezi opens her hands.

I reach for my quiver, gripping one of the arrows. "Somehow, it will."

Amnon's obsessions were entirely carnal. But Absalom's ambition, coupled with his charisma and the calculating persistence of his Aramite blood, make him much more dangerous. He's been feeding his resentful sense of entitlement in exile all this time, but now he's taking the path of least resistance, making it seem like his father has wounded him.

It'll tear David's heart out and give the scheming prince whatever he wants.

David sends for me, but the moment I reach the palace, I know my arrival is going to be completely overshadowed.

Joab is ahead of me in the throne room, and his vitriol carries down the corridor.

"*I told you?* Is that all you can say to me after I brought your son back? After I've endured his messages for years while you ignored him?"

David sounds weary. "I meant that it was poor judgment to ask for the field next to his. You should have expanded your property on the other side, next to Abishai's."

"How was I supposed to know your own son would burn it!"

David's voice is muffled, like he's speaking through his hand. "You shouldn't have taken him under your wing so much at the training grounds. He didn't learn how to handle disputes from me."

"This isn't funny! Do you know how much barley he ruined?"

I don't hear David's response, but Joab shouts, "Oh, there will be restitution, will there? I look forward to seeing what you…"

He's cut off by the king's relieved sigh. "Mephi. Thank God." David stands up, beckoning to me.

Embarrassment burns my chest until the heat spreads up my neck into my face. The king has always approached me before, understanding that I can't move from the chair unless my servants carry me forward. But he's just standing there now, waiting without expression.

"I didn't realize you were back. How's Machir?"

My mouth goes dry. I imagined this so differently. "He's well. He should be coming soon, with Ama. They have news for you."

"Good news, I hope. It's been in short supply these days."

A shiver of pity eats through my wounded pride. David sounds so tired. Older than his years, like Joab said. All the more reason he should have been glad to see me. At least I returned to him willingly.

"Not as good as the news of Sar Absalom's return, but yes. Good news," I say tightly.

David tilts his head to the side, regret darkening his brow like a cloud. "I don't know why I didn't just send for him. Punishing myself, I suppose." He trails off, staring at something between us.

"Did he seek your favor all this time? Or did he just send messages to Joab?"

The sharpness leaves my tongue sore. But I can't take the words back. A sickly shade of pity colors David's expression. "Sometimes seeking a father's favor is harder than it should be. It's not something you've ever had to struggle with."

Because my father's dead. I see. A heavy cloud pushes between us, and I have to squint to see David through it. Fumbling, he tries to amend his words.

"I meant that it was never complicated between you and Jonathan the way it is with Absalom and me. You always knew your father loved you. There was never a question about that."

*Oh, no?* I lift a shoulder. "You knew him better than I did, so…"

David lifts his chin. "Yes, I did. I also know Absalom better, so you shouldn't question me. I know jealousy when I see it, Mephi."

Now I'm jealous of Absalom? That's what's happening here? Not a word about why I came back. I'm just an ungrateful subject questioning the king? The flames are filling my throat now. I'm not sure I can say anything else. It won't be respectful if I do.

Fortunately, Absalom's voice breaks the unsteady silence behind me.

"Abba?"

David's face changes so swiftly and completely that I feel my heart turn over. His breathless smile as he brushes past leaves me speechless with hurt.

Absalom collapses on all fours, but David heaves him up into his arms, kissing both his cheeks. Joab bends over to me. "And you would deny him this?"

I can't look away from David. My eyes are burning as though smoke has been blown into my face. I turn to my guards. "Get me out of here."

David won't realize I've left. I shouldn't have come back. He has the son he wants. Refusing to watch them, I grip the edges of the chair while the servants lift the poles on either side to carry me out. We've almost made it to the guarded front doors when Absalom's voice follows us.

"Mephi."

Azarel stops the servants, and I glare at him before turning around. What I wouldn't give to be able to walk away from someone.

Absalom's face is filled with some unreadable emotion, and I'm annoyed that I can't interpret it. Hands clasped, he gushes, "I'm sure your encouragement had something to do with this. You don't know how the king favors your opinion."

"I didn't say anything," I respond stiffly, and Absalom pretends to look surprised.

"Oh. I thought surely…"

"I've been in Lo Debar for a few years," I inform him. "You can save your effusion for Joab."

Absalom's eyes spark strangely, and I feel vindicated. He is covering something. But how can I possibly prove it?

"Didn't I hear that your…well, the woman who raised you is betrothed or something?"

I narrow my eyes. "You knew?"

Absalom bares his teeth, placing his hands on my shoulders. "Mephi, it's my business to know. If you want me to speak to the king about it, I will. I'm sure he'll need to provide some kind of incentive for Machir to marry Jonathan's…what was she, a concubine?"

I ease my shoulders out from under his hands, my teeth gritted. "I can speak to him myself, thank you." I force the last words. His courtly contempt is no less offensive than his old open hatred. Pretending to care about Ama when he knows very well that he just played the king like his own harp.

I look straight at Azarel. "Let's go."

Absalom laughs gently. "You're a bold one, Mephi. Not many men would walk away from me, let alone a man who can't."

The insult claws the back of my neck, but I refuse to respond.

I can't stand him. I hate the way his eyes flash when he smiles. I hate his powerful form, his ridiculously-thick hair. It's like a curtain on his shoulders. He's such a perfect deceiver, it's sickening. There has to be something dangerous about him. I know it.

But David doesn't. Even if he saw it, he'd look the other way. And Absalom knows. That's why he's smiling, letting his triumph eat its way through me as I leave. Because no matter how much David claims to love me, I'm not his son.

# THIRTY-NINE

## *Mephi*

———— •• ◆ •• ————

*Three years later*

My servants tie my crutches to the back of my mule, and I fumble with the reins, feeling both guilty and inept. I've felt the pull of my father's house before, only I didn't know how to interpret it. Now my father's ring glowers at me in the late afternoon sun. Accusing me.

After today's events, nothing will be the same.

In all my days, I'd never thought that the sons of Benjamin would seek me out. I was nothing to them—the crippled boy they'd dismissed as unfit to rule. But a few hours ago, they were all in my house, uninvited. Twelve elders of my father's tribe, some of them men who'd sat around the fire at Ramoth with Ziba.

Ziba himself hadn't joined us, which puzzles me. He's usually at the center of any new developments. But this time, Shemei and the others had come to me. Without the king's knowledge.

I watch the well-worn road beyond Saul's courtyard, trying to locate the pride I should be feeling. I'm the grandson of Israel's first king, and the sons of Benjamin finally see me that way. But since they left, a cold sickness has been gaping in my stomach like hunger.

I've never been sought out for solutions before, and I don't have any now. I wasn't able to answer their concerns, and now I wonder if I've wasted my years preparing for the wrong future.

My ears still sting with Shemei's insistent warnings.

"What portion do we have with David? Our inheritance has never been with the son of Jesse. We could do no less than support him when all Israel was behind him, but things are changing. Every day, his son steals away more of the people's hearts, and before long, he will have the kingdom."

Troubled, I had tried to placate him. "If there is any deceit in Absalom, the king will search it out." But I hadn't believed my own words, and Shemei had seen right through my uncertainty.

"David sees what he wants to see, and you know it! Most matters of state don't even reach him before Absalom handles them at the gate, and that's not a coincidence. The prince will grab as much power as he can until everyone is behind him. After all we sacrificed to crown David, he's just going to let the throne slip from his fingers? Not on our watch."

At that point, I couldn't help scoffing. "I never knew you had this much zeal for David's throne."

"I don't!" Shemei had bristled violently. "He's a shepherd who never should've crawled out of his cave. But this is the reason we have come to you, son of Saul."

The name had reached into me and seized something, commanding my attention. Twelve pairs of eyes were fixed on me, so I wasn't sure who said the words.

"We are well aware of Nathan's prophecy, but prolonged violence will harm the kingdom. If the throne does depart from David's house, we want your word that you will help us claim it for Benjamin."

I'd expected to feel shocked by the request, but instead, I'd stared back at him as though we'd spoken about this before.

"You're asking me to go against David?"

Shemei had rolled his eyes. "We're asking you to defend the throne of your father if David loses his grip on it."

"You would want a cripple to rule?" I had forced myself to look him in the eyes, hoping he'd remember that night in Ramoth when they'd all sneered at the idea.

But Shemei had fallen silent at that point, allowing the other elders to weigh in.

"Israel's position was precarious when you were a boy. No one could have challenged David back then. But you have fought past your limitations and regained your position. We would rather a Benjaminite on the throne than Absalom."

Shemei had grabbed my arm. "There's a man named Sheba, the son of Bichri. He's willing to help us fight back if David doesn't stop Absalom."

Kezi's voice floats after me now, and I straighten in the saddle, trying to shake free of the conversation. The conspiracy had left me in a fog even though I hadn't promised anything. They're all assuming far too much. Absalom might be an ambitious man, but why should he take the throne by force if he's next in line for it? Chileab has no interest in ruling, and Absalom has been in court more often than I have.

My face flushes, my heart skipping beats. I haven't seen the king in months. Not that I've been counting the days, but since

I returned from Lo Debar, nothing has been the same. Since Absalom also returned.

I adjust my grip on the reins, trying to push the previous hours from my mind. I have to find out what's going on before my father's kinsmen make any more decisions for me.

Kezi comes up behind me, the first I've seen of her since the elders left. "What did Shemei want?"

I inhale right as the wind shifts, pushing dust into my mouth. My cough covers the hesitancy of my answer. "It's nothing. I was going to ride into the city to find Mica."

He's been spending more time there lately, sparring and studying with the younger princes. They're safe at least. At eleven years old, Solomon is turning out to be everything I'd imagined a son of David would be. The king finally has a child who favors him in every way, from his musical abilities to his affinity for language. But in that regard, he's already surpassed David, writing his own songs and poems until even the king is exhausted hearing about them.

Bending down to kiss my wife, I stop when I see her face. "What's wrong?"

She holds up a parchment. "Did you hear about this? Ziba showed me."

I scan the list of figures on the paper, assuming it's another tax document. But this one bears Machir's name, with a hefty sum next to it. "What is this? David exempted Machir from taxes years ago." And Machir never mentioned anything about that changing when he was here for his wedding.

Kezi nods. "I thought so, but Ziba says that he's reimposing them on all the nobles he's exempted in the past. Barzillai, Shobi, Machir. The order has David's seal."

"And Absalom's signature." I crush the paper in my hands. I'll wager David hasn't even seen this. Any of the princes can use their seal ring to sign an order, but Absalom's been doing it the longest. The snake! I shove the parchment in my belt, lifting my brows at Kezi. "I'll be back."

I kick the mule, urging it down the road toward the city. Fresh agitation is fueling me now, and I'm eager to dispel it on the open road. I feel as though I've been handed a burning arrow, and I need to determine what I'll do with it. Where I'll aim it.

Maybe I should just find the nearest river and douse the flame before it burns out of control. That's what my father would do.

I fix my eyes on the widening horizon, watching for the towers of Jerusalem. It's been so long since I've sought the face of the Lord. Would He give me counsel if I asked? Perhaps I should ask Ahimaaz or Jonathan to send one of their fathers to me so I can inquire of Adonai. They often spend time among the young princes. Jonathan is the son of Abiathar the priest. He's named after my father, and the king trusts him.

I squint into the dust as it races past me, sticking to the sheen of sweat on my face. I can't forget how I used to crawl through it as a beggar. "You brought me out of all that and placed me here," I say into the open air, hoping Yahweh's listening. "Why?"

Shemei's plots crawl my skin, and I want to shake them off like insects. My father's throne, he'd said. But it's not my father's throne. Yahweh gave it to David, and He never said He was going to take it from him.

"Are you displeased with David, Adonai? What do you want me to do?"

I hear nothing in response. Just the dust kicking up under the mule's hooves. The sun's heat bending the air. Maybe my dream about the lion was some kind of answer. But it's old news at this point. And why does it point away from Jerusalem?

"I'm tired of the riddles, Adonai. I just want to know what to do."

I'm more honor bound to David than to the house of Benjamin. But how can I prove that without exposing the men who came to me? I'm not ready to call them traitors, but if I wait much longer, they could make a rash move and take me down with them.

As much as I hate the idea, I know I need to go straight to Absalom. See for myself what he's been doing. I've heard his name more than David's of late, but my own father was more involved in the people's concerns than Saul was in his later years. Still, Jonathan had never tried to seize power. And he'd never built a monument to himself.

According to Shemei, Absalom has set one up in the King's Valley. His vanity disgusts me, but I'm more jealous for David's sake than for my own. It disturbs me that Benjamin's desire for the throne still burns hot even after all these years.

The sun is setting by the time I ride into Jerusalem, heading through the market to the front gate. Perhaps I'll see David when I circle back to the palace in search of my son later.

Near the front of the city, I have to push through a small crowd. Absalom's at the center as usual, clasping hands and gushing over every person who approaches the platform where he's seated. Since his return, it's become more customary for people to see him there, hearing cases of individual need rather than letting people bring them to David's court.

I stop at the fringes of the crowd, counting fifty men in the prince's retinue, with chariots blocking the road on the left side. I'm wondering whether to approach when Ahithophel steps down, noticing me. The king's advisor threads his way through the onlookers and greets me. "Shalom. Looking for your son?"

I blink, startled. "Is he here?"

Ahithophel points, and all the blood cools in my face. Mica is standing at the front of the crowd on the prince's platform. At thirteen, my son is almost eye-level with most of the princes, something I can see now that Absalom's arm is draped across his shoulders.

The sight strikes a flint in my gut, and I ride past Ahithophel, pushing into the crowd. Several of the men step away from me, looking up sharply when I shout, "Mica!"

Mica straightens, and a strange look crosses his face. I feel sick when I understand it. He's ashamed.

"What are you doing here?" I ask him. "Has the king also made you a judge over his people?" I slide my eyes up to Absalom, who laughs comfortably.

"Mephi." Stepping forward, he clasps my shoulder and leans in to embrace me, but I edge away. "What's wrong?" The prince backs off slightly, keeping his grin firmly in place.

"This." I remove his hand from my arm and slam the paper into it. "Why would you impose back taxes on the king's most trusted friends? Is it possible that your father doesn't know about this?"

Absalom's face turns white, his eyes like glowing coals within ash. He speaks through the same false grin. "Now, now. You've crossed a line, and there's no going back if you proceed. Come and talk to me about this in private."

"No," I say loudly. "We're not talking in private. We're talking now. Better yet, I'm going to the king. Why am I wasting time with you? Come, Mica." I beckon to my son who moves toward me with his head lowered. "What are you doing here anyway?" I ask him again. "I thought you were with Solomon."

Absalom folds his arms. "You think I'm trying to lure your son into some crime? As though I need him to accomplish what I mean to do?"

"And what is that?" I stare at him, hoping he reads every bit of distrust in my eyes.

Absalom spreads his hand at the crowd. "I plot nothing here, Mephi. All these people have come here to pay homage to me. Because they know I will hear their disputes and judge fairly. Why should I make them wait for the king to hear cases that I can handle now? This is merely the job of a Hassar, which you would know if you were any use to the kingdom at all."

Whispers ripple through the crowd, and I watch Mica's head drop lower. I hold Absalom's attention. "Don't talk to me like that."

He flashes his teeth, lowering his voice. "Giving orders now? You know, it's no secret that you haven't eaten with the king since you returned. I, on the other hand, dine with him every night. His acceptance means very little to you, it would seem."

Mica looks at me, but Absalom continues before I can respond.

"The king never mentions you. In fact, after your five years hiding in the north, I'd say he wouldn't notice if you left for good. Would you like me to prove it?" His fingers tickle the sword at his side.

"Are you threatening me?" I demand, tightening the reins.

"Call it a command, son of Jonathan. Hopefully one you prefer over the taxes." Absalom lifts his chin. "I want you to leave. Take your wife and your spawn, and get out of Jerusalem. Go back to that garbage dump you crawled out of, and don't come back. You left before; it should be easy for you to do it again."

I stiffen, my hand gripping Mica's shoulder. "You will repeat this before the king."

Absalom shakes his head. "No, I will not." He steps closer, speaking right into my face. "Here's what will happen. I will send servants to your house to get your wife. My guards will take you and your son to the north gate to meet her, and you will leave the way you came. With nothing."

"Abba," Mica begins, but I clamp down harder on his arm, restraining my temper.

"The king brought me here. You have no authority to command me from his presence."

Absalom's brows tilt. "You think not? He's always said that open rebellion will not exist in his house. It's no secret that you've entertained sons of Benjamin who still speak openly against the king."

My stomach twists. How did he know? "They're kinsmen. They mean no harm."

"Shall the king wait for harm to come of it?" Absalom's tone bites. "Can you control their actions from your crutches? I don't think so. I'm tired of your arrogance, and so is the king. Now, are you going to obey me, or shall I send you from this place under guard?"

My pulse drums in my throat, burning my eyes. But I'm backed into a corner. My son will have to see me defeated this once. "As you command," I say tightly, refusing to address him as my lord. "Let's go, Mica."

Absalom touches my son's shoulder. The gesture is gentle, but it feels like a fist in my chest. "Perhaps I'll keep the boy here with me."

"What?" I yank the reins so sharply that the mule jerks its head back.

Absalom shrugs. "Apparently, there are plenty of rogue Benjaminites who are desperate enough to follow even a cripple against the king. But not if your son is with me."

My stomach turns over, and flames sting the edges of my vision. "You can't take my son!"

"It's all right, Abba. I'll stay," Mica murmurs, his eyes jumping nervously back and forth.

He can tell I want to spring at Absalom, regardless of the consequences. There's no way I'm leaving Mica here.

But Absalom's chuckle shreds my nerves. "Don't worry. I want no part of your kind." He shoves my son toward me and gestures to his guards. "Get them out of here."

My head pounds as Mica and I approach the north gate, surrounded by Absalom's soldiers. I don't want to believe David would really allow this. What have I ever done to have him send me away empty-handed?

I grind my teeth, resisting the urge to release my frustration in front of my son. *Adonai, why is this happening? I have tried to honor David. I have accepted him as king.*

I've counted on David's provision. Now everything is being stripped away from us again. As I feared. My family will suffer dishonor forever, cast aside by Israel's most benevolent king.

I shiver, every hair on my neck standing on end. Perhaps the Gibeonites have surfaced again, and the king would rather find an excuse for me to leave than deal with punishing me openly. The thought carries an evil presence that I can't shake.

Desperate to escape it, I urge the mule faster. If I leave without a fight, maybe David will relent.

My noble resignation vanishes when armed soldiers deliver my wife to the gate. She's trembling, hurrying along to avoid being touched by the guards. Tears streak her face.

It's been years since I've felt grief over what it's cost Kezi to marry me. David's kind reception has been the only pride she's known as my wife. Now it's all gone.

One of the guards shoves her toward me, and my voice cracks the air like a whip. "Leave her! She's done nothing wrong."

"Hold your peace and be gone," Absalom's guard Amasa orders me gruffly. "The Sar has ordered you to leave before the sun sets."

I pivot to face him. "We are to travel at night with no protection?"

Amasa snorts. "Aren't you protection enough?" He nods at my bow, slung over my shoulder. "He wants you gone as quickly as possible. Three of our company will see you through the gates to the first milestone. Then, you'll be at Yahweh's mercy."

Kezi clutches at her mule's saddle, restraining sobs. "Why has he done this?"

I reach for her, praying for strength. "Kezi, we'll be all right. Machir will welcome us. You know that."

She gulps, wiping her eyes with the edge of her veil. "I've praised Yahweh every day for His kindness in bringing us here. Why does He let us leave with nothing?"

I wince. Yahweh will have to forgive me for failing to justify His plans this once. It's hard to believe David will correct this after the months of silence between us. Absalom might make him think we left willingly.

When the guards leave us a mile outside the city, Kezi breaks down, weeping. I ride in silence, grateful that Mica is far enough ahead that he can't see the shame staining my brow. It's all I can do not to ride back to Zion and demand to see David. But we've only been a few hours outside the gates when someone shouts after us.

Kezi whirls around in the saddle. "Look! It's the prince's guards."

Squinting through the dust, I make out the emblem of the king's household on the soldiers' mounts. But they aren't

Absalom's men. Solomon is riding in front, sunlight shimmering on his blue cloak. I keep forgetting he's old enough to ride out on his own.

"The king wants to see you at once." Solomon reins in next to me.

I swallow, stung by resentful hope. "Have we offended him, my lord?"

Solomon's breathless smirk is strangely encouraging. "He is offended, but not with you. My brother has gone too far this time. Come back with me. You will see justice done."

# FORTY

*David*

⸺⸺•◆•⸺⸺

I pace in the throne room, waiting for my sons. I hadn't wanted
to believe Ahimaaz when he'd told me what happened at the
gate, but Solomon had volunteered to go after Mephi before he
could get far. I'm immensely relieved to see Mephi's servants help
him through the doors into the throne room, but the moment he's
inside, I feel anger returning, my pulse spinning beneath my skin.

"Mephibosheth, what is the meaning of this? Why did you
leave unprotected?"

How could he assume I would order something like that?
He's kept aloof from me since he returned, and now this? Arguing
with my son in the street and then trying to leave?

Mephi bows his head, but he isn't covering guilt or shame.
His temper is smoldering, barely held back. "Sar Absalom ordered
us to leave. I could not disobey a son of the king."

Absalom's expression shifts slightly, but otherwise, he keeps any emotion covered.

"What has he done?" I demand, my voice thundering toward my son.

Absalom's eyes blaze. "He defied you, my lord king. He accused me point-blank in front of the crowd at the gate. And I have seen men of Benjamin returning from his house. Who knows what they've been plotting against you?"

Annoyance crackles inside me. I'm so tired of men twisting each other's words, finding reasons to paint one another as traitors. I look into Absalom's face.

"Mephibosheth is the son of the man I made a covenant with before God. As long as I live, no son of Jonathan's will be turned out of Jerusalem. My vows before the Lord are more important to me than a whim from you."

I turn around, and Mephi drops his eyes again. "Do you have any wish to leave here, Mephibosheth?"

Mephi stays silent for too long. "I don't want to grieve you, my lord."

Good enough. I'll wonder why he didn't answer me directly later. "You will never be sent away like this again."

I follow Mephi's eyes over to Absalom. Deep tension smolders in my son's face. "Is there more you'd like to say?" I ask him.

Absalom blinks, waking up. "I have a request to make of you, my lord."

I sigh, rubbing my temple. "In a moment. Wait here." I lift my chin at Mephi's servants. "Bring him into my antechamber."

I haven't been alone with Jonathan's son in a long time. Perhaps it's been a mistake to give Mephi so much freedom, allowing him to live in Gibeah with little supervision. I've never viewed him as someone who would subvert my rule, but plenty of devious men have access to him. And for the first time, I realize that I don't have absolute confidence to answer the shivers of doubt inside me.

Seated at my table, Mephi stares me down, refusing to blink. I sigh heavily. I'm so tired of fighting my own family.

"Mephi, why did you accuse Absalom? Why do you feel the need to antagonize him?"

Mephi locks his jaw, and I pace, continuing. "I know my own sons, and I know you. I know you haven't plotted anything with the men of Benjamin. Absalom lashes out with the information he obtains. But he only does that when he feels threatened."

I stop, bending to grip the edge of a chair. "I don't understand why you persist in shutting me out. I opened the doors of my kingdom to you. I gave you Saul's house, his wealth—everything that would've been yours if he had lived."

"Who asked you to do that?"

Mephi's answer throws my sincerity back in my face, and I bristle.

"I was honor bound to do it, but I also wanted to! All those years, I persisted in searching for you because you were lost and needed my help. I wouldn't rest until you were found. Do you find that so hard to believe?"

Mephi lifts a shoulder. "Somewhat. As Jonathan's son, I had value to you, but as a cripple on the fringes of Israel, what did I matter?"

I shake my head, confounded by his coldness. "There's something else at work here, Mephi, some other force determined to turn you against me."

Mephi tilts his head, his eyes changing. "And what would that be? Saul?"

I drop my arms, incredulous. Why do I feel like I'm talking to a stranger? "Do you need me to talk about him? I thought you understood everything that happened."

"I understand it," Mephi responds icily. "I had plenty of time to figure it out all those years, hearing stories of how noble you were to my monster of a grandfather."

"He was a monster!" I shove the chair out of my way, my voice turning hoarse. "He threw a spear at me when I was just a boy! Do you know how many innocent people he killed to try to get to me?"

My tone slants abruptly when the anger in Mephi's face shifts, letting me see a hint of Jonathan again.

"I'm sorry," I amend. "He was like my father for so long, and it killed me to see him so determined to destroy me. He cast me out and drove me from Adonai's land like a criminal. Do you have any idea what that was like?"

Mephi's expression settles. "You know I do."

I move closer to him, softening my tone. "No matter what anyone's told you, I've never been Saul's enemy. I'm not yours either, but I refuse to stand against my own son at your whim."

"My whim?" Tension squeezes back into Mephi's face, twisting the muscles in his neck. "You said you knew jealousy when you saw it. Your son has hated me from the day I set foot in this house. He hates anyone who might steal what he believes is his. And he hates you, but you refuse to see it."

"Watch your tone with me, son of Saul." I wince before Mephi does. Why did I say that? I search for ways to take it back, but it's too late. Mephi's face is drawn tighter than Jonathan's ever was around me. His eyes aim a cold challenge into mine.

"I believe you like having me with you. Because as long as you look at me, you can tell yourself you haven't failed Jonathan, even if you've failed everyone else." His chest lifts, and he rushes to finish. "You give Absalom his own way because you're afraid you've failed him. As you failed his sister."

The moment he mentions Tamar, I can't see. My vision smears with the rage I only use in battle, and I fold my fists, desperately trying to control it. "What do you want from me, Mephi? Do you want me to hate you? You're making it easy."

Mephi's mouth drops open, and he struggles in silence for several moments. Azarel chokes on a strange laugh, glancing at the door. Mephi flinches, staring at something I don't see on the table.

"Don't call for me again," he says when he can speak. "I won't come."

I lock my tongue onto the roof of my mouth, refusing to say anything in response. I'm already regretting everything about this exchange. But what have I done to deserve his contempt? As offensive as it was to say, it does seem as though something is pulling him away. Something beyond both of us. And I can't tell whether he has the strength to fight it.

Absalom loiters in the corner of my throne room, watching Mephi's servants help him out into the street. When the doors close, he pushes off the wall. "Rather harsh, Abba. He's only a harmless cripple."

I wince, thinking of all the hidden insults I've caught being passed between my sons since Mephi arrived. "Now you're being harsh," I mumble. "But harmless would never be a word to describe Saul's sons."

*Or yours.*

I hear it in my head in Mephi's voice, and I try to shake it off. Something's eating Mephi alive, causing him to see enemies where there are none. He has no need to take on burdens that are mine.

I sigh, remembering. "What did you want to ask me, Absalom?"

My son straightens, wasting no time. "I wanted to ask your permission to go to Hebron. When I was in Geshur, I vowed that if Adonai would bring me back to Jerusalem one day, I would go to Hebron and offer a sacrifice. I have yet to make good on my promise."

My back is turned, and my son's words are rolling over me, sounding strangely hollow in my ears. I should call Mephi back. But what would I say to him? He wants to hate me.

"Do I have your permission, my king?" Absalom bites through the last two words.

I nod, moving slowly toward the side door. "Go in peace, my son." My limbs are weighted, my thoughts sluggish, as if I'm in a dream.

But then I notice Absalom watching me. And everything turns cold. I don't know how to answer it, but I haven't seen that look in any man's eyes since I was fifteen, sitting across from Saul with a harp in my hands. And a spear aimed at my chest.

<hr />

*Three months later*

*You are beloved by Yahweh. Your kingdom will endure.*

The promises wind through my mind, compensating for the heavy weight of betrayal. It's creeping closer by the day, trapping me in a place I never thought I would find myself. The Mount of Olives fills my window, and I stare at it, afraid to put my questions into words. Afraid to hear the answer.

I breathe deeply, steeling myself against the sting behind my eyes. *Yahweh, you promised that your steadfast love would always dwell with me. Is that over? Is this how you mean for my kingdom to fall?*

I've failed in so many ways, but I never imagined things ending this way.

The door to my private chamber opens quietly, but the sound still sends needles of alarm through my chest. I can feel my inner control tensing, shaking, like a house about to collapse. Gripping my elbows, I turn around, praying it isn't Joab.

It's Abishai. And the news is written in his eyes.

I swallow. "Say it."

Abishai's face wears the same tight calmness that he's displayed since my youth, since we hid out in caves from Saul. Now, he's about to tell me someone else is against me.

"My spies came back from Hebron. It is clear that the hearts of Israel have gone after Absalom. At least two hundred supporters followed him there initially, and now the number has more than doubled." Abishai's chest lifts, and something settles on him that I never thought I'd see. Fear. "We're ready to do whatever you decide."

I turn to the window, grab a glimpse of the mountains, and trap it behind my eyes while the news leeches into me, souring into the worst pain I've ever experienced. I had thought nothing could be worse than Saul's hatred, but this is it. This is an enemy from my own house, my own body. Absalom's careful smile sears into my heart, and I have to force breaths in and out. Waiting for battle fury to rush in to cover the pain.

But something else surfaces instead. It's the old instinct that told me to run from Ramah, from Keilah, from a dozen other cities before I brought Saul's wrath upon them. The impulse crawls back into view, and I'm as disappointed as I am relieved to see it.

I turn to Abishai, testing my voice. "Summon the household, all my wives and children and their servants. And assemble the mighty men. Gather them at the north gate, and we will flee. Quickly, before Absalom besieges Jerusalem and strikes the whole city with the sword."

"You won't fight?" Abishai has never questioned a command of mine before. Except for sparing Saul.

I chew on my lip. "It's not the time. It's me he hates. If we leave, we'll spare Jerusalem, draw the fighting away from here."

I'm not ready to say my son's name. Not yet. How I'd yearned for him when he lived in Geshur. It had felt like a part of me was still in exile. And now, I'm heading into it again. Because of him.

Dizzy, I shove Abishai. "Go now! Hurry. We have to be out of here by nightfall. I don't know how close he is."

Abishai springs into action, and I follow him, sensing the familiar sweep of adrenaline rushing in to protect my mind. I breathe it in deeply, glad for a distraction from the pain. I can feel the thorn edging up under my heart, shortening my breath. But it can push through later. Once we've left.

I walk blindly down the hall that connects my chambers to the harem, trying to think, trying to measure my steps. But my thoughts are riveted on Yahweh. The God I still love. Once again, it's all on Him. It's no use raging or blame-shifting. All I can do is face my failures and hope for Adonai's mercy.

*If I still find favor in your sight, bring me back to this place. If I've fallen short too many times, then I am willing to accept your judgment. But make your will plain, so that I may walk in it and not offend you again.*

The words find rhythm in my head like a song, pushing toward my lips. I repeat them in whispers, over and over. Because as long as I do, I'll have something to light my way. And because the moment I stop, I know I'm going to break.

# FORTY-ONE

## *Mephi*

———◆◆◆——

This is wrong.

It repeats in my mind with every word out of Azarel's mouth. The air is singing in my head, the high-pitched whine drowning out everything I'm being told. Shoving coherent thoughts to the corners of the room.

Mica tries to weigh in, and the urgency in his voice wakes me up somewhat. "David wouldn't just leave. Surely, he's going to Hebron to fight Absalom."

Azarel shakes his head. "No, he's leaving. Ten concubines will stay to keep the house, but the rest of his family is going to hide beyond the Jordan."

"Why?" Kezi gasps, and the air in the room tightens.

Zarethan shrugs. "He thinks Yahweh intends to punish him, maybe answer the sins surrounding Bathsheba or Amnon."

559

"What do the priests say about that?" I hiss, finally figuring out how to talk.

"They're staying too," Zarethan responds. "David told Zadok and Abiathar to remain here with their sons. And he's keeping the Ark of the Covenant in Jerusalem. He seems confident that Yahweh will bring him back if he still finds favor with Him. But in any case, he's not willing to fight to hold onto the throne if Yahweh is removing it from his grasp."

Ziba's sons look almost pleased at my confusion. My thoughts are a painful tangle of protests that I want to fling in each of their arrogant faces. These are assumptions at best, and not good ones. Yahweh has not clearly said that David has lost the throne, and the king has no right to give it up without a fight! It's the last thing I'd ever expect of the man who's slain giants and subdued every other enemy in this region.

Except this one is his son.

"I don't care," I snap angrily. "He may be David's son, but he's a manipulative deceiver, and Yahweh cannot mean for the throne to go to a man like that."

I refuse to believe it. But it's worse than that. Beneath my anger, I can feel the pull of my connection with the king. Once, the cords binding me to David had drawn me back to Jerusalem, but now, they're dragging me toward the edge of a cliff. David isn't thinking. He's leading with his heart, as Joab has warned me, placing trust where it doesn't belong. And this time, he's going to drag us all down with him.

"So, what do we do? What does David want us to do?" Mica asks.

I glance at him, at Kezi, and my eyes start to burn in the smoke of their fear. This is the development I've dreaded, the one I knew I couldn't protect them from. David stepping away from the door of the sheepfold.

"Someone will have to fight, even if David won't," I mutter. But how many of us will be alive when it's over? Is it worth all this to keep the king's conscience intact? I pull my bow across my lap and grip the wood until the shaft starts to shake in my hands.

Ziba's been waiting silently in the corner, watching me. Now, his back scrapes the wall as he pushes off of it. He directs his sons in a gentle voice I've never heard before. "All of you, go. Leave us a moment."

His sons slowly stalk from the room, followed by my wife and Mica. It's been years since I've been alone with Ziba, and now an undefined change sits between us. His face has always been unreadable, but now it's softening. Opening some unknown door.

I avert my eyes, shutting him out. "How can David leave Jerusalem to that pretender?"

I don't like the way I feel saying it aloud to Ziba. He's hardly family. Since I came to Jerusalem, he's been aloof, living his own life.

I rake a hand through my hair, thinking of the moment when I'd thrown everything back in David's face in the palace. He might forgive me for that, but there's little chance he sees me as he used to. Yet, no matter what demons of the past lurk between us, I don't want to believe this is the end of his kingdom.

I sit forward, reaching for my quiver. "He doesn't have to do this. I have to go after him. I can make him understand…"

"No. You can't. Even Jonathan couldn't at this point."

Ziba's sorrowful manner unnerves me.

"He's our king, Ziba. Until Yahweh Himself anoints another, we should go with David."

I'm hesitant to approach David after our last meeting. But I can't imagine being safe with anyone else. My life is bound up in his. It has been since before I was born.

"You don't have to trust me," Ziba ventures, his hand against the wall over my head.

"I don't." But trust is becoming a foreign concept. I don't understand it anymore.

Ziba looks down at me. "Why do you think it took so long for David to find you?"

"You were hiding me in a cistern." The words taste bitter.

Ziba doesn't blink. "I could have told him anytime I wanted. Your father's letter instructed Machir to bring you to David. When he questioned me directly, I thought it would be wrong to deceive him when he evidently wanted to find you. But I kept you back initially because I wanted to spare you all this."

If I wasn't so sick, that would make me laugh. I shake my head.

"You don't have to believe me. But it's true." Ziba angles closer. "You may have been born a prince, but you weren't raised as one. Lo Debar was better for you. You didn't need to come here and have David flaunt everything that was taken from you."

"He didn't flaunt it. He gave it back."

"So that you could watch his sons murder each other and take the kingdom by force while he did nothing? So that one of them could snatch your inheritance away again?" His voice hardens. "I saw years ago what you're seeing now. David dragged you into the court for his own selfish reasons, with no regard for what it would expose you to. Now every safeguard he's built around you is coming apart. Everyone knows who you are. And David will not protect you."

He shakes his head. "It would have broken your father to see how weak David is. He's not strong like you are. Like Saul was."

I frown. Ziba never had anything good to say about Saul before.

Reading my confusion, Ziba sighs. "Saul hunted David for you. Because he was jealous for your father's kingdom, the one that would have been yours. David won't even fight to protect what is now rightfully his. He'll risk the lives of all his faithful followers rather than kill Absalom. And I would rather not be another Benjaminite casualty of David's wars. That is why Shemei and the others came to you."

I didn't realize he knew about that. But then, Absalom did. I would never have considered aligning myself with Ziba years ago. But desperation drove me to David. Why shouldn't I look to my kinsmen now that the king has abandoned me?

My next words are outside my chest, like they don't belong to me. "Do you believe what Shemei says? That David's an imposter who stole the kingdom from Saul?"

Ziba shrugs. "Who can know? But the irony is too pointed to be ignored. Absalom is merely repeating David's actions. David pretended to be an innocent victim, a hunted wanderer persecuted by your grandfather. He collected supporters under that guise, waiting for Saul's failures to pile up, and in the end, Israel gave him the throne." He spreads his hands. "That's all Absalom has done. Stolen Israel's heart."

"And Yahweh will let that happen?" It angers me that He might. Doesn't He realize that Absalom will kill anyone who doesn't support him? He won't be another David.

Ziba's mouth twists. "Yahweh is always at work, but men also choose their own ways. David may have given up, but we don't have to."

The chill of danger sweeps back over me, lifting every hair on my arms. It's the same sickly sense I got from my earlier meeting with the Benjaminites. Treachery hovers over Gibeah like a plague, and I'm tainted by it, the same as Shemei and the others. Even if I haven't lifted a finger against David.

Ziba steps in front of me. "Years ago, in Ramoth-Gilead, our brothers saw another solution. It didn't make sense at the time, but they mentioned it because they knew it was valid."

*The night you were keeping me in a pit like an animal? When you called me a dog, unfit for the throne?*

I try to recoil from the memory, but Ziba pushes closer, planting his hands on the bench on either side of me. "Even back then, they knew that you could garner enough support to challenge David, simply by virtue of your blood."

*No.* The word sits behind my teeth, but I don't say it. I just keep staring at this stranger I've known my whole life.

Ziba straightens. "Benjamin's elders plan to fight this if David won't. They will fight with or without you, Mephi. But they know your lineage. We all thought it was foolish of David to give you the position he did. But now, it's clear that there was a reason beyond what even he could see. Your father knew that David would protect you. But now, you can do more than survive."

I push air through my lungs, hardly breathing. Ziba must be truly desperate to come to me. But then, David's put us in this position. At least standing with the sons of Benjamin would provide me with support. Otherwise, I'm alone. But Ziba is taking so much for granted.

I swallow hard. "Joab will fight to the death before he lets Absalom get to David. If Absalom dies and David doesn't, then we've become the traitors."

Ziba's deathly calm expression chills my heart. "David isn't invincible. No matter how he chooses to look at it, this is war. Someone will die."

I'm gripping my bow so hard, the feeling is leaving my hands. We're back where we started when I was a boy. Saul's death had thrown the tribes into bloody chaos while David grappled for control. Surely there's a better way. But not if David won't fight.

Ziba backs off, confident he's made his point. "If you want my advice, stay here and lie low. Pretend to be neutral. Let the battle play out, but keep the sons of Benjamin close."

"And then?" The words freeze on my tongue.

Ziba's eyes darken with the coldness I remember. "Then, seize your moment to take back what is yours."

Ziba leaves me to myself, and no one else enters the room. For hours. On the bench by the west window, I watch the walls of my father's weapons turn red with the sunset, and I try to imagine myself doing it. Taking one of those spears and turning it against David. Out of zeal for the house of Benjamin. Isn't that what the elders said?

But what about zeal for our country, for what binds us together? Israel is Benjamin's covering. It's Judah's. And Ephraim's and all the others. Saul's misplaced zeal killed my father, made me a despised orphan. And as hard as I try, I can't hate the man who lifted me out of that.

David might be weak, but if weakness sought me out for good while strength would've killed me, which is better?

I reach down and grip my ankles, thinking of how much they used to hurt. How Ziba mocked me when I couldn't stand on them. How disgusted Michal looked when she saw me on the crutches. My own family left me in the streets. David's efforts to elevate me had offended them. Because they didn't see a prince when they looked at me. They still don't. They see a way out from under Judah.

I set my bow upright in my hands. I wish I had my father's, but at least I've grown to be a fighter. It's Jonathan's legacy I was meant to carry out, not Saul's. Not the vengeful, power-hungry campaigns that led to his torment.

*When Yahweh is with you, your arrows will fly on the wings of the wind.*

Passion surges into my throat. My father wouldn't be using David's darkest hour as a chance to grab revenge for a house that had already fallen. All I have to do is remember the way David worshipped at the fire in Lo Debar, and the way the *hakkodesh* was there, listening.

Yahweh hasn't forsaken him simply because Absalom has dazzled the people. David's sins aren't greater than our God's mercy poured out on his repentance. Rebellion will only spell death for my family. David is the direction of life. It's as true now as it was in Abba's day.

Pushing off the bench, I slide onto the floor. "Ziba!"

He might not agree to help me pursue David, but I can always have Kezi find Jonathan or Ahimaaz to assist us. I'd rather not make my wife and son leave Gibeah, but they'll be safer with David.

"Ziba! Azarel!" I'm not used to silence when I call out. Not anymore. At the very least, Kezi always answers. "Ziba!" I take one of the swords and tap the metal gong in the corner. Nothing. Where is everyone?

I crawl to the door and grasp the handle to pull myself up, but it jams against a cedar plank on the opposite side. I try again, for whatever it's worth, but ice shoots into my veins when I realize what's happened. The door's been barred, trapping me in my father's armory in Saul's fortress.

# FORTY-TWO

## *David*

———◆◆◆———

I recognize this road. It runs over the Mount of Olives, sloping upward to the east before opening into the Jordan Valley. Outside Gibeah, the memories start pounding with each step closer to Nob. As a youth, I'd run from Saul to this very city in much the same way as I'm traveling now. Torn robes. Barefoot. Disgraced.

I'm moving faster than the others on purpose. Letting my heart bleed along with my feet. Up ahead, I can groan aloud to Yahweh without worrying my children. Though I'm sure they can still hear me. The moans are trapped under my ribs, throbbing.

"Will you not arise, Adonai? My own household has risen against me, but you see it all. You're still my God. Will you not help me?"

My shoulders quake, and a wave of pain nearly sends me to my knees. I grip the edge of Nob's mile marker, trying to see past the rubble of my life. Back when I fled as a boy, I'd been able to look to the future. I was anointed and had yet to see how Yahweh would give me the kingdom. If I'd known then that I wouldn't be able to hold onto it, that my own son would steal it from me, I might've have let Saul kill me.

Running footsteps pound the ground, and a man sprints outside the gate.

"Get out!" he bellows, flinging a stone directly at me.

Ducking out of the way, I shade my eyes. "Shemei?"

The son of Saul's armorbearer has always disliked me, but he's livid now. He springs at me, spitting, railing, grabbing rocks and handfuls of dust.

"Get out, you worthless man of blood! This day, Adonai has finally avenged the blood of Saul's house. He's cast you back into the dust where you belong!"

"Be quiet!" Abishai roars, running up behind me. "Insolent dog! Who do you think you are?" His sword is halfway out of its sheath, but I grip his arm.

"Let him alone, Abishai." I swallow, tasting dust. "We don't know that he's wrong."

Startled, my nephew faces me. "You're serious?"

My sight blurs again. "My own son hates me. How much more should this Benjaminite? Let him curse. Maybe Yahweh will take pity on me and repay me good for all this evil."

"Will He?" Sorrow shifts the fury on Abishai's face.

My voice turns to gravel. "I'm willing to hope."

The effort is turning me inside out, ripping my heart down the middle, but it's better than trying to rage and fight like Saul did. I saw what that cost everyone. Better to put your mouth in the dust and hope for mercy. It's all I know.

Turning, I stagger up the slope, leading the others into the forest skirting the town. It's evidently not the time to pass straight through. Shemei follows us halfway up the rise, throwing stones, cursing, and spitting like an animal.

Once we reach the cover of trees, I wipe sweat from my brow and notice Solomon walking beside his mother. He's steadying her with one arm, helping her over the rocks, but his jaw is trembling.

"Solomon." I reach over and grip his arm.

He sucks in a shaky breath, and a tear rolls down his face. "Why didn't you make him stop?"

My heart wrenching, I pull his face into my shoulder. He matches my stride, moving farther up the trail while Bathsheba drops behind us.

"Do you remember what Adonai called you when you were born?" I ask him, hoping to shut out Shemei's vitriol.

Solomon sniffs. "Jedidiah."

I smile, savoring the sweetness of the memory. "Though our foes rail against us, we know the truth. Adonai is our glory, our shield, and the lifter of our heads. If we cry out to Him, He will answer us."

"And break all the teeth in our enemies' mouths." A muscle tightens along Solomon's jawline.

"Easy," I chuckle, squeezing his shoulder. Solomon is already known far and wide as a sweet psalmist. I so rarely see fierceness take hold of him. But there will be time enough for hard decisions. He'll have plenty of them waiting for him when I sleep with my fathers.

"My lord, someone's coming," Abishai shouts, pointing down the slope.

I glance back through the screen of trees. "Shemei?"

"No. It's a man with provisions. I think it's Ziba."

I step into the clearing, relieved that Shemei has dropped back. Ziba's servants are driving an army of donkeys laden with wineskins and packs of food. My wives and their maids approach them, visibly relieved. Ziba rides out ahead and dismounts, dropping to one knee.

I spread my hands. "What's all this?"

Ziba dabs his forehead with the edge of his cloak. "You will need the food and wine for your journey, my lord, and you can ride the donkeys. Truly, I'm shocked that you've traveled all this way on foot."

The surprise is so welcome, I almost laugh. "*I'm* shocked that you brought all this from Jerusalem without Absalom's men stopping you." I study the servants and notice that Ziba's sons are missing, along with someone else. "Where's your master's grandson?"

How could I have forgotten to summon Mephi? I should have made sure he was with me! He did say he didn't want me to call for him. Yet, surely such a danger to the kingdom would have made him reconsider.

Ziba's tight grimace stirs my defenses.

"He stayed in Jerusalem, my lord. Your son was right about the men of Benjamin who have been meeting with him. Mephi believes that enough of the house of Israel will resist Absalom, and once the disarray passes, they will restore Saul's kingdom to him instead."

My throat curls shut on itself. "You heard him say this?"

Ziba lowers his eyes. "He summoned me on the day you fled. He asked if you had really been anointed, or if you had stolen the throne from Saul." His shoulders drop. "My lord, you don't know Jonathan's son the way I do. I didn't want to disrespect you by saying it, but he's not what you've believed him to be. All these years, you've been searching for someone who didn't exist. Jonathan was a faithful friend to you, but Mephi doesn't have the same vision. Too much of Saul's bitterness runs in his veins."

Flames twist my gut. "But why should he be bitter? I've never sought his life. I took him from nothing and gave him everything."

My voice dies, hurt staining my vision. My fists are squeezing at my sides as the truth pounds into me. Again. Along with Mephi's curt response to my generosity. *Who asked you to do that?*

Why do I do it? Why do I continually pour myself out for people who hate me?

I held back from dishonoring Saul. When he was in trouble, I mourned and prayed as though grieving for a father. While Absalom was stealing the people's affections in front of me, I'd determined to believe he wouldn't rebel. I had loved them both while knowing they both hated me. But I'd always expected Mephi to be different.

I had dragged him to Jerusalem, desperate to believe that Jonathan was still alive within his son. All the while, I was just delaying the inevitable. When am I going to learn?

Ziba lifts his eyes, and I wince at the pity in them. He has fifteen sons who would never turn against him. Why do mine scheme and plot against me?

"All he sees is what you've taken, my lord," Ziba continues sadly. "And now he has a chance to take it back."

"That doesn't make sense. Does he really believe the sons of Benjamin would follow a cripple over my son?" My voice turns hard.

Ziba shrugs. "Perhaps he's counting on Benjamin's vengeful nature, the schemes of men like Shemei. You see how they revile you with no regard for what you have done for Israel. Mephi has grown up around those men. And you know better than anyone how pride can blind a man to the truth."

I look at Ziba sharply, but whoever he's referring to, he's right. I cannot pretend Mephi is someone he isn't. As much as I wanted him for a son, he doesn't want me for a father. Like Absalom.

I turn away, but the pain is waiting for me wherever I look. No more. No more giving gifts that men will trample on. No more seeing friends where enemies are determined to dwell. Setting my jaw, I face Ziba.

"All that belonged to Mephibosheth is now yours. The land, the houses, everything." It should have been his to begin with. He and his sons were serving my kingdom from Gibeah for years before I even found Mephi. And Mephi's never said that he wanted his grandfather's property.

Ziba bows low, his face hidden. "I pay homage. Let me ever find favor in your sight, my lord king."

"You will always have it," I promise him with the last shred of control I can muster. "Go back to the city and get your sons. You can catch up with us." Turning away, I mount one of the donkeys and summon my commanders.

It may be too late to reconcile with Mephi, but Absalom is my true son. Perhaps I can still salvage whatever connection we have left. Once Jerusalem is safe.

Abishai rides up beside me, keeping his eyes on the trail. "What's your plan, my king?"

"Our friend Hushai has agreed to remain in Jerusalem as a spy. But I've sent two units of warriors ahead of us to Mahanaim." I pant over my jumping pulse. "Machir is ready to welcome us, along with my friend Barzillai."

"And then?"

I swallow the thorn in my throat. "Once we've counted the fighting men, I'll divide our forces into three companies. One will follow Joab, one will follow you, and the third will go with Ittai. I will ride out with Joab's company."

Joab opens his mouth, but Abishai cuts in faster. "Forgive me, my lord, but I can't agree. Absalom's men don't care whether we live or die. But you're worth ten thousand of us. Better for you to stay in Mahanaim and send us help from there. Ahimaaz and Jonathan are fast riders; they can reach us with any news Hushai learns back in Jerusalem."

"I agree," Ittai folds his huge arms. "You shall not go out with us."

I have to clench hard against more tears. Ittai's loyalty has remained as stark and obvious as the old Philistine tattoos circling his arms. Once again, Yahweh hasn't left me completely alone.

Joab's fierce scowl hasn't moved since we left Jerusalem. His anger is building beneath the surface like fire within rock. "You know where I stand, my lord," he mutters.

"Very well. I will do whatever you think is best." They know I wouldn't be able to strike my own son. Something shudders in my chest, and I tighten my grip on the reins. "You will deal gently with Absalom for my sake."

If he's defeated and brought back to me under guard, perhaps I might eventually restore him. In time.

Without waiting for a response, I ride over to join Solomon, answering the question in his eyes. "It's going to be all right, my son. We will join our brothers in Mahanaim and refresh ourselves beyond the Jordan." I reach over and tip his chin. "We will sleep in peace and wake again, sustained by Adonai."

And then I will send out my fiercest warriors into the forests of Ephraim.

After my son.

# FORTY-THREE

## *Mephi*

———————— ◆ ————————

I strap on my father's armor, piece by piece, refusing to believe I'm as trapped as I feel. By the time darkness chokes the room, I'm sure I know what's happened. They've left me. Ziba has taken his sons and gone after David, no doubt preparing some excuse to offer the king for my absence.

What I can't figure out is what they've done with my family. I never should have let them out of my sight. I'm an idiot, letting Ziba spin some story about reclaiming the throne. Recrimination fuels the fire in my chest, burning hotter each hour I'm left alone.

I'm no traitor to David. I should be with him. Why am I here?

When someone opens the door in the morning, I'm waiting with my bow aimed at it. But I don't recognize the man who enters. When he sees me, he drops the food he's carrying and flattens himself against the wall.

"Who are you?" I shout, making him cringe. "Where's Ziba?"

"I'm only his servant," he mumbles, staring down the shaft of my arrow. "He'll return soon."

"Where's my wife and my son?" I rise up onto my knees, and the servant edges into the hall, catching my arrow with the door.

I curse, sitting back on my heels. If I'd shot the man, I'd be free right now. But then what? The doors downstairs are probably guarded, and I can't crawl to the stables with soldiers everywhere.

I lean back against the wall and cover my self-hatred with prayers for my family. I refuse to see them suffer for my inability. We should've stayed closer to David. We should've left with him the moment he decided to go. Why didn't he summon me?

The question weakens my resolve the longer I consider it. Even if David no longer favors me, he still had to know what he was doing leaving me behind. I grind my teeth. I can't walk. He always forgets. Even I forget, allowing myself to believe I'm as capable as I've always wanted to be. But I'm not.

No one opens the door again for three days. The servant left plenty of food, but I only eat to keep my strength up. I force my scattered thoughts into a plan, rehearsing it until confidence emerges. With the bow, I can fight my way out of here and hide until I reach the stables. Once I can get on a mule, I'll ride after David, and he'll help me find my family.

It's madness. But I have no choice. I fill my quiver with as many arrows as it can hold, and sleep with my bow across my lap.

The next time the door opens, it crashes into the wall, flung aside. Japhia, Shaphat, and Azarel march into the room, wearing heavy royal robes. Their golden armbands flash the sunrise into my face.

I sit up, startled. "What are you doing here?" They should be halfway to Mahanaim by now.

Japhia folds his arms, burying his hands within thick purple sleeves. "We stand with whoever Israel has chosen, and right now, I would think it's obvious. Absalom has sent for you."

My stomach drops. "He's not pursuing the king?"

Offense tightens Japhia's face. "Absalom is king now. He's come back to Jerusalem to consult with Ahithophel."

"David's advisor?" This isn't good. Ahithophel's counsel has been esteemed like the advice of a prophet for decades. If he's helping Absalom, then David could be in serious trouble.

Japhia's eyes darken. "Ahithophel is Bathsheba's grandfather. What do you think is coursing through him right now?"

I rotate my bow, pulling my quiver close. "I have no allegiance to Absalom."

Azarel's calmness mocks the desperation squeezing the room. "He's more similar to you than you think. You both know what it's like to live in exile, cut off from what should have been yours. I would go now, peacefully. He only wants to speak with you."

Then why lock me in the fortress? I hesitate, but Azarel's next words set me on fire.

"His general Amasa has already brought your family before him."

"Take me to him, then." If Kezi and Mica are with Absalom, the decision's been made for me.

I ride to Jerusalem surrounded by Ziba's sons, but their father is nowhere in sight. Zion wears a heaviness I've never seen before. A wailing chorus smears the city walls, and men in sackcloth huddle in their doorways, heads bowed. A few of them glare at me, spitting when I ride past. "Traitor," one mutters.

I tense in the saddle, keeping one hand on my bow at all times. I have to prove them wrong. A strange thunder rumbles at the edge of the city, and I shudder. *Are you seeing this, Yahweh? Are you listening?*

At the door of David's house, Absalom's Ishmaelite general waits with half a battalion to greet me. His black eyes take in my armor, snapping dangerously. "He won't need all of that. Take it off him," he orders the guards who strip my weapons, carrying them inside behind me.

Amasa's men haul me up the stairs circling David's throne room. Absalom is waiting in an upper antechamber where a glass etching takes up most of one wall. I'm repulsed to see him wearing one of his father's scarlet robes. He's deep in conversation with one of David's closest friends, an older man I've seen in court many times. Absalom is chastising him in that honeyed tone I despise.

"I don't know how I feel about having such a double-minded man at my side, Hushai. Why didn't you go with your friend, the king?"

I'm disgusted by Hushai's answer. "I will stand with whomever Adonai chooses. As I have served your father, so I will serve you. I can only assume that's what he wanted after leaving Jerusalem."

My stomach clenches, protests warring behind my lips. Hushai speaks as though Yahweh approves of Absalom's rebellion. Why would He? Why did David leave?

Ahithophel's gaze shifts, and Absalom follows it to me. He waves the two men off, but Hushai's face turns as gray as his beard when he notices me.

Absalom lifts his hands. "You don't bow?"

The soldier at my back shoves me, and my knees crash into the floor. Absalom's approach makes my skin crawl. "Unlike Hushai, I know you're not here for me." Stopping in front of me, he calls, "Guards!"

Three armed men push my wife and son into the room, and a sharp pain explodes behind my eyes, spinning my vision out of control. Their hands are bound, but what's worse is the terror eating through their expressions.

I rise up onto my knees, shouting, "Let them go! They've done nothing to you!"

I look into Absalom's face, and fear grips every vein in my body, laying each one raw. It was the worst mistake of my life to stay here with him. He's dead behind the eyes. There's absolutely nothing in him that wants to show mercy. A raging tempest rushes into my face, and I hiss against tears. *"What do you want?"*

Absalom lifts his chin. "From you? Nothing at all." Without moving his gaze, he orders the guards, "Take them."

"Abba—" Mica shudders, on the edge of panic.

I push toward him, tension biting through me. I can't let them go.

Absalom's hand in my chest forces me back against the floor. "Where are you going, Cripple?"

"You'd be surprised," I snarl. Burning like two coals trapped in my face, my eyes go past him to the bow on the floor. I'm enveloped in fury, but in the center of the storm, I'm trembling, pleading. *Yahweh, spare them! They've done nothing!*

"Look at you." A disgusting laugh shudders through Absalom. "You hate me. As useless as that is."

I catch a wild breath between my teeth. Maybe I can still reason with him. "I don't hate you. You confuse me. Your father loves you. He wants to spare you."

"How merciful of him." Absalom's laugh drips bitter poison. We both know if he survives his own rebellion, he'll live in exile or under house arrest, and eventually, it will be Solomon who determines his fate. *God, let it be Solomon.*

Absalom carries that for several paces, back and forth, before looking back at me. "If my father was really able to control his soldiers, then your uncle and Abner would still be alive. Joab would have made you like one of them without blinking."

"I know that."

His teeth emerge in a knowing smile. "That's why you love my father. Because your life would be nothing without him."

"You're wrong." The old pain broods in the dark corners of my heart, but I know better now. David's taught me better. David and Yahweh.

Absalom paces, his hands folded behind him. "What have you ever given my father, apart from a broken image of the friend he idolized? You're the fulfillment of a debt. Nothing more."

"What if I am?" I force it over the bitterness in my throat. Absalom has never experienced the alternative. That's why he's so able to despise what he's always had. "Is that supposed to make me wish for his death?"

His eyes go dark, blackness smearing over the deep brown. "You think I'm trying to win you over? Mark my words, son of Jonathan, you have nothing that I want." He turns and kicks the bow across the floor toward me. "Go ahead. Shoot me for the honor of Benjamin. Save your family. And the king will never see your face again."

Powerful dread grips my stomach, battling with the anger building there. I want to do it. But he's right. Nothing would be the same. Even if David forgave me, our bond would be destroyed.

Absalom's foot pushes a loose arrow up against my knee, circling like a vulture. "Go on, clumsy filth. Take your best shot."

I breathe in deeply, my teeth set. *He's baiting you. Don't give in.*

He steps around in front of me. "Wake up, son of Saul. That Benjaminite rage must be in there somewhere."

Somewhere? It's consuming me. I feel its breath in every inch of my body—the teeth of a wolf ready to strike.

Absalom glances over his shoulder. "Maybe I'll take your wife to the roof with the other concubines."

Fire devours my senses, and my arms stretch over my head, pulling the bow taut in his direction. The shot should be easy, but I have to wait for the flames to subside. They're pushing into my vision, blurring my focus.

Absalom edges to the side of the room. The glass etching takes up most of the wall to his left, giving him the appearance of an evil spirit in double. A frantic breath pushes through the grind of my teeth, and I blink, trying to see him.

*David's son. David's son. David's son.*

But I can't see that. I only see evil. Two evil eyes glittering through the curtain of his hair.

He spreads his arms, clearly unafraid. "Don't worry. You'll miss. And then I'm going to kill David and send him to sleep with his fathers, a forgotten, meaningless relic. Like yours."

The shout that tears through me releases the arrow. But my shaking arms wobble the shot to the right, and it sails over Absalom's shoulder, spearing the glass. The piercing sound explodes in the room as millions of tiny shards splinter onto the floor like pieces of a frozen waterfall.

My shaken pride grabs hold of the instant of shock on Absalom's face and devours it. Seconds later though, he's laughing. Heartily. Gasping with confidence.

His guards enter without being summoned. They grab my arms and bend me forward to bind my wrists behind me.

"Aide?" Absalom calls outside.

My heart is still galloping out of control, but it freezes in my chest when Ziba walks into the room.

Absalom waves his hand. "Take this traitor to the roof. I'll deal with him after my father knows what he is."

"He knows." Ziba's voice sends lightning through my head.

Absalom places a hand on Ziba's arm. "I've ordered no one to pursue you. Ride in the morning with your sons and stay in one of Benjamin's cities until I return."

Ziba's eyes barely touch me before snapping back to the floor. But it's long enough for me to see all the years unfolding to this moment. He didn't know how it would happen, what king would give him the opportunity. But he planned how to be on the opposite side, looking down at me like this.

Halfway out of the room, he pivots to face Absalom. "I would advise you not to waste his death. Use it."

The guards drag me into the hall, restraining my fury while Ziba stalks through a side door.

"May the God of David judge between you and me!" I shout after him, blinded by rage. Yahweh sees him. He always has.

A man's knee in my back flattens me and other hands yank me back up. It keeps happening until I've been dragged down the outer corridor, across the battlements, and up the stairs to the palace roof. The unknown guards drop me near the top, letting my jaw collide with the stone step.

I've never seen these men before, but they must be the traitors Absalom's been amassing in his secret gatherings. Why didn't I realize that Ziba would attend those meetings? He always knew or at least suspected Absalom would come out on top.

Now, Ziba will paint me as the traitor, and if David withdraws his favor, I won't survive this. Absalom has no reason to keep me alive. My only hope is if David doesn't believe the lies. But who am I fooling? David's already seen Ziba ride out to meet him while I stayed behind. How did that look?

A large tent takes up most of the palace roof, its heavy canvas walls bending and snapping in the unsteady wind. Absalom's guard opens a short wooden door to a narrow partition in the opposite corner. Another man seizes my hair and manhandles me through the slanted opening, kicking me over onto my side.

Beyond him, I see women being brought up onto the roof, one by one, and all the blood leaves my face when I recognize the ten concubines David left behind. When I see Absalom step onto the roof with his robe over his arm, I realize that he doesn't plan to torture me physically. Nathan's prophecy burns in my ears, and Absalom's brought me here to listen to it unfold.

He turns to the nearest trembling woman and points at my cell. "If any one of you touches this door, you'll hang on the wall with him tomorrow," he threatens before Amasa slams a wooden bar over the front, trapping me inside.

"Let them go, so help me God!" I shout, my voice breaking. "You miserable, Godforsaken son of…" *David!*

How can David's son be causing all this torment? How can this be happening?

My wrists writhe, but the ropes just pull tighter. I claw at them anyway, my fingers bending unnaturally to pick at the knots. My wife's and son's faces scorch my mind the way the women's cries are scalding my ears. Bound, I can't even cover my face. I can't tear my clothes. I can't free myself or anyone else.

"Yahweh!" I scream, unleashing every inch of unsatisfied rage that's trapped in my feet. It burns my jaw, breaking open into anguish that barely drowns out what I'm hearing.

*Yahweh, what can I do? Just tell me what to do!*

I force my knees under me and ram my shoulder into the rotting door, fully aware of what will happen if I get it open.

I'll die.

The reality hits me hard, chilling my resolve. To die fighting would be more honorable than waiting for Absalom to finish with the women and turn on me. But, the thought of leaving my family defenseless freezes my blood.

*David!*

I want to curse him, and I want to cry out for him. He should have killed Absalom when he had the chance, not flee like an outlaw! Ziba was right. He's weak! I've pledged myself to a weak king, and now I'm suffering for it.

I pull violently at the ropes again, my wrists aching from the unnatural bend. David deserves to watch me die. He deserves to come back and find everyone dead and know that he did it. He failed us.

I hate him! I hate the anger that's turning me against him. Everything in me wants to fight rather than give in to it, but what else do I have? I cry out again, ramming my useless ankles against the door until it finally breaks open. But not because of me.

The guard behind it bends through the opening and buries his foot in my side until my lungs flatten and my breathing turns jagged in my chest. Finished, he strikes my head with the butt of his spear and leaves me with pain erupting in my body and the sounds of *Sheol* still clawing through my brain.

My head against the stone floor, my heartbeat pumps through my temples, and I gasp with relief, anticipating the loss of consciousness. Welcoming it. I can't breathe enough to scream anymore. The anguished cries just wander around the caverns inside me like harassed fugitives. My mind pulls strangely, and my sight blurs around the grinding of my ribs.

But when the sounds mute, my sight doesn't disappear. I'm immersed in a strange brightness, surrounded by forest. The low hum of distant battle lurks on the periphery, but I can't see the fighting. All I see is a tree, its thick bark bleeding. And myself, bound against it. Blood smears my side, flushing the edges of my garment.

Upright without crutches, I stand there looking at myself at thirteen. The most desperate and helpless I'd ever been up to that point. But my attackers are nowhere to be found. The moonlight is filling my face, and I'm watching it through the trees. My lips move, saying the Name of the One who'd saved me that night. The One who's standing at a distance now.

*Yahweh.*

"He's right here, Mephi," I hear someone say. "All this time, He's had His eyes on you, and He reached ahead of all of us to save you."

It's David's words. But it's not his voice.

The branches part, and a six-foot warrior steps into the clearing. A thick tangle of hair sweeps his shoulders, and a dark beard spreads in the widest smile I've ever seen. The boy at the tree is gone. The man is looking directly at me.

"Abba?" I lose my breath around the word. I don't know how it's possible, but I know it's him.

He reaches out a hand, and I see the seal ring. "Mephi."

What happens next is strange. I see myself run to him. Still watching from a distance, I don't feel his arms come up around me. And yet, it's the most satisfying embrace I've ever known.

I breathe in, smelling spices. In that moment, I spot the arrow wound in his shoulder, and I remember how he used to touch it in prayer. It's really him!

I grip his shoulders, every muscle shaking. "Abba, don't leave. I need you." Such simple words for the yearning that's tearing me apart. I can't do this without him. I can't fight for my people the way he could. I couldn't even ride out after my king in his moment of trouble. I'm terrified that I might be as worthless as Ziba always said.

My father looks at me, eye to eye, and I realize that I'm almost his exact height. He holds the sides of my face as I've seen David do with his sons. "You don't need me. Not anymore." He sounds immensely relieved, not an ounce of regret in his voice. His words are warm and sweet, like honey.

I cling to him, afraid he'll go. "But what can I do? Who am I to be here with David?" My voice breaks, and I feel the fissure in my chest widening. "It should have been me on Gilboa. You should have stayed."

Pain enters Jonathan's face like a flicker of firelight. Gone in a flash. He smiles again. "Moses said the same. *Who am I?* Yahweh's answer put his focus back where it belonged. On Him. The One who is with you now."

My chest is heaving, but I'm afraid to breathe. "Yahweh's with me? Truly?"

The moment I ask, His presence pours into the forest, filling the trees with the sound of armies marching. Abba hears it too. Tilting his head up, he closes his eyes around a peaceful grin. "I love that sound."

So do I. The *hakkodesh* unlocks my heartbeat, spinning it free. In that moment, I know it was the unction that called my father into his battles. It was the rushing in David's veins at Elah. And now, it's come for me. If I have the courage to answer.

I press my forehead into Jonathan's, holding onto my father one last time.

He disappears the next time I blink, but someone is still holding onto me, keeping me on my feet.

Then, I feel the floor. I hear the harsh hissing of night insects, smell the sharp breath of incense riding the evening breeze. Several women's voices fold together in soft weeping.

My lungs fill, forcing me awake. I'm back. But David isn't. He's far away on the hills, running again. The way he did when my father helped him escape. But this time, he can't stay away. We need him to come back.

I roll over onto my knees, pain swimming in my head. "Please, Yahweh! Rescue him. Shield him. Bring him back to the city you promised to give to his descendents."

It's not like it was with Saul. Our God has treated David like a son, promising him a kingdom that would continue forever if he kept after His heart. And as far as I can see, David has not departed from pursuing Adonai. He has crashed and burned, but he's still holding onto the God of Israel, trusting Him for what's ahead.

"You won't fail him, will you, Yahweh?" I clench against unbelief, tears anointing my fists before dripping onto the floor. "He's more than my king. He's like an angel of God. No one else could have done what he did for me. I can't lose him too!"

Prostrate on the ground, I let my heart bleed into the floor. "Forgive me for turning away from him. Away from you." Yahweh and David both refused to leave me, even when I thought they had. Lifting up onto my knees, I present my resolve to God as the only offering I have.

"I vow to you, Adonai, if you bring David back safely to Jerusalem to rule Israel once more, I will spend the rest of my life in his service. With no fear. As a son."

Without Saul's bitterness trying to claim my future. Without Ziba's voice in my head urging me to grasp at what doesn't belong to me. My father's grin warms my mind, the wind of Yahweh's armies filling every aching corner of it.

I'm not what I was. I'm not a wounded beggar fighting for scraps, or a jealous prince scheming for position.

And I'm not an orphan anymore.

# FORTY-FOUR

## Mephi

———◆———

The scraping of wood against stone rouses me. I turn onto my side, and sunlight stabs my eyes before being blocked by a woman's body. A tear-stained face appears above mine, and one of David's concubines bends over. I hear her short, tight breathing while she slides something sharp under the ropes, freeing my hands.

"Tikvah, what are you doing?" I look behind her for the guards, but the roof is empty.

"Hushai sent me." She wrings her hands, barely holding herself together. I try not to stare at the bruises climbing her arms.

"Hushai betrayed David." I sit up, anger rising with each throb of my head.

"No, he's been helping us," she hisses, shaking. "The king left him here to learn Absalom's plans. He lured the guards away so I could help you. They're out chasing Ahimaaz and Jonathan. You have to leave before they return."

Tears roll down her face, and the terror in her eyes eats into me. "What Absalom did was for my lord's benefit. Flaunting his control over what belongs to the king. He wants to do the same with you. I heard him. He'll slaughter you on the city wall for the king to see if he returns. You have to get out, now."

The door to the roof opens, and Hushai appears, followed by several servants. "Tikvah, get downstairs," he beckons, but I catch her wrist.

"Thank you," I say into her eyes before she skitters off.

I'm already being lifted up, supported by two giant Ethiopian men. Hushai points toward the palace. "Your mule is in the courtyard. We'll get you down to it, and then I'll take you to my house. Your wife and son are hiding there."

Gratitude sears my lungs. "Where's Ahithophel?"

Hushai grimaces. "Hanging himself. One of my servants followed him. I didn't leave until I was certain Absalom would take my advice and not his, however unlikely that was. David must be praying."

"He's not the only one." I look into the old man's face, deeply shaken. "Thank you."

Hushai's eyes flood. I know he wishes he could have done more. But there's no time.

"What will happen when Absalom discovers I'm gone?" I ask him as we ride to his house at the edge of Joab's property.

Hushai shakes his head. "He's ridden out after David with the units he's armed. The king may remain in hiding, but he will not fail to answer a deliberate challenge. Joab won't let that young man return here except in chains."

*Yahweh, let it be so!*

The fierce hope pushes pain through my bruised ribs. How foolish I was to believe the king wouldn't fight! He'd refused to kill Saul and still won. Yet, the subsequent battles had dragged on for years, opening our lands to foreign enemies. *Not again, Adonai. Let this be won quickly!*

I'm unprepared for the sudden sweetness of Yahweh's presence rushing my veins. I'll never forget the powerful peace that had taken hold of me in my dream. My eyes flood in response, but I know what I have to do now.

Hushai brings me down to the basement chambers of his house, and Kezi and Mica burst into tears, flinging themselves at me. We embrace on the floor, my heart breaking with joy that they're safe.

"I can't believe you're here!" Kezi sobs, and I touch her face, dreading to tell her what I've planned. But I know it deep in my bones.

I hid during the war between Saul and David, believing I had no purpose. But I've learned different. I'm not meant to sit quiet during this one.

"Hushai, where's my armor?" I ask him while his servants bind my bruised ribs.

"It's still in the antechamber where Absalom arrested you," Hushai answers, frowning.

"Have someone bring it here."

"Mephi—" Kezi protests, but I reach for my son.

"Mica, come here." My heartbeat scatters as Mica kneels in front of me. The tremor in his face makes me sick. I take both his arms and look into his eyes. "My son, do you believe that Yahweh is with David?"

Mica nods, his eyes huge.

"Do you believe Yahweh is with me?"

He nods again, pressing his lips tight. He looks so much like his mother, but in that moment, I'm able to find someone else in his eyes. If only Abba could have met him. But Yahweh has given me a father in the king of Israel, and it's time for me to stand with him. As best I can.

I press my forehead against Mica's. "Then, do you believe I will come back safely?"

This time, he just throws his arms around me. In the tightness of our embrace, I remember how my father hugged me goodbye. Before Gilboa. Now, I know what it was like for him to do that.

But it's different this time. Yahweh's *chesed* is at my shoulder like the warmth of the sunrise, promising that this is the right course. Sunrise. I have to move.

"As soon as I find out if Ahimaaz and Jonathan are safe, I'll follow you with some of my guards," Hushai promises, his face calm. "The more weapons at your side, the better. Either way, try to stay clear of the fighting."

Still weeping, Kezi kisses me. "What are you going to do?"

I finger her face, memorizing it. "I'm going to find my father."

———————◆◆◆◆◆———————

I should relax once I've cleared Zion's walls without being spotted, but the fist of fear is tight around my throat. Gibeah is next, and I'll have to keep to the hills if I don't want to meet any Benjaminites. I cross a low point in the stream and ride hard across Saul's back fields, heading straight for the rocky wilds that broke me as a child.

The ground tilts sharply, and my mule scrambles up the steep embankment, sending pain through my ribs. I lean forward, adjusting my weight while the uneven terrain crumbles beneath us. At the top, there's a semblance of a path, but water rushes nine feet below me, and sharp boulders push up from the riverbed. This is what Ama had tried to traverse in the dark, holding me. But I can see my way now. And Yahweh's leading me.

I've never believed that before, but it's fueling me now, guiding me up toward the side of the hill to avoid the drop-off. In another mile, the landscape plunges into valley before lifting toward the mountains again.

Hugging the Mount of Olives to avoid the main roads, I push north into Ephraim's territory, every grisly war story riding out to meet me. My own kinsmen fell in these forests, fighting David.

The sounds of battle wind through the thicket, reaching me before I'm ready. Screams and clashes pierce the air. Arrows slam into trees. It's like I'm riding into my own dreams. But this time, David won't be there.

I tug the mule left, then right, trying to listen, trying to decide where to go. I have to get around the fighting, find my way to the road that follows the river north. The wailing up ahead twists my nerves, and the mule sidesteps, nearly sending me out of the saddle to avoid a heavy tree branch hanging over the path. It sounds as though the forest is devouring men.

Bowing flat, I duck between two cedars, but a wild, terrible scream pulls my attention to the east.

I whip the mule's head around and thread between the clinging branches. How is anyone fighting in this tangle? The giant oak to my right is thicker than two of me, but on the other side of it, a heavy body swings into view. A man is hanging from the tree by his hair, armored legs kicking, mouth open screaming. His thick black locks are twisted around a low branch, and his hands are clawing at them. It's Absalom.

The jolt of horror is almost enough to break my balance. I ride into the thicket as fast as I dare, my pulse driving up under my ribs. Trapped up there, he's an easy target. But David doesn't want him dead. The soldiers can capture him and end this right now!

The two armies spill over the next rise, iron and bronze slamming into each other for half a mile. I draw my sword and bend low, searching for faces in the fray. I can't stay exposed for long, but the commanders can't be far. A few feet off, a man leaps from a higher rock, only to be impaled on a long spear. Twelve armorbearers swarm him, finishing him off.

"Joab!" I shout over the sounds of battle.

Joab curses, whipping his horse around. "What are you doing here?"

"Following David."

Blood drips from beneath Joab's helmet. "David is safe. Do you think he needs a crippled man to defend him? Get out of here before Absalom sees you."

"He already did." Eleazar grimaces, riding up behind me. "He's back there, hanging from a tree by his hair."

His words freeze the rage on Joab's face. "You saw him?" he screams, his eyes bulging. "Why didn't you strike him? Do you know how much I would have given you for taking him down?"

"How could I do that?" Eleazar's face twists with offense. "Even if I felt in my hand the weight of a thousand silver pieces, I wouldn't strike the king's son. David commanded us to spare him. We all heard it."

The memory of my arrow sailing over Absalom's shoulder claws my throat. Thank God I'd missed. David's lost too much. He'll never forgive the man who strikes Absalom.

"Is no one able to think clearly anymore?" Joab roars. "He's an *enemy!* Our lives mean nothing to him. Just kill him!"

Eleazar's response oozes sarcasm. "I suppose if I had turned against David himself, you would have stood aloof."

Dread pierces my chest. "He's right, Joab. Send your men to capture him, but spare his life."

"Enough!" Joab's eyes have turned to fire. "You think I rode out here to waste time with the likes of you?"

He pulls his horse around, ready to charge into the thicket.

Gripped with alarm, I shove my mule in his way. "Don't be crazy, Joab. The king loves him!"

I lift my sword to deflect his aim, but his spear strikes my weapon from my grasp. With my reins in a death grip in one hand, I reach for the spear on my back, but the flat of Joab's javelin slams into my chest instead. My ribs crack, and I jerk from the saddle, hitting the ground hard, every bit of air crushed from my body.

Light and dark spin the forest into inconceivable shapes, and my heartbeat turns into an anvil, slamming into the bones Joab broke, driving me further and further into the ground.

The last thing I hear is Absalom screaming.

Jagged pain combs through my sides, crowding out every other sensation, but gradually, I feel the pine-needled grass under my hands. Folded cloaks are bunched under me, one covering the rock under my head. The sinking sun is wrapped around the tree trunks, and smoke stains the air. A fire crackles nearby, and David's men are moving back and forth across the clearing, tying weapons onto horses, lifting the wounded onto biers.

If I didn't know better, I would think we suffered defeat. No one gives orders, no one celebrates. Every man who walks by is either limping or bleeding. Several are still stretched out on the ground.

I turn my head, groaning, and Hushai leans over. He's crouched against a tree next to me. "Don't sit up," he says. "Your ribs are broken. So is your collarbone. It's going to be a painful ride back to Jerusalem."

"Jerusalem?" I squint. "Isn't David up in Mahanaim?"

Hushai's face is drawn down, all the sparkle gone from his friendly eyes. "We're going back to Zion. It won't be long before the king returns now that…" He clasps his hands around his knees, and a fist folds into my chest.

"Absalom's dead?"

Hushai tightens his lips, nodding. "They tossed him in a pit and covered it with stones. He was…not to be seen." The old man breathes twice, tears appearing. "I was there when he was born. I'll never understand why he did this, but the king loved him." He wipes his eyes with his sleeve.

My swallow sticks in my throat. "Joab?"

Hushai nods again. "He sent a Cushite servant north with the news. It won't be long before David knows." His gaze hardens into the clearing. "Odds are, someone else will be leading the army by the time we return." Shaking free of whatever gruesome image imprisons him, Hushai pushes to his feet. "I'll get my servants to pitch a tent. Try not to move too much. We'll leave in the morning."

I couldn't agree more. David will have enough to bear with this news.

And I won't be the one to tell him.

# FORTY-FIVE

## *David*

—————◆◆◆◆◆◆——————

In the upper room above Mahanaim's gate, tattered breaths pull from my lungs. In and out. Refusing to stop, even though I have no more strength. The tempest that's chased me down since my youth has finally found a way inside me, and nothing has been left standing.

After losing Jonathan, I'd thought I was finished with grief. Nothing worse would hurt me that deeply ever again. But I was wrong. This is it. This is the wound that will never heal.

*Absalom, my son. My son!*

Even after what he did, I can't see him as anything else. This wasn't how his life was meant to end. And I'm afraid of my own going on like this. When they told me Absalom was dead, everything else dropped off a cliff inside me. Every reason to live was dragged out of sight, crushed under the news.

Amnon's death had been softened by the wickedness of his crime. Absalom had reason to be angry. Back then, I'd lived on the hope that my fierce son would come back to me.

But now, he won't. And such a large part of me has died with him that I don't know how to take my next breath. I'm terrified to live like this. I don't even know how to pray. I can't form any words except his name. Absalom. My son. *My son.*

I barely notice the door crashing open, but I recognize the vehemence behind it.

Joab's voice cuts through the room, striking my bowed head. "What are you doing?"

I drag myself from the ground, my swollen eyes struggling to focus.

I haven't seen anyone since the news came. Machir and the others have left me alone. But my oldest nephew's vitriol has always been able to uncover me wherever I'm hiding, find a way to force me into the open. His expression volcanic, Joab storms across the room and stands over me.

"Don't you realize that your kingdom has been returned to you? No. You don't care. You'd be happy if Absalom were alive and all of us were dead."

I don't even have the strength to flinch, let alone argue. Everything has been crushed out of me. I have nothing left to offer him. And Joab knows it.

He paces, his teeth grinding. "For years, I have been silent. I was silent while you risked our lives to spare Saul. I was silent when you brought his grandson to the palace. But this is going to cost you, David ben Jesse." He gestures between us, incensed. "Every servant and soldier who fought for your life is now burdened by your grief, crawling back in shame to *your city!* The city they reclaimed for you."

He flings his arms. "Even that cripple pursued you after you abandoned him. But how long do you think that loyalty will last when you love those who hate you and hate those who love you? Now, get up on your feet and say something to the men before they leave, or mark my words, you will have no one left by nightfall!"

I stare at him and let the coals in his eyes burn me. I've seen this coming. For years, I've felt all the fuel building between us, waiting for the day it would sweep into a blaze that would scorch us both. I'd seen it in his eyes. Everyone he wanted to eliminate to pave the way for my kingship.

I'd thought commanding him would be enough to subdue his rage, or at least redirect it. Even now that his brutality has finally caught up to me, it's still so hard to fathom that my own general would have deliberately pushed me over the edge.

But he has.

A brief shiver of insanity pierces my mind, and I wonder whether he plans to kill me too. Right here. Take the kingdom the way he threatened to take Rabbah when I wouldn't fight. But the thought passes with a maddening flash of resignation.

I am king. Even broken, I have to keep going. For Israel. This is part of what kept Jonathan moving through all the torment, what kept Saul clinging to an illusion of power, even as it faded.

Except, I have Yahweh.

The thought should bring more comfort than it does. He's given me back the kingdom, but how does He view me now? Is there anything left inside me that pleases Him?

Jonathan's voice groans in my mind. *When you fail, repent. Cling to Yahweh and don't let go.*

I lean into my hands and knees, trying to stand. I'll do what I must. I'll remember Adonai's voice. I'll return to Jerusalem, stand before the Ark, and hear Yahweh's acceptance in the cries of Israel. I'll learn how to sing again, except the songs will be different.

Songs. Soft musical notes touch my ears, and I glance around Joab, wondering why I didn't hear them before.

Joab slaps the door open with his hand and leaves, nearly knocking Solomon down in the hall.

When I see my youngest son standing on the threshold with my harp, the grief that spins through my head nearly flattens me again. With the last ounce of strength I have, I open my arms and he comes into them, holding onto the lyre behind my back. He's worried, terrified even. But how do I explain? Being a father has hurt me worse than anything else I've suffered.

"Adonai is your glory, the lifter of your head," my son whispers into my shoulder, and I hold him closer, raindrops of gratitude trickling down into the pit of my despair.

I thought I knew how to prepare Solomon for his time on the throne. Now, I worry that the mantle is less about nobility, fighting skills, strategy. It's more about wisdom. The ability to discern friends from enemies, to acknowledge Yahweh's voice over any other.

And it's about endurance. Staying faithfully fixed on the path ahead even when you have to pick up the pieces of your own heart and keep moving.

Completely broken.

# FORTY-SIX

## *Mephi*

———◆———

*A month later*

I don't need to be told when David returns. Jerusalem erupts with joyful praise, exuberant songs lifting over the walls to greet the king when he passes through the gates.

Weak from fasting, I don't move from the chamber in Hushai's house until he comes for me. The relief filling the old man's face is enough to erase most of the anxiety and pain I've suffered for weeks, staying hidden while my ribs healed and the tribes argued about bringing David back.

The priests had confronted the men of Judah, asking why the king's own kinsmen would be so hesitant to help him return. Pressured, the elders had finally traveled beyond the Jordan to accompany David home, along with a considerable group from Benjamin.

Apparently, Shemei had met them at Nob and begged David's forgiveness. The last I heard was that David had promised to spare him, vowing that there would be no more death now that he was returning to Zion.

Hushai struggles against thankful tears. "He's with the priests now, offering sacrifices before the Lord. It would seem our prayers have been answered."

Behind my cracked ribs, my heart tightens. Kezi and Mica have gone out to join the celebration in the streets, looking for Machir and Ama, but I won't be seen in public until the king and I have made peace.

"I need to see him." I lift my eyes, tentative. "Do you think he'll receive me?"

Hushai chews his lip. "I think he will. But you know Ziba and his family went ahead to bring him back over the Jordan. He gave them everything, Mephi."

"I heard." I swallow. It won't be easy to convince David out of whatever lie Ziba has spun concerning me. Not after what he's seen. Fortunately, I'm a fighter, and this is one battle I plan to win. "I want to see him."

Hushai's servants bring me around the back way to the palace, cutting through the fields to avoid the main roads. But my first obstacle is the new general the king has appointed in Joab's place. Amasa serves David now, but the sight of him still sends lightning through my body.

"What are you doing here?" he demands, blocking my way.

"I'm here to see my king."

"Like that?" Amasa eyes me scornfully.

My robe is still torn from the battle, but I haven't changed it. I haven't washed or eaten since I rode out after David. But what does it matter? This is exactly the way I arrived in Jerusalem years ago.

Swinging my leg over the mule, I lean on a servant, only to lose my balance and land hard on my knees on the stone porch. It's a while before I can breathe around the knife-edged darts of pain.

"Let me see him, please."

Amasa rotates his spear, touching my broken collarbone with it. "You have no right to speak to the king. After what you plotted with Shemei, you should be in prison."

"Let the king put me there himself, then." I look down the spear into Amasa's eyes. After what he's already done, he won't spill any more blood without David's permission.

His mouth twisting, Amasa gestures for the servants to help me. The walls close over my head, and I let myself remember being carried over this same threshold more than a decade ago. Back then, I hadn't needed to prove myself. It was enough to be Jonathan's son. But now, I'm facing the king as myself.

No tribal affinities, no covenantal heritage, no gifts. Just me.

The main corridor is empty. Notes from a harp drift into the hall, and David is sitting on the top step beside his throne, bent over, playing. My heart leaps in my chest, speared by a joy I've only felt with one other man.

"My king?"

David's fingers stop, but the melody echoes, sliding into the walls around him. He descends the rest of the steps while the servants help me forward, placing me at his feet. I swallow my fear, bowing with my face hidden. We've come full circle.

David doesn't waste any words. "Why didn't you go with me, Mephibosheth?"

My heart folds in half, hearing how much that hurt him. I haven't planned what to say, and I don't know what I'll do if he doesn't understand. I breathe a few times into the floor, and David's tone softens.

"Look at me, son."

I sit up, forgetting to cover my wince. The pain in my collarbone still takes my breath.

Frowning, David touches my bandages, visible through my torn robe. "What happened?"

"Joab," I say without thinking.

Anger wrestles aside the anguish in David's eyes. He looks down. "He said you came after me. Why would you do that when you failed to go with Ziba?"

I fist my hands against the floor, wishing I could crush Ziba's lies with my grip. The truth is so much simpler than everything he tried to spin in my mind before abandoning me. I force myself to look up.

"I never wanted to stay with Absalom. You're my king, and I belong at your side."

David nods several times, chewing the inside of his mouth while tears gather in his eyes. "Ziba said you conspired against me with the sons of Benjamin. That you wanted revenge on me. For Saul." He looks like he hates saying it. He folds his arms. "You won't defend yourself?"

Anger rushes into my eyes, but I refuse to break his gaze. *Yahweh, help him see!*

"Ziba deceived me, my king. I thought he would help me ride out after you, but he left me and I was unable to follow him because…" I sigh, gripping one ankle.

I won't be able to forget that night on the roof anytime soon. But my ride into the forest also glimmers in my mind. David knows my legs don't hold me back anymore. Not like they used to. I played into Ziba's hands. He exploited the weakness he found in me.

I breathe in sharply and pain bends my vision. "I never planned to conspire against you. But I was so angry when you wouldn't fight. I thought you were abandoning Jerusalem to Absalom. I thought you didn't care if I lost another father." The words cut my breath in half. "I thought we were losing you. But it was me. I was the one who was lost, and you…you went after me even though you had many other sons."

I'm rambling, grappling for what I really want to say. Whether he believes me or not, this is the truth.

David lifts his brows. "Is there any chance you're trying to get Saul's land back? You know I gave it all to Ziba."

I drop my hands. He still thinks this is about riches?

"What right do I have to cry to you about wealth, my king? My entire family was doomed to death at your hands, and yet you lifted me up to your side and made me like one of your sons. You've been a messenger of God in my life, and that's more than I ever had any right to hope for."

I pause while David broods in the silence, struggling to believe. When he answers me, it's not with the confidence I was hoping for. "Why speak of it anymore? You and Ziba can divide Saul's land."

He turns away, but I shake my head. "No."

I didn't risk my life for another badly-mended truce. I reach out and catch the hem of David's robe. There's only one way to prove what my words can't.

"Let Ziba keep it all, my lord. It only matters to me that you've returned safely."

David turns around, and his eyes grab hold of mine. "Mephi…is that true?"

"It is. Abba."

David's face fills with emotion, like a river about to overflow its banks. He pulls it back, eying my bandages again. "Eleazar said you came upon Absalom in the forest and didn't strike him. Thank you."

His words are balanced at the edge of his control, and I watch him stumble over it. His shoulders shove forward, and he sinks to his knees, tears rolling down his face. Giving in, he slumps over onto the throne steps, sobbing heavily.

Pain chews through my side as I crawl up behind him. I lift his head onto my knee, letting his tears fill my hands. After several moments, his fingers move to my wrist, and his sobs twist into words that he repeats over and over. "Thank you. Thank you. My son."

Anguished relief leaps up inside me, and I bend over him, tightening my grip on his shoulders. I could never replace the sons he's lost. But I'm here, and he's grateful for that. He sees the miracle that's rescued us both, returned us to Zion, kept Israel united.

And I'm grateful.

Because I finally know where I belong, where I need to be. And my father, the king, finally knows that I'm not going anywhere.

# EPILOGUE

## *Mephi*

———————◆◆◆————————

*Three years later*

M y windows are shut.

For days, I've kept them closed, blocking out what's happening beyond them. I wouldn't see anything if I looked. I'm in Jerusalem, and the seven men facing execution are more than a mile away, in Gibeah. But the image of the deaths I won't witness still pushes into my mind, hardening the rock in my throat.

I've never met any of them. But I feel like I know them. Seven men guilty of the same thing I'm guilty of. Association with Saul. My aunt Merab's five sons. The two sons Rizpah bore to Saul as a concubine. One of them even shares my name. Saul's blood. My blood. And by nightfall, they'll hang on the walls of my grandfather's old city.

Since I heard the news, I've stayed locked away in my new house in Jerusalem, staring at the tiny spear of light cracking the shutters. Stunned into silence, even though I won't be joining them.

After Absalom's rebellion and the ensuing threats from Benjamin were quenched, the Gibeonites had emerged from hiding. They'd approached David and demanded the lives of Saul's remaining descendents. The wandering remnant of the Amorites was only one target of Saul's hatred. But the Canaanites have long memories. And Yahweh holds men to their vows.

For three years, famine has held the land in a pitiless grip. As with every crisis he's ever faced, personally or nationally, David sought the face of Adonai and discovered that Saul's bloodguilt against the Gibeonites still remained and would strip the land of its life until the broken vow was answered.

The Amorite elders had admitted their lack of authority to take lives at will, something their rogue followers hadn't understood when they'd taken me.

Bound against that tree with Becorath's knife at my throat, I'd thought Yahweh wanted me dead. I was afraid to face being cursed for Saul's sin, afraid to feel my life drain away in the dark. But Yahweh was watching that night. I didn't understand that His hatred for bloodshed was guarding me, as was the vow that my father and David had kept at the risk of their own lives.

That night, Yahweh had used my father to save me. Just as He's using David now.

Propped on a bench against the wall, I twirl my father's ring around my finger and stare at the two rubies David gave to Jonathan and then to me. Symbols of a decades-long covenant resting in my hand. It still amazes me how David and Jonathan thought ahead, but now I'm certain that it wasn't their own strength that held them to their promises. It wasn't their own honor that made them *neshama sheli.* It was the Lord our God.

Even though Saul chose to cast off Adonai's protection, Jonathan and David stayed under it. They stayed there because our God is worthy and good. But they also stayed there for me. Even without knowing I'd be crippled, they knew it would be a struggle for me to stand in the quicksand Saul had created. So, they'd given me a hand up, supporting me with their faith before I was ever aware of it.

I close my hand around the rubies, utterly amazed. Nothing's been wasted or coincidental. Nothing about Abba or David. Or me. Yahweh's had a plan for our good all along. That has to be enough.

Fatigue pulls at me, but I know I won't sleep until this night passes. I haven't even noticed how the light's disappeared from the shutters. The shadows have left the corners and consumed the room, and now the floor rumbles under me. Something crackles through the whole house, shuddering the walls with a deep, mountainous moan.

The sound fills my ears and chest, so I don't hear the footsteps approaching until the door opens. David stands there in riding clothes, a heavy black cloak draped over his red and gold robe. He's drenched, his wet hair tangled around the usual jeweled band. The lion medallion hanging over his chest glimmers in the dark, washed clean by rain.

Then it hits me. It's raining. For the first time in three years.

I look in David's eyes and something moves in my chest like a boulder breaking off a mountainside. The part of me that believed he might still sacrifice me. I had no idea it was still there, but it's gone now. The ache in my chest doubles, gratitude rushing in, and I close my eyes briefly, allowing it to cover any remaining survival guilt. Yahweh spared me for a reason.

I lean into a crutch to try to stand, but David crosses the room and lifts me up himself. I fold my fists in his robe and lean my head against his chest, every breath crashing through me like a wave.

David's arms tighten around my back. "It's done. I had the men of Jabesh-Gilead bury them with Saul and Jonathan's remains in the tomb of your great-grandfather Kish. The Gibeonites have no other claims on Israelite blood."

A tremor goes through me the same moment thunder grips the house. David tilts my face up, his voice shaky with relief. "Do you hear me? It's over. Look..."

Wrapping his arm around my waist, he turns me toward the window and throws open the shutters with his other hand. The wooden planks hit the stone sides of the walls, letting in a furious shower of rain. We're standing close enough to feel the spray, see the huge raindrops soaking the floor at our feet.

David smiles, a hint of youth playing around in his eyes again. My lungs ache with gratitude to see it. The years have broken us both, but Yahweh's fierce, joyful grip hasn't let us go.

David's arm encircles my shoulder. I slip my hand up behind his back to hold onto him. And we stand there marveling. None of us have been doing this alone. We haven't been victims of circumstance, lost sheep struggling to find our way.

Yahweh's been guiding our pursuit, opening the path before us and equipping us to follow Him when our strength failed. We always had everything we needed—safety, weapons, an Advocate. Even when enemies assailed us, we were on the winning side because we had Him.

Clinging to David, supported by his strength, I find I can actually brace with my feet against the ground and hold steady. For a few precious moments, I barely breathe, drinking in the feeling of my own height beside the king's. My own strength. Finally, I get up the courage and stretch out my free hand.

The rain strikes my palm, filling it, and I swear I hear Him in the rushing sound of water. The real Giant-Killer. The expert Bowman. His armies marching in the thunder.

Tears flash like lightning in my eyes. The Warrior of Israel didn't only want my father and David. He wanted me. And it's taken me this long to believe it.

For years, others had forced Saul's yoke onto me, and I had chosen to remain bound by it, assuming it had to be mine. But I always had the ability to cast it off. I'd thought different for so many years, believing Jonathan and David were strong and I wasn't.

But the same power that built them has been strengthening me. Whenever I stopped fighting. Whenever I stopped letting my past dominate the future Yahweh had planned. It's the one the king has talked and sung about for years. Israel's future. Mine, David's. A blessing that will touch the world for one reason.

David catches his breath, because he knows it deeper than I do. The truth that it's taken me years to believe.

Yahweh's listening.

CPSIA information can be obtained
at www.ICGtesting.com
Printed in the USA
LVHW031102221221
706910LV00005B/168/J